CREATING THE JAZZ SOLO

American Made Music Series

ADVISORY BOARD

David Evans, General Editor
Barry Jean Ancelet
Edward A. Berlin
Joyce J. Bolden
Rob Bowman
Susan C. Cook
Curtis Ellison
William Ferris
John Edward Hasse
Kip Lornell
Bill Malone
Eddie S. Meadows
Manuel H. Peña
Wayne D. Shirley
Robert Walser

CREATING THE JAZZ SOLO

Louis Armstrong and Barbershop Harmony

VIC HOBSON

University Press of Mississippi
Jackson

www.upress.state.ms.us

Designed by Peter D. Halverson

The University Press of Mississippi is a member of the
Association of University Presses.

Portions of Chapter 15 have appeared in a different form in *Jazz Perspectives*, 10, no. 1, 2017, 97–116.

Copyright © 2018 by University Press of Mississippi
All rights reserved

First printing 2018

∞

Library of Congress Cataloging-in-Publication Data

Names: Hobson, Vic., author.
Title: Creating the jazz solo : Louis Armstrong and barbershop harmony / Vic Hobson.
Description: Jackson : University Press of Mississippi, [2018] | Series: American made music series | "Portions of Chapter 15 have appeared in a different form in Jazz Perspectives, 10, no. 1, 2017, 97–116." | Includes bibliographical references and index. |
Identifiers: LCCN 2018017427 (print) | LCCN 2018020876 (ebook) | ISBN 9781496819796 (epub single) | ISBN 9781496819802 (epub instititional) | ISBN 9781496819819 (pdf single) | ISBN 9781496819826 (pdf institutional) | ISBN 9781496819772 (cloth : alk. paper) | ISBN 9781496819789 (pbk. : alk. paper)
Subjects: LCSH: Armstrong, Louis, 1901–1971—Criticism and interpretation. | Jazz—Louisiana—History and criticism. | Jazz musicians—United States. | Jazz—1921–1930—Analysis, appreciation.
Classification: LCC ML419.A75 (ebook) | LCC ML419.A75 H63 2018 (print) | DDC 781.65092—dc23
LC record available at https://lccn.loc.gov/2018017427

British Library Cataloging-in-Publication Data available

This book is dedicated to the memory of my mother
Jessie Olive Hobson

CONTENTS

ACKNOWLEDGMENTS   IX

PREFACE   XII

CHAPTER 1: "Singing Was More into My Blood, Than the Trumpet"   3

CHAPTER 2: "Singing Was My Life"   11

CHAPTER 3: "Always Had Music All Around Me"   18

CHAPTER 4: Church Is Where "I Acquired My Singing Tactics"   25

CHAPTER 5: "When I Was at School, I Played All Classical Music"   33

CHAPTER 6: "My Brazilian Beauty"   39

CHAPTER 7: "Me and Music Got Married in the Home"   47

CHAPTER 8: "I Was Singing Selling Coal"   55

CHAPTER 9: Did Bunk Teach Louis?   71

CHAPTER 10: "Going to the Conservatory"   81

CHAPTER 11: "Dippermouth Blues"   97

CHAPTER 12: Fletcher Henderson: "That Big Fish Horn Voice of His"   110

CHAPTER 13: "The Pride of Race": When Louis Sang with Erskine Tate   126

CHAPTER 14: Lil's Hot Shots   136

CHAPTER 15: The Hot Five and Seven   145

CHAPTER 16: "I Figure Singing and Playing Is the Same"   153

NOTES   174

BIBLIOGRAPHY   216

INDEX   230

ACKNOWLEDGMENTS

SINCE WRITING MY FIRST BOOK, *CREATING JAZZ COUNTERPOINT: NEW Orleans, Barbershop Harmony, and the Blues* (2014), and despite the best efforts of senior lecturers Jonathan Impett, Simon Waters, and Sharon Choa, the School of Music at the University of East Anglia has been closed down. I am currently not lecturing, and the absence of an academic affiliation has made me particularly aware of the importance of the research network that made writing this book possible.

I should begin by mentioning the people who assisted with my first book who, because things were already at the proofreading stage, didn't get a mention at the time. They include my sister Ingrid Harvey, Heather Munson, Shane Gong Stewart, John Langston, and Anne Stascavage. I am grateful for the work of William Rigby for copyediting this book.

Some of my early research on Louis Armstrong surfaced at the 2014 conference of the Jazz Education Network. I am particularly indebted to John Edward Hasse (Jazz Education Network), and David Robinson (Traditional Jazz Education Network), for their help and encouragement at the conference. This conference paper was expanded and submitted for publication in *Jazz Perspectives* under the title "'I Figure Singing and Playing Is the Same': Louis Armstrong and Barbershop Harmony." My thanks to Ken Prouty who is assisting me as editor to work through copyright difficulties.

It is through the foresight of archivists, jazz enthusiasts, journalists, and editors that jazz research is possible. The William Ransom Hogan Jazz Archive in Tulane University began interviewing the jazz musicians of that city in the 1950s and today holds a treasury of recordings and transcripts of oral history dating back to the earliest years of jazz. Bruce Raeburn and Lynn Abbott have assisted me in too many ways to enumerate to access these collections and guide and advise me. It was through these connections that I came to know David and Sandi Wright, and David Krause of the Barbershop Society of America. I was pleased to be invited to their 2015 midwinter convention in New Orleans. It was good too to revisit the Historic New Orleans

Collection (HNOC)—I was a Dianna Woest Fellow in 2009—in connection with this research, and my thanks to Daniel Hammer and Rebecca Smith for their interest in my research. The Institute of Jazz Studies (IJS) at Rutgers University holds the manuscript of Louis Armstrong's autobiography *Satchmo* (1955) and the notebooks that Armstrong wrote that were used to write *Horn of Plenty* (1947), by Robert Goffin, one of the earliest biographies of Armstrong. These notebooks are not complete. There is one notebook for 1918 and then a gap up to 1922 and the years beyond. In an effort to remove some of the uncertainty around Goffin's book, I contacted John Chilton, who secured the notebooks that the IJS do have; unfortunately, John had no new information, and the earlier notebooks have not surfaced. Sadly, John will not see this book go into print as I learned with regret that he died as I was putting the final touches to the manuscript. The IJS also holds a manuscript written by Armstrong toward the end of his life that he intended to be a last autobiography. It was never published but nevertheless contains interesting and sometimes contradictory information. I am grateful to Dan Morgenstern, Christian McFarland, and Vincent Pelote of the IJS for their help and assistance in accessing the original and advice on the Goffin notebooks.[1] I am also grateful to Ricky Riccardi for his introduction to the Louis Armstrong House Museum in Queens. While in New York I took the opportunity to meet up with Lewis Porter (Rutgers), who has taken an interest in my work for some years now, and also Jeff Nussbaum of the Historic Brass Society (HBS). It was a joint conference of the HBS and the IJS in 2005 that I consider a cardinal point in my research.

I am a trustee for the National Jazz Archive (NJA) in the UK. I have made use of this collection in the preparation of this book. It is through the foresight of Graham Langley, founder of the British Institute of Jazz Studies, who with Digby Fairweather and Clarence Blackwell went on to establish the NJA, that we have today such a valuable resource in the UK.[2] My thanks to David Nathan (NJA research archivist) for his help in accessing the collections, and to the trustees, Paul Kaufman, Nick Clarke, David Goodrich, Alex Wilson, Alis Templeton, Maria Regan, Roger Cotterrell, Jane Hunter-Randall, Penny Hutchins, Nathan Granger, Pedro Cavinho, and Jez Collins. The NJA could not function effectively without the support of our volunteers. Many thanks to Mike Rose, Alan Quaife, Christine Smith, Steve Carter, George Wilkinson, Judy Atkinson, and Louis Malcolm. The NJA has recently completed a second project funded by the Heritage Lottery Fund to support jazz research in the UK. Building on "The Story of British Jazz," the Intergenerational Jazz Reminiscence Project collected oral history interviews from communities in the

UK that developed to support the music. This was conducted under the guidance of Angela Davis (project manager) and Layla Fedyk (project archivist).

This is my second book for University Press of Mississippi. My thanks to Craig Gill and David Evans, who above and beyond their role as editors have been of great assistance in establishing connections to other UPM writers. I hope to be able to work more closely with Gerhard Kubik in the future, and my thanks to Karl Gert zur Heide for keeping me abreast of his research.

I came to academia somewhat later in life than is usual. I was fortunate to receive AHRC funding during my doctoral years and a scholarship to the Kluge Center of the Library of Congress; I am still drawing on the fruits of this in my ongoing research. In the absence of any present-day academic support, I have been fortunate to have been able to work freelance in the glass industry. My thanks to Malcolm Reynold (Penelectro) and Andrew Reynolds (Fives UK) for the opportunity to combine my research with a flexible working life that has made this book possible.

PREFACE

IT IS A DAUNTING PROSPECT TO WRITE A BOOK ON LOUIS ARMSTRONG. There is a wealth of literature about Armstrong's life. So much has been written about him that it might seem there is little more to add. Although Armstrong's contribution to twentieth-century music making has been widely discussed, surprisingly little has been written about *why* he played *what* he played. In recent years, the availability of transcriptions of Armstrong's recordings and analysis of his playing has increased. This has enabled analysts to describe *what* he played—to identify "blue notes" and recurring motifs—but why he played as he did is less explored. In order to consider Armstrong's development as a musician, this book does not get beyond the 1920s, and I have made no attempt to cover all aspects of Armstrong's life during this period. I have only considered those aspects of his life that may have significantly affected his development as a musician.

In *Creating Jazz Counterpoint*, I attempted to bring together the historical record, oral history, and musical analysis to show how barbershop harmony is at the root of blues tonality and jazz counterpoint. At the time, this seemed a controversial claim. It is far less so only a few years later. Lynn Abbott had argued back in 1992 "A Case for the African American Origins of Barbershop Harmony."[1] In the intervening period, few researchers have followed up on Abbott's research. One notable exception is James Earl Henry in his PhD thesis: "The Origins of Barbershop Harmony: A Study of Barbershop's Musical Link to Other African American Musics as Evidenced Through Recordings and Arrangements of Early Black and White Quartets."[2] Despite the paucity of research since Abbott's essay, the consensus has decisively shifted. I was fortunate to be present at the 2015 convention of the Barbershop Harmony Society held in New Orleans when Lynn Abbott was awarded life membership in the organization for his work in understanding the origins of barbershop harmony. Given that there is growing evidence that barbershop harmony is of African American origin, and that barbershop harmony played a significant role in blues and jazz tonality, the focus of this book is not to argue *whether* barbershop harmony influenced the emergence of jazz and blues, but rather *how* it influenced the emergence of jazz; in particular, how it influenced Louis Armstrong as the first great soloist of jazz. To do this it is necessary to use music notation, music theory, chord symbols, and barbershop theory and practice. This too brings challenges.

I am conscious that not everyone is musically literate. I am also mindful that not many people know how barbershop harmony functions. For this reason, I have decided to transpose many of the musical examples in this book into the key of C. I justify this for two reasons. The first reason is that it makes the argument easier to follow for readers who do not have a grounding in music theory. Jazz has always been a music that is approachable to musicians with very little understanding of music theory. It seems reasonable that it should be possible to explain how it functions in an approachable way too. The second reason for transposing most musical examples into the key of C is that early jazz musicians were not concerned with absolute pitch; they were, however, concerned with relative pitch. All schools in New Orleans used a common music syllabus based on the solfeggio system where each pitch is assigned a syllable. In this system, *Do* is the first note of the scale, *Re* is the next, and *Mi* is the next, and so on. Any note could be the start note of *Do*, and therefore absolute pitch was not as important as the relationship between the pitches.

Louis Armstrong made many recordings. Some have been transcribed in full, others in part, and some not at all. A transcription of a recording can only be an approximation of what was played. It would test even the most skilled transcriber to notate every nuance and inflection of even just a single note; a complete solo would be impossible. To what extent a transcription is acceptable depends on the type of analysis required. If a transcription is to be used to analyze how a musician imparts a swing feel in his or her playing, it may be necessary to introduce finer subdivisions of time from simple eighth, sixteenth, or thirty-second notes and instead consider percentages of swing. In a similar way, ethnomusicologists often divide pitches such that 100 cents are equal to one semitone of conventional music theory. This level of detail is not necessary for my purposes. My reason for using transcriptions is to explore the relationship between melodies, countermelodies, obbligatos, solos, and harmony. To avoid any possibility of prejudicing the evidence, I have decided to use wherever possible published transcriptions by other people. The only exception to this is Armstrong's vocal chorus on "Basin Street Blues" (Example 47), as I know of no published transcriptions.

There is a difference between the notation of popular music and jazz in the early twentieth century and the way it is written now. Contemporary jazz musicians tend to use chord symbols. These chord symbols provide a shorthand way of relaying a lot of musical information. Chords are constructed by selecting alternate notes of a scale and sounding those notes together. A chord of C major seventh (Cmaj7) informs a musician that the chord contains the notes of C (the root), E (the major third), G (the fifth note of the scale), and B (the major seventh note of the scale). Early jazz musicians did not think in terms of chord symbols and they rarely appear in sheet music of the early twentieth century unless for ukulele or other stringed instruments. For the benefit of readers who may be more familiar with chord symbols than with notation, I have added chord symbols to the musical examples where required to make it easier for contemporary musicians to follow the argument.[3]

CREATING THE JAZZ SOLO

CHAPTER 1

"SINGING WAS MORE INTO MY BLOOD, THAN THE TRUMPET"

LOUIS ARMSTRONG IS PERHAPS THE MOST INFLUENTIAL INSTRUMENtalist and singer in the history of jazz. He is credited as being the first great soloist, one of the earliest jazz singers, and reputedly invented scat singing.[1] On the occasion of his seventieth birthday (based upon the belief that he was born on July 4, 1900, when it was actually August 4, 1901), tributes from the greats of jazz arrived in the offices of *Down Beat*.[2] Cootie Williams observed, "Louis Armstrong is the greatest trumpet player I ever heard in my life."[3] Fellow trumpeter William "Cat" Anderson said, "Louis Armstrong is the greatest horn player that ever played."[4] Speaking for his later generation, Dizzy Gillespie argued Louis was "the cause of the trumpet in jazz. . . . He's the father of jazz trumpeting."[5] This was supported by Thad Jones: "I think he's probably the greatest living influence in trumpet playing today."[6] The saxophonist and trumpeter Benny Carter acknowledged, "He influenced so many instrumentalists—and not just trumpeters."[7] This point was emphasized by saxophonist Cannonball Adderley, who claimed Armstrong as "our first important jazz soloist."[8]

Armstrong's contribution to jazz was not only as an instrumentalist. As reed player Herb Hall opined, "He started it—both trumpet and jazz singing."[9] For reed player Franz Jackson, Armstrong "seemed to make everyone sing, even people who could never sing. He made it sound so natural. Nobody ever did anything like that with their voice."[10] Saxophonist Harry Carney said simply, "The sound of his voice makes you happy."[11]

Today Armstrong's singing is appreciated in equal measure to his playing, but while much has been written about Armstrong's playing, rather less has been written about Armstrong as a singer. One of the reasons for the initial resistance to acceptance of Louis's singing is that his singing has been rather more controversial. In his early career, both Joe Oliver and Fletcher

Henderson, according to Armstrong, were "afraid of letting me sing thinking maybe, I'd sort of ruin their reputations, with their musical public."[12] In April 1923 Armstrong began his recording career, cutting forty-two sides with Oliver.[13] He did not sing on any of these recordings. Later he joined Henderson, and ignoring the fact that Joe Oliver did not let him sing either (at least on record), Louis complained, "Fletcher didn't dig me like Joe Oliver. He had a million dollar talent in his band and he never thought to let me sing."[14] Armstrong had more opportunity to sing when he began recording under his own name as Louis Armstrong and the Hot Five in 1925. Less clear is how his recorded output from these years is representative of the music he was performing and singing in the dance halls, clubs, and vaudeville shows. Although he probably had more freedom to sing in live performance after leaving Fletcher Henderson's band, it was not until he was performing at the Vendome Theater in Chicago around 1926 that singing is known to have become a mainstay of his live performances.[15]

By the late 1920s, Armstrong had already expanded his Hot Five to the Hot Seven, and by 1929 he was recording under the name Louis Armstrong and His Orchestra. The Great Depression of the 1930s fundamentally changed the music industry, and Armstrong had to adapt. In the 1920s Armstrong recorded for record companies that catered to the expanding black populations of the cities of Chicago and New York, and the African American population in the South. With the Great Depression, a focus on niche "race" marketing was less attractive to record companies that preferred to sell to the mass market. The rise of radio as a cheaper alternative to costly phonograph records and the decline of vaudeville also began to affect the type of material that was recorded. With the rise of the mass market, and with radio providing a cheaper alternative to records, lyrics needed to be suitable for a wider audience of all ages.[16] It is no coincidence that blues songs in Louis's recorded output reduced dramatically after the Wall Street Crash. In the years 1929 to 1931, Armstrong did not record a single twelve-bar blues.[17] The advent of "talking" pictures in 1927, with *The Jazz Singer*, also hastened the decline of the touring vaudeville shows. Armstrong was quick to capitalize on this trend. His earliest films were *Rhapsody in Black and Blue* (1932) and a Betty Boop cartoon of the same year. In his first film he sang "Shine" dressed in a leopard skin with the opening lyric "Oh, chocolate drop, that's me." He also appeared in the Betty Boop cartoon in a jungle scene dressed as a cannibal. The question that these films raise is the extent that racial attitudes have hindered serious investigation of Armstrong as a singer. While it can be argued that Armstrong's trumpet playing in these films "transcends the racist trappings" of his environment, to make the same argument about Armstrong the singer and entertainer is, on the surface of things, a little more awkward.[18]

Succeeding generations of commentators have approached Armstrong's role as an African American in segregated America somewhat differently. It is likely that many African Americans of Armstrong's generation would have viewed Armstrong as something of a race champion. The song "Shine," for example, was written by black composers Ford Dabney and Cecile McPherson, and its lyrics can be interpreted as an assertion of black identity.[19] This could explain Terry Teachout's observation that, in the film *Rhapsody in Black and Blue*, Armstrong "comes out less like Uncle Tom than Superman."[20] However, this assessment would not have been universally accepted by African Americans at the time. Hampton Institute educator and author Robert Russa Moton in 1929 claimed that "shine" and "darky" were only slightly less offensive than "nigger," and by 1933 the *Chicago Defender*, a black newspaper, considered all three to be equally offensive.[21] However progressive the song "That's Why They Call Me Shine" may have been when it was first performed in 1910, by the 1930s some black intellectuals rejected popular culture and took a different view.[22] After World War II, the bebop generation also took a different view of Armstrong's role. Although he would change his mind later, Dizzy Gillespie initially criticized Armstrong for being an "Uncle Tom . . . grinning in the face of white racism."[23] For some in the bebop generation it was possible to confront racism more directly than it had been just a few years earlier. In recent years there have been attempts to cast Louis as someone who transcended the racist society of his time: through "subversive comic art . . . disrupting from the sidelines," as though a "trickster, 'winking' at the audience."[24] Postmodern scholars may argue that Armstrong's scat singing "points at something outside the sayable . . . evading or going beyond the racial and political structures of the time," but published lyrics were very much of their time.[25] Minstrelsy and "coon songs" were a mainstay of American entertainment for both black and white audiences in Armstrong's early years. And more than anything else Armstrong wanted to entertain.

There is little evidence in what Armstrong said about the lyrics that he sang that he saw them as either offensive or conveying subversive messages. Armstrong responded to his critics: "There you go! See, now what's wrong with 'Shine'? I mean, the people are so narrowminded, they're worrying about the title, they forgot to listen to all that good music! . . . And I think if we just take it in a little easier stride, I don't know—a lot of people worry about a whole lot of unnecessary things and they don't do nothing about it."[26] One song he recorded many times was "When It's Sleepy Time Down South."[27] In his early recordings, he sang the published lyric "darkies are crooning." When he was persuaded to change these lyrics to "people are crooning," at a subsequent recording session, he is remembered to have asked, "What do you want me to call those black sons-of-bitches this morning?"[28] In a radio interview in 1956, Armstrong discussed his views on the lyrics and titles of some of his songs: "Now pertaining to titles and things, I remember the time we made a record called 'Shine,' 'Black and Blue,' things like that, why people would—you know, especially our people, the Negroes—they'd probably get insulted a little for no reason at all."[29] There seems little reason not to take Armstrong at his word. He was brought up in a period when racism permeated all aspects of show business, and Armstrong saw himself as an entertainer whose job it was to please the public. For him, the lyrics of his songs were not significant, but for others they have been, and this may have prevented Armstrong's singing being explored with the same rigor as his trumpet playing.

And then there is the question of Louis's vocal style: white audiences, in particular, needed persuasion to accept Louis as a singer; this is evident from Armstrong's first autobiography *Swing That Music* (1936). Rudy Vallée wrote an introduction praising Armstrong's trumpet playing before describing the "utterly mad, hoarse, inchoate mumble-jumble that is Louis's 'singing.'"[30] But, Vallée encouraged readers, if they studied more closely they would come to see that his singing is "beautifully timed and executed," and acknowledged that he had "perfect command of time spacing, of rhythm, harmony and pitch."[31]

John Petters has argued, "Satchmo more or less invented the art of jazz singing." He would go on to say, "the body of work Louis laid down in the 1930's for Decca, where he performed mostly pop songs of the day, amply showcased this unique talent."[32] However, Armstrong's eagerness to please the public with popular song throughout his career often distanced him from those promoting the acceptance of jazz as an art form, and this too affected study of Armstrong's singing.[33]

Music critics often judged Louis's singing inferior to his playing. In 1962 jazz writer Leonard Feather reflected on how to explain Louis Armstrong's contribution to music to a generation reared on modern jazz. He concluded that it "might be easier" were it not that the "personality who, as a singer and comedian rather than a trumpeter . . . had already [by the 1930s] forsaken the blues almost entirely in favor of popular songs." He went on to complain, "Singing once incidental on his records (many of the Hot Five sides had no vocals), became indispensable."[34] This was written before Louis Armstrong's biggest hit: "Hello Dolly." *Melody Maker* headlined this recording as "The Hit

No One Wanted."[35] On one level, the *Melody Maker* story was a celebration of the persistence of Armstrong's manager, Joe Glaser, to get the record made.[36] But the headline can also be interpreted as a prediction of the reaction of many jazz critics. As Gunther Schuller lamented late in Armstrong's career, he "embraced singing as a full-time commitment, equal in its allocation to his trumpet-playing. And it was as a singer—of songs like 'Hello Dolly' and 'Mack the Knife'—that a large public was finally to know Armstrong in the last decade or so of his life. One cannot help feeling that his genius and art somehow deserved better than that!"[37]

Louis's singing also had a utilitarian role. Barney Bigard remembered that in the late 1940s and early 1950s "Louis worked so hard that his lip gave out—just like that. It lasted for about two weeks and he got mighty worried. But you know him, he just went along, did a lot of singing and eventually his lip got back into shape."[38] From the 1930s onward, singing provided a way to rest his lip between playing trumpet passages.

In his lifetime, the abiding image is of Louis Armstrong as a man of two exceptional talents. His first talent was as a trumpet player—the first great soloist of jazz—and the second a singer whose unique approach to singing was generally appreciated in its own right, but due to commercial pressures and the effects of age on his lip, had come to dominate Armstrong's later years. After his death on July 6, 1971, a one off special collector's magazine was published. Stanley Dance summed up the prevailing view: "The original Louis Armstrong was a trumpeter *par excellence* who threw in humorous vocalizations as a kind of bonus."[39]

After his death opinion on the significance of Armstrong the vocalist began to change. Gunther Schuller, writing in 1986, observed:

> To the listener orientated to "classical" singing, Louis's voice, with its rasp and totally unorthodox technique, usually comes as a complete shock. The reaction is often to set the voice aside as primitive and uncouth. Actually, Louis's singing is but a vocal counterpart of his playing, just as natural and inspired. In his singing we can hear all the nuances, inflections, and natural ease of his trumpet playing, including even the bends and scoops, vibrato and shakes.[40]

Some writers would acknowledge Armstrong's influence on other singers. In a chapter titled "Armstrong the Celebrity," in their book *Jazz: From Its Origins to the Present* (1993), Lewis Porter, Michael Ullman, and Edward Hazell observe, "His singing while continually entertaining, is not to be dismissed artistically: It influenced Billie Holiday, Ella Fitzgerald, Bing Crosby, Frank Sinatra, and a host of others."[41] By 2001 Gary Giddins felt that he was being redundant in saying that the genius of Louis Armstrong "can be relished in 'Hello Dolly!' as well as in 'West End Blues.' But there I go again making an argument I just said no longer needed to be made."[42]

Although Armstrong's vocal contribution is now generally seen as of equal significance to his cornet playing, with very few exceptions the prevailing view is that his singing and playing are not related. Brian Harker's otherwise excellent assessment of Armstrong's recordings of the 1920s argues that Armstrong's "singing had little direct effect on the transformation of jazz in the 1920s from an ensemble based music to a solo based music."[43] It is this assumption that this book challenges. I argue that Armstrong's singing did have a direct influence on Armstrong's ability to transform the earlier ensemble jazz to a solo based music that he played on his cornet.

The connection between Armstrong's singing and playing will be developed, in part, through Armstrong's own explanations for his musical development. Armstrong believed singing was the nexus of his musicianship. He proclaimed flatly, "Singing was more *into* my blood, than the trumpet."[44] The reason, he explained, was "I had been singing, all of my life. In Churches, etc. I had one of the finest All Boys Quartets that ever walked the streets of New Orleans."[45] This is an important point in understanding Armstrong as a musician. He thought of himself first and foremost as a singer who played the cornet. However much he loved his horn, to Armstrong his instrument was an extension of his voice. What is more, when he said "I figure singing and playing is the same," he meant that he applied the same principles to his phrasing and note choices as a singer that he did when he played cornet.[46] He explained in some detail the relationship between his singing and his playing in an interview in 1960. Armstrong was asked about how all of the members of his band could be improvising at the same time. His answer to this question makes it clear that when he said that playing and singing were the same he was not speaking figuratively. In essence, what the questioner asked was how collective improvisation functions. This is a question that has confounded musicologists, but Armstrong's answer was very clear: "In the early days in New Orleans they always had one in the band that could read. Either the trumpet player, or the cornet player, or the piano player maybe, we always had one."[47] The reason for this, as Armstrong explained, was that somebody in the band needed to play the lead part: the melody as published. He continued, "So we'd go down to the music store, in the days before radios, and get the new piano copies, tunes that just come in New Orleans, and all you'd do is just run the lead down once."[48] Once the lead part was mastered, "We'd woodshed on the weekend just blowing."[49] He went on to explain how the other instruments would find their harmony parts: "If you'd sing in a quartet, you ordinarily get your harmony, if you sing baritone, you sing tenor, and I'm gonna sing the lead, you bass. Do you understand? So if I sing 'Sweet Adeline,'" (sings the melody), "right now you gonna sing 'Sweet Adeline,'" he then sang a harmony part, and that's "the same every number. So you've got to practice."[50] Having discussed the methods used by a vocal quartet to find their harmony parts, he then explicitly related this to instruments: "If you do it on the instrument then love the instrument."[51] What Armstrong described in this single interview was how a barbershop quartet rehearses and how the same practices were applied in New Orleans to a jazz band and its instruments. This also explains why singing was "more into" Armstrong's blood than the trumpet. His formative years were spent singing in quartets. It was in quartets that he developed his ear for music and learned how to construct the lines that he would go on to play on his horn.

In part the argument made in this book for the connection between Armstrong's singing in a quartet and his cornet solos will be developed by analysis of his recorded solos. In his solos, Armstrong often played "blue" notes associated with blues tonality. These blue notes are characteristic of particular voices in a barbershop quartet. Armstrong often sang tenor in his boyhood quartet. The tenor voice sings a third above the lead voice, often alternating between minor and major third. This gives rise to what later theorists would describe as "blues thirds." Similar distinctive progressions in the baritone voice in a quartet result in flatted seventh notes in this voice. The flatted third and seventh are the two most common "blue notes" identified in Armstrong's cornet playing. Armstrong also often arpeggiated chords, implying harmony that is not commonly found in European music. Later jazz musicians would describe this practice as chord substitution: where one chord could be replaced with another. Given that improvising the harmony around a melody is foundational to barbershop practice, chord substitution in Armstrong's playing also provides evidence of the connection between his singing barbershop harmony and features evident in his cornet playing.

In the early chapters of this book, the connection between Armstrong the singer and Armstrong the musician will be made by placing him in context with other musicians who also used the same barbershop principles to inform their playing and compositions. When Armstrong was young, barbershop singing was a mainstay of recreational and professional music making. People sang in quartets, at home, in bars, on street corners, and on minstrel and vaudeville stages. People sang as they worked and they sang in their worship. This was the culture that Armstrong grew up in, one he knew well, and one in which he excelled. Singing was his musical foundation: it was his *life*.

CHAPTER 2

"SINGING WAS MY LIFE"

IN HIS LATER YEARS, LOUIS ARMSTRONG LOOKED BACK ON HIS LIFE IN New Orleans and remembered that "singing was my life."[1] In his heavily edited first autobiography, Armstrong recalled "Some of my friends liked to sing, so on warm nights we would go down to the Mississippi and sit on the docks and sing together."[2] Louis told of how they would swim among the banana boats, and when they got tired they would get out of the water and sing some more. On reflection, Louis came to realize that this was a good way to spend the evenings of his boyhood because it kept him "out of a lot of mischief."[3] He later recalled at age thirteen, "I started up a singing quartet with three of the best singing boys from my neighborhood. Believe me, we four were, 'singing fools.' No Kiddin'! We went out big" for what he retrospectively described as "new jazz songs." The term "jazz" to describe a type of music was not used at the time.[4] In fact, Louis was at least two years younger than he remembered when he organized his first quartet because he was singing with his quartet at the end of 1912. Everything was going well with his quartet, according to Armstrong, "until that New Year's Eve of 1913. Our quartet was out hustling, as we called it, and the city was celebrating." Louis and his friends were expecting to make "a lot of change" before the night was out.[5] What happened was that Louis let off a gun in the street, he was arrested, and was committed to a Waifs' Home for around eighteen months. Because these events are verifiable we can be sure that he was at most eleven years old when he first sang with the quartet.

In *Swing That Music*, Louis did not identify the members of the quartet, but in *Horn of Plenty* (1947), a book written (based on notebooks that Armstrong sent to him) by Robert Goffin, a Belgian lawyer, Armstrong is quoted as saying that the members of the quartet on New Year's Eve 1913 were "Little Max," "Red Head Happy," and "Georgie Gray."[6] Later in his second

11

autobiography, *Satchmo: My Life in New Orleans* (1955), Armstrong remembered, "Little Mack, our lead singer, later became one of the best drummers in New Orleans. Big Nose Sidney was the bass. Red Head Happy Bolton was the baritone."[7] Armstrong told the editors of *Jazzmen* (1939), "I sang tenor" and "Mack was the leading tenor." He would later claim, "I used to sing tenor when I was twelve years old—with my hat around my ears—hit those big high notes like Caruso."[8] He would also claim, "I sang lead sometimes."[9]

The quartet probably started out in the spring or early summer of 1912 and practiced in a disused yard in Freret Street.[10] They rehearsed for around a month, with Louis beating out time on a soap box, before they sang publicly.[11] Once ready to perform, "They walked as far as Poydras and stopped before Maylie's Restaurant . . . lined up against the wall and began to sing, beating time with their right heels."[12] If these events did take place in the early summer of 1912, the confidence of the quartet grew rapidly. Another sighting of Armstrong singing comes from the drummer Zutty Singleton.[13] "The first time ever I saw Louis was when he was about 12, 13 years old. He was singing with three kids in an amateur show at Bill and Mary Mack's tent show in New Orleans. Louis was singing tenor then, and they broke up that night. The other three boys were Red Happy, Little Mack, and a guy by the name of Clarence."[14]

Billy McBride (born 1883) and Mary McBride (born 1891) played in theaters throughout the South, Midwest, and Eastern United States between 1908 and 1959. They appeared as Mack and Mack or as Mack's Merry Makers.[15] They usually spent the summer in Bay St. Louis which they described as a "kind of a resort for the colored people who came from New Orleans and Mobile." From there they took their "show to the little towns up and down the coast—Pass Christian, Biloxi, [and] Bay St. Louis."[16] There was a theater that they could rent in Bay St. Louis but not in the other towns; instead they would use "a tent and played in a lot." Billy Mack recalled, "In New Orleans one lot was at Louisiana and Howard, and then we had lots in Algiers and Gretna."[17] Billy and Mary McBride remembered Louis's quartet, and they told jazz researcher Bill Russell, "Louis and Little Mac and Little Georgie Grey, and Happy, they had a quartet . . . and they'd go up there [an airdome at Jackson and Robertson streets] and sing amateur-night songs, you know."[18] It seems likely that Zutty Singleton heard Louis and his quartet singing at an amateur night with the Mack and Mack tent show when they were in New Orleans doing their summer circuit in 1912. Zutty remembered that after seeing Louis at the Mack and Mack show, "I didn't see him for a while. But I heard about him at the home. Some of the fellows that were sent there [the Waifs' Home] would come back and say how fine this Louis Armstrong was playing."[19]

It is significant that in these accounts Louis sang tenor in the quartet, and the other voices are identified as lead, baritone, and bass. These voice designations are particular to a barbershop quartet. The musicologist Sigmund Spaeth, who published widely on American popular music, becoming known as a "Famous Tune Detective," was also an avid barbershop singer.[20] Spaeth wrote two books on barbershop singing: *Barber Shop Ballads: A Book of Close Harmony* (1925) and *Barber Shop Ballads and How to Sing Them* (1940). In these books, he described the role of the four voices in a barbershop quartet: "First comes the second tenor," Spaeth explained, "who generally carries the air and is therefore the outstanding singer of the four."[21] Because this voice sings the melody it is often referred to as the "lead" voice.[22] "The first tenor," according to Spaeth, "should have a lighter and higher voice than that of the lead, and an occasional bit of falsetto will do no harm."[23] Of the baritone voice, Spaeth commented, "The first bass, or baritone, should be the best musician of the four, as his part is generally the most difficult . . . The 'bary' is consistently called upon to sing the trickiest intervals."[24] Finally, on "the low bass, a solidity of tone and impressive resonance are needed."[25]

In his barbershop quartet, Louis sang first tenor, and therefore he would have sung above Little Mack singing lead. This is unlike a European quartet where the lead is usually sung by the top voice. The role of the top tenor voice is to find a harmony line above the melody. To find his notes, Louis said, "I used to put my hand behind my ear, and move my mouth from side to side, and some beautiful tones would appear."[26]

Quartet singing was a common pastime in New Orleans when Louis was young. In New Orleans around 1910, "it was typical, almost, for any three or four Negroes to get together and, they say, 'Let's crack up a chord! Let's hit a note!'"[27] For Louis's quartet to "crack up" a chord, they would first have to form it. This would have been done by the lead singer, Little Mack, singing a particular pitch. If, for example, he sang a note of C, the bass singer (Georgie Gray according to most accounts) would sing a note of C an octave below him. The baritone singer (Red "Happy" Bolton) sang a note a perfect fifth (G) above the bass. Louis, singing tenor, would find a note a major third (E) above the lead, and collectively the quartet would form a C major chord.[28] The object then would be for tenor and baritone voices, and sometimes the bass too, to slide their voices to other notes and form other chords before returning to their original notes. In this way, they would "crack up a chord" before resolving back to the original chord. This practice lives on in barbershop endings. As Spaeth observed, "No barber shop quartet in history has ever been guilty of landing right smack on a tonic chord and staying there for the three, four, or five beats of the final harmony. The least it can do is to let the tenor and baritone move a half-tone up or down, while the lead and bass hang on to their key notes."[29]

One of the songs that we know Louis and his friends sang was "Swanee River."[30] This title comes from the opening lyric to "Old Folks at Home," written by Stephen Foster. The song had been in circulation in the minstrel shows for more than half a century before Louis and his quartet learned to sing it. It was published in 1851, described as an "Ethiopian melody," as sung by Christy's Minstrels.[31] In 1887 a version of "Old Folks at Home" was arranged and published for "male quartet."[32] The song's arranger, Wilson G. Smith, was clearly familiar with barbershop harmony and the practice of cracking up a chord. The final cadence is an example of what would become known as the "barbershop chord": this is a chord on the flatted sixth of the scale.[33] The arrangement was notated in the key of A major but in order to demonstrate the principles used in a barbershop cadence I have transposed it to the key of C major.

Much of the quartet arrangement of "Old Folks at Home" is typical of European harmony, but in keeping with barbershop tradition it is the final cadence (the chord of A♭ to C) that has the most interesting harmony. As Spaeth explained:

> Barbershop harmony really begins at the end and works backward. If a quartet is well equipped with "wicked" endings, the body of its music may be fairly conventional. It is the close that leaves the final fragrance of the barber shop, and if this be beautifully flavored with nostalgic aroma, it matters little what went before. The most obvious harmonies are forgotten in a really subtle finish.[34]

The final measure of "Swanee River," as arranged for a quartet (see Ex. 1), shows a clear example of the practice of cracking up a chord. Both the bass voice and the lead voice stay on the principal (key) note of C. If Louis and his friend sang this ending as written, the only voices that needed to change their notes are the baritone voice ("Bass 1," Bolton) and the first tenor (Armstrong), and both would have sung a note that is not usually sung in the key of C major: Bolton would have sung a note of A♭ (the flatted sixth), and Armstrong would have sung a note of E♭ (the minor third). Armstrong previously sang a

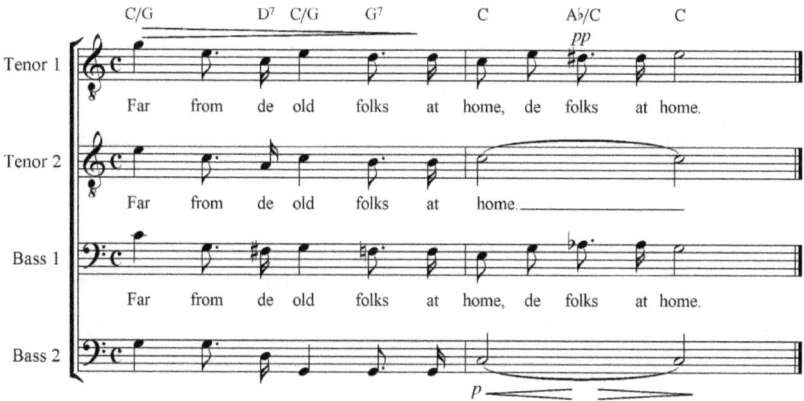

Example 1: Stephen Foster, arr. Wilson G. Smith, "Old Folks at Home (Down on the Swanee River)" (1887)

note of E♮ (the major third). In this instance, the alternate major and minor thirds result in a change of chords. When alternate major and minor thirds are sung as a melody, these intervals became known as "blue note" melodies. The term began to appear in sheet music while Armstrong was still young. The 1913 reprint of "The Memphis Blues" (1912) claimed it was "founded on W. C. Handy's World Wide Blue Note Melody."[35] This was with reference to the use of a minor third in melody that was written in a major key. Because the tenor voice usually sings a major third above the lead voice, and then slides to another note to form a new chord, one of the most common note choices of the tenor voice in a barbershop quartet is to descend by a semitone to the minor third thereby imparting a bluesy quality.

It was not only the final cadence of "Swanee River" that could be adapted to barbershop harmony. This song was particularly suitable for barbershop embellishment, and it is likely that Armstrong and his friends would have reharmonized other parts of the song. John C. Cavendish wrote an article for the *American Mercury* in 1925 where he attempted to challenge the "two-part doctrine, first, that a body of folk tunes . . . constitutes a profound and authentic contribution to art music, and second, that folk tunes in general lend themselves most aptly to musical treatment and have thus proved an invaluable inspiration to the great composers."[36] To make his argument, Cavendish used "Way Down Upon the Swanee River" as an example. Whether this tune is a folk song, in the sense that most people would have understood the term to describe music that was not composed and transmitted orally, is open to question: it had been published in many forms with different arrangements. But in the sense that it was still undergoing folk adaptations in street quartets

Example 2: Stephen Foster, arr. John C. Cavendish, "Swanee River" (simple harmonization)

more than half a century after its publication it had clearly become music of the folk. This is a definition of folk song that Armstrong would have agreed with. Asked about what he thought of folk music Armstrong replied, "Folk music, Why, Daddy, I don't know no other kind of music but folk music—I ain't never heard a hoss [horse] sing a song."[37]

The first arrangement that Cavendish gave was "simply harmonized."[38] There are a number of characteristics typical of European harmonization in this example. The first is that this version contains no accidentals. This is because all of the notes in the melody and all of the notes used to harmonize this melody are notes from the scale of C major. This key has no sharps or flats in the key signature. In European musical practice, a melody is harmonized using notes from the appropriate scale: if a melody is in the key of C, the harmony notes will be in the key of C as well.[39] The second observation is that the harmonic rhythm (the number of chord changes in each measure) is slow: there is just one chord of C for the first measure and a half. Although there are notes in the first measures that are not found in the chord of C, these are just passing notes; the underlying harmony does not change. A third observation is that all of these chords are triads: there are just three different notes in each chord. The triad is the foundation of European harmony. Although more extended chords can be found in European art music of the nineteenth century, for simple melodies three note chords will usually suffice. Because the rules of counterpoint and harmony in the European tradition had been codified and taught in a prescribed way for more than two centuries by the time of this article, the author found it quite difficult to reharmonize this song using European musical conventions and produce anything substantially different. As one reviewer of the Cavendish article commented, "To show how hard it is to devise harmonic and melodic variants of folk tunes, he [Cavendish] introduces a stupid and inappropriate 'barber shop' harmonization of 'Way Down Upon the Swanee River.'"[40] In order to produce a reharmonized version Cavendish had to abandon European harmonic practice and instead use barbershop harmony.[41] Instead of simple diatonic harmony with no accidentals, the barbershop version has many

Example 3: Stephen Foster, arr. John C. Cavendish, "Swanee River" (barbershop harmonization)

accidentals. This is because the harmony notes are selected from notes that do not belong to the key of C. Notice also that there are many more chord changes. In this barbershop arrangement, the harmony changes with every note of the melody. The result is that the harmonic rhythm is much quicker than in the previous version. Finally, most of the chords in the barbershop version have four notes in each chord.

What this suggests—and this argument will be developed further—is that European harmonization and barbershop harmonization are based on two different musical systems. They can both be expressed using conventional music notation; the harmony can be analyzed using the same type of chord symbols; the same songs can be sung with their melodies unaltered; but there is a fundamental difference in the principles that underlie the two different harmonic systems. This difference by 1925 was already having a significant impact on American music. An insightful observer commented, "Negro folksongs differ from the folksongs of most other races through the fact that they are swung [sic] in harmony, and as Negroes harmonize instinctively, each performance differs in some particular from every other performance, although the melody retains its general integrity."[42] In a letter that was published in the *New York Telegram* at the end of the same year that the Cavendish article appeared, Spaeth wrote: "America is gradually producing a curious folk music of her own, in the midst of highly civilized surroundings—a phenomenon which has no parallel in human history. In this music the jazz rhythms, ballad melodies and 'barber shop' harmonies play an important part. It is still in a primitive stage, but so was all folk music at one time."[43] Spaeth wrote this letter on November 4, 1925. A week later, on November 12, Louis Armstrong and his Hot Five would begin recording in Chicago. These recordings began what many have viewed as a critical stage of the development of jazz as the new music developed from collective improvisation into a soloists' music.

CHAPTER 3

"ALWAYS HAD MUSIC ALL AROUND ME"

LOUIS AND HIS FRIENDS WERE JUST A SMALL PART OF THE MUSIC THAT could be heard on the streets of New Orleans in the early years of the twentieth century. Armstrong remembered that there was "music all around you. The pie man and the waffle man, they all had a little hustle to attract people. Pie man used to swing something on the bugle and the waffle man rang a big triangle."[1] We know something of these street cries between 1877 and 1890 from the writing of Lafcadio Hearn and from a little later in *Gumbo Ya-Ya: Folk Tales of Louisiana* (1945).[2] Examples of these street songs include the pie peddlers who would cater to the longshoremen on the docks of New Orleans "with a monotonous cry of 'Hot pies—hot pies—hot pies—hot pies!'"[3] There was also a song about the waffle man. It is remembered that children "ran out at the shrill blast of the Waffle Man's bugle" to buy hot waffles powdered in sugar.[4] Bugles and tin horns were common among the street peddlers. Armstrong recalled: "The junk man had one of them long tin horns they celebrate with at Christmas—could play the blues and everything on it. Called him Lonzo. I used to work with him and we'd go in all the rich neighborhoods and buy a lot of old cloths. And I'd be yelling 'Old rags and bones, lady! Old rags and bones!'"[5] Thomas Brothers, in writing *Louis Armstrong's New Orleans*, had access to Armstrong's typescript for *Satchmo: My Life in New Orleans*.[6] In the typescript Armstrong identified the junk man as "Larenzo" who publicized "his wares with a real bugle."[7] Larenzo, Armstrong wrote, would play without a mouthpiece but could somehow "play a tune on the darn thing . . . he had soul too."[8] As Brothers comments, "Most writers have been more interested in lineages of great masters passing on genius, one to the other, than in the entanglement of jazz with everyday life."[9] According to the New Orleans pianist and composer Jelly Roll Morton, there were many traders who played on

Example 4: The Buttermilk Man's Cry, *Mellows* (1925)

toy horns: "The town was full of the best musicians you ever heard. Even the rags-bottles-and-bones men would advertise their trade by playing the blues on the wooden mouthpieces of Christmas horns—yes sir, play more low-down dirty blues on those Kress horns than the rest of the country ever thought of."[10]

According to Armstrong, "There was so much music when I was growing up in New Orleans that you couldn't help but hear it."[11] Among the street music that Armstrong heard was the banana man: "he'd be hollering 'Yellow ripe bananas, lady, 15 cents a bunch! Yellow ripe bananas!' Oh, yeah, always had music all around me of some kind."[12] Some of the songs and calls of the street peddlers of New Orleans were transcribed by R. Emmet Kennedy (1877–1941). One of the cries that Kennedy transcribed was that of the Buttermilk Man. Kennedy described this cry as "one of chromatic pleading, enticing you buy in spite of yourself."[13] This chromatic melody (see Ex. 4) would be difficult to explain using conventional music theory.[14] This melody has been transposed to C major, and, as can been seen, there are two notes that are not in the key: B♭ and G♯. Both of these notes require the use of an accidental, and therefore the song of the Buttermilk Man is not based on a simple diatonic European scale. However, an understanding of the voice leading in barbershop singing does offer an explanation for these chromatic intervals. This appears to be a barbershop practice of a minor third "swipe" in the baritone voice as described by James Earl Henry: "The swipe is a typical barbershop convention for coloring a major chord with a dominant seventh. The baritone leaves its position on the fifth and sounds the minor seventh."[15] If we consider the song of the Buttermilk Man to be a solo baritone voice, instead of coloring a chord the baritone voice sings a single melodic line. The third note of the phrase is a G (the fifth of a chord of C major). The long-held B♭ that follows is a minor third above the note of G and sounds the flatted (or minor) seventh relative to the tonic note of C. The note of B♭ is then, as Henry describes, "compelled to lead toward the submediant of the key," which in this key is A♮.[16] This in turn is compelled toward the flatted submediant (G♯/A♭) before a return to its usual position on the fifth of the key (G♮). Spaeth called this minor third swipe in the baritone voice a "blues progression."[17] Spaeth clearly recognized that there was a relationship between barbershop harmony and

Example 5: Spaeth's "Blues Progression," *Barber Shop Ballads* (1940)

blues tonality as he also provided a number of "blue and modern endings" in his second book on barbershop. As he acknowledged, these blue and modern endings were "breaking all the rules of conventional harmony."[18] Spaeth's "Blues Progression" is one of the simplest ways to crack up a chord because it only requires the baritone voice to change note. In this progression (see Ex. 5), the baritone voice starts on the fifth of the chord G.[19] It ascends a minor third to B♭ before descending through the major sixth (A) before a return to its starting note of G, in this case, missing out the flatted sixth (A♭). Spaeth also commented that "the *baritone* can sing a whole progression starting on his regular interval of a fifth . . . and working his way to the minor seventh and back again."[20] If a baritone singer sings a whole progression he would sing all of the chromatic intervals between the flatted (minor) seventh and the fifth inclusive of the flatted sixth, as the Buttermilk Man had done.

Another street trader's song that Kennedy transcribed was that of the Chimney Sweep. A similar understanding of barbershop voice leading may also explain his song. In the local dialect of New Orleans, chimney sweep is "rom-ma-nay" from the French word "ramoneur."[21] Superficially, Example 6 appears to be a conventional melody in the key of C major. But where this melody differs from conventional diatonic practice is in measure 6 were both the major and minor third appears. This is a characteristic of barbershop voice leading, but in this instance it is in the tenor voice. As Spaeth commented, "On the simpler endings the 'swipe' is achieved by a gentle slide upward on the part of the *baritone*, and downward on the part of the *tenor*." Because the tenor voice usually begins on the major third (E♮ in the key of C), if it descends it may sing either the minor third (E♭) or a note of D. All of these notes are found in this melody.

Example 6: The Chimney Sweep's Song, *Mellows* (1925)

Example 7: Charcoal Man's Cry, *Mellows* (1925)

At an early age, Louis Armstrong began work filling coal buckets on a round between Tulane and Rampart.[22] "The well trained mule would halt of its own accord, and Louis, standing on his chariot as proud as a Roman dictator, would chant between cupped hands: 'Stone *coal, ladies, five cents a water bucket!*'"[23] As Armstrong described it, "Hell, I was singing selling coal."[24] This profession was closely associated with the Charcoal Man, who visited twice a week to supply the washerwomen who do "de w'ite-folks washin' an' i'nin on de primisis." The Charcoal Man also had his own cry.[25] Example 7 has the same non-diatonic intervals found in earlier examples. There are the characteristic alternating thirds (E♮ and E♭ mm. 3 and 11) associated with the tenor voice. There is also the flatted sixth interval (A♭) in measure 6, a brief B♭ appoggiatura, and the flatted seventh in measure 9. These intervals are associated with swipes in the baritone voice.[26] Many of these notes are slurred, suggesting that, as in barbershop singing, this cry was sung with slides between the notes. The appearance of these flatted intervals, particularly thirds and sevenths, has been widely associated with blues tonality, and a number of New Orleans musicians recall that street traders played blues-inflected melodies. Johnny St. Cyr (born New Orleans 1889), who would play with Armstrong in the 1920s, remembered a waffle man that he called "Buglin' Sam" who played the blues.[27] This could be a reference to "Buglin' Sam" Dekemel, who has been described as a "New Orleans institution in the early twenties, when his colorful horse-drawn wagon would ply the streets of New Orleans selling hot waffles."[28] Ed "Montudi" Garland (born January 9, 1895) recalled that "a man who dealt in old bottles, rags, etc., had a tin horn on which he tried to play everything the bands played." John Wiggs (born New Orleans 1899) reported that when he was around seven or eight years old, the tinhorn men were "the most gifted people in the world for playing the blues."[29] While it is possible that Armstrong may have been influenced by the blues inflected melodies he heard all around him on bugles and tin horns, he also sang barbershop and knew this tonality well. Armstrong remembered the quartet "went all over and would put on long pants and go up to the district, and all the old gammies and pimps, they'd call us to sing. I used to sing tenor, had a real light voice, and played a little slide whistle, like a trombone. I could feel the positions so beautiful."[30] A sliding whistle would have been ideal for playing swipes as it could slide between notes. Conversely, Armstrong could have used his voice to imitate an instrument. Goffin relayed how Armstrong and his quartet sang "Jack Cary"; this was a tune that would become better known as "Tiger Rag."[31] "In this song Louis took the part of the clarinet by whistling through his fingers to the great amusement" of a small crowd of twenty or so passersby that stopped to listen as they performed outside of Maylie's Restaurant.[32] There are also reports of Armstrong's friends trying to play ragtime: "Redhead Happy beat on a dish pan for a drum while Georgie Gray was playing a crude tin horn."[33] It is possible that this process of applying vocal lines to toy and homemade instruments, or conversely imitating instruments with the voice, could explain the role that "spasm" bands had in the early years of jazz: blurring the line between vocal quartets and instrumental bands.

The most famous of the New Orleans spasm bands was the one led by Emile "Stale Bread" Lacoumbe (born 1885).[34] In one of the earliest books on jazz in the English language, *So This Is Jazz* (1926), the author Henry O. Osgood believed that the origins of jazz centered on "a colored newsboy known by the picturesque cognomen of Stale Bread."[35] Stale Bread, whose real name was Emile Lacoumbe, was actually white.[36] A good number of New Orleans musicians began playing in spasm bands or in bands that used homemade instruments. Albert Glenny (born March 25, 1870) made his first bass from a cheese box when he was around twelve years old.[37] Montudi Garland played homemade instruments at an even earlier age.[38] Edmond "Doc" Souchon, who would go on to write *New Orleans Jazz: A Family Album* in partnership with Al Rose, recalled from his youth a "spasm band of four colored boys" that played on the pier at Pass Christian. They played from seven to ten o'clock in the evening for two dollars. They played homemade guitar and bass and used tissue paper with a comb as a harmonica. Souchon said that they also sang. One repetitious song from their repertoire was "Yonder Come the Hoodoo Conductor Man."[39] Trumpeter "Kid" Thomas Valentine remembered how he started out on homemade instruments. They used a wooden box and some fishing line to make a bass, flutes made from bamboo, a zinc tub for a drum, and Thomas himself played a homemade kazoo "like a trumpet."[40] The ukulele player, Clarence "Little Dad" Vincent, remembered "field bands" using tin fifes, homemade basses, guitars, and tin pans.[41] Sidney Bechet, who would become one of the few New Orleans musicians who could claim to be the equal of Armstrong, started out with the René brothers (Joe and Henry) on homemade musical instruments.[42] Jelly Roll Morton began playing chair legs and a tin plate, and he remembered there were a lot of "bad bands" that were called "spasm" bands. These bands "played any job they could get in the streets. They did a lot of 'ad-libbing' in ragtime style with different solos in succession, not in regular routine, but just as one guy would get tired and let another musician have the lead."[43] Preston Jackson (born circa 1902) bragged about hanging out as a teenager "listening to a band and then having whistling contests among his friends the next day in an attempt to duplicate the event. 'I could whistle anything anyone played.'"[44] Some of the white musicians also started out using homemade instruments. Papa Jack Laine organized many of the early white jazz bands in New Orleans. Although he had a proper field drum himself, he remembered that the other kids had cane flutes that their fathers had made and homemade stringed instruments before they graduated to secondhand instruments.[45]

Another musical feature on the streets of New Orleans were the bands. The most famous was the band led by Charles "Buddy" Bolden. It is doubtful that Armstrong ever heard Buddy Bolden play. Bolden was committed to an insane asylum in June 1907, and given Armstrong's age, and because Bolden played mostly in bars and saloons, there would have been few opportunities for Armstrong to have heard him. Armstrong's claim falls well short of a positive sighting: "When I was about 4 or 5, still wearing dresses, I lived with my mother in Jane Alley . . . And right in the middle of that on Perdido Street was Funky Butt Hall . . . If I ever heard Buddy Bolden play the cornet, I figure that's when."[46] Edmund Wise (born 1888) was a friend of Buddy Bolden who remembered that Bolden's trombone player, Willie Cornish, sang in a barroom quartet. He recalled, "You see, in them days, there used to be quartets and all like that, you know. Well just like all them fellows would be singing, 'cause he had Cornish was playin' the trambone [sic] with him, he could sing, well they'd be singing around them bar rooms, well, just this was what they was singin.'" He also recalled Bolden's guitarist Brock Mumford singing too: "Mumford 'n them, well just what they was singing, Buddy Bolden going to play it . . . Well if they'd sing it right, well, he'd learn how to play it right . . . See, that's the parts he played it right."[47] What Wise had witnessed was the transformation of the lines sung by a quartet being played on Buddy Bolden's cornet and the process by which barbershop quartet singing became jazz.

Bolden and his band were not alone in developing jazz using the principles employed by a singing quartet. Louis Keppard (born 1888) explained how a brass band would organize. One band member "would give us an idea, and we would memorize [i.e., harmonize] [sic] behind them. Of course, we could only do that because we could chord with one another. That's what made it sound good; we'd organize like a quartet, like about six or five or four mens. Bass, baritone and alto. Everybody got their own parts."[48]

The tonality of the blues, and the practice of barbershop quartet singing, had by the late nineteenth century become part of a common heritage shared by street traders, quartet singers, spasm bands, vaudeville minstrels, ragtime bands, and professional arrangers of sheet music of tunes such as "Swanee River." Male quartets and singing families were a mainstay of minstrelsy and vaudeville for both black and white performers in the late nineteenth century.[49] Recordings of these quartets survive from the 1890s and confirm how widespread the practice was.[50] Many of the musicians who would go on to become prominent jazz players began their musical apprenticeships in spasm bands and informal quartets. The distinction was not clear-cut. Some spasm bands played instruments and sang; some quartets used instruments like slide-whistles as well as singing; some singers imitated the sounds of instruments with their voices and whistled too. Many of the songs they sang and attempted to play on their homemade instruments would have been published as sheet music. Some of these songs would have been arranged specifically for quartets to sing.

But it was not from sheet music that Louis Armstrong and his contemporaries learned these songs and their harmony parts. As Armstrong remembered it, "We sang the new jazz songs, and got to learn how to sing them 'hot.'"[51] To learn to sing or play these songs "hot," the lead singer, in the case of a quartet, or the lead instrumentalist (usually a violinist) in the case of a spasm band, need only pick off the melody, and the others could find their parts by experimentation. This is the same process that barbershop quartets use. What the other voices (or instruments) need to do is find a suitable harmony part. Given the propensity of the tenor voice to descend from the major third to the minor third of the tonic chord, it is almost inevitable that the tenor singer (or the instrumentalist who takes this role) will sing or play a blue note melody. Given the tendency of the baritone voice to perform a minor third swipe, it is also almost inevitable that this voice, or instrument, will sound a flatted seventh, and other intervals that are associated with the "hot" tonality of the blues and jazz. Armstrong and his friends were immersed in this culture. But no one could have known at the time how Armstrong and his contemporaries would use this musical heritage to transform popular music.

CHAPTER 4

CHURCH IS WHERE "I ACQUIRED MY SINGING TACTICS"

MANY NEW ORLEANS MUSICIANS DREW A CLEAR DISTINCTION BETWEEN religious and popular music. Ann Cook, a blues singer, remembered as one of the "toughest sporting women in the District" and "a hustling woman," was in later life "a singer and church worker" who would not sing the blues.[1] Another singer, Lizzie Miles, gave up singing in later years to devote her time to the church, and she turned down an opportunity to sing ragtime songs on a national television program.[2] Sister Berenice Phillips (born 1894) remembered in her youth "singing concerts" in church including spirituals such as "Go Down, Moses," "Wade in the Water," and a song that she would later record: "I Couldn't Hear Nobody Pray."[3] She said that at this time [church] people were not able to sing "sinful songs," and she was concerned that in her later years love songs and religious music was all "gumboed up together."[4]

Singers often made a distinction between the lyrics of popular songs and hymns, but in terms of the music there was less of a distinction. Joe René, the brother of Henry "Kid" René, who was at the Waifs' Home with Armstrong, observed that "Baptists all sing in a blues style."[5] Guitarist and banjo player Johnny St. Cyr, who played with Armstrong in the 1920s, made a similar observation saying that "Baptists had the same rhythm and style as the blues."[6] Steve Angrum believed "all the church hymns come from blues."[7] Conversely, jazz musicians were influenced by church songs. Joe Oliver, whom Armstrong idolized, used church music in some of his compositions. Oliver's widow, Stella, said, "Joe didn't belong to any church, but his parents were Baptist, his father being a Baptist preacher. Joe was fond of the hymns, however, and joking, would say he would take some of the hymns and make up some songs."[8] An example of a religious song used by Oliver is "The Holy City" (1892), quoted in "Chimes Blues" (1923) and "Canal Street Blues" (1923).[9] Like many of her generation, Stella objected to this practice.[10]

The first African American Baptist church in New Orleans was founded in 1826.[11] Although from the late 1850s a city ordinance technically made all black religious organization unlawful, by 1883 black churches in Louisiana had around seventy thousand members attending some five hundred Baptist churches.[12] An early description of singing at the African Baptist Church in Port Royal, South Carolina, in 1863 commented on a performance of a published hymn with "crooks, turns, slurs, and appoggiaturas, not to be found in any printed copy."[13] Recollections of singing in black Baptist churches in New Orleans also confirm the improvised nature of the singing and point toward a similarity with early jazz. While not specifically citing Baptist churches, Steve Brown (a white bass player from New Orleans, born in 1890) remembered, "For harmony, we used to love to pass by these Negro churches and hear 'em sing."[14] Buddy Bolden is also believed to have "got most of" his tunes from "the Holy Roller church."[15] The Holy Roller churches were also not Baptist. The New Orleans cornet player Mutt Carey remembered, "That music was swinging all the way back in Bolden's time and before him in the Holy Roller churches he got it from. You know, all those churches, like Baptist and Methodist, got hot now and then—but the Holy Rollers were hot all the time."[16] The guitarist Bud Scott believed that it was through going to church each Sunday that Bolden "got his idea of jazz music."[17] Edward "Kid" Ory, who would be one of the first bandleaders to employ Armstrong, remembered some churches not only sang but used instruments: "Oh yeah, they had drums and piano while they sang, clapping their hands. Even the Baptist Church had it. They'd have guests; invite a trumpet player, trombone player to come play with them . . . They'd get to swing you know."[18]

Armstrong's earliest recollection of going to church was "Elder Cozy's" church just across the road from where he lived.[19] He recalled:

> Elder Cozy started to get warmed up and then he hit his stride. It was not long before he had the whole church rocking. Mama got so happy and so excited that she knocked me off the bench as she shouted and swayed back and forth. She was a stout woman and she became so excited that it took six of the strongest brothers to grab hold of her and pacify her.[20]

It is likely that "Elder Cozy" is the Rev. William M. Cosey. He is listed as the pastor of the Mt. Zion Baptist Church at 512 Howard (now LaSalle) Street in 1915.[21] Inspired by this stout preacher from Natchez, Mississippi, Armstrong remembered, "mama really got religion. I saw her baptized in the Mississippi where she was ducked in the water so many times that I thought she was going to be drowned. The baptism worked: Mayann kept her religion."[22] Armstrong's sister, Mama Lucy, unlike her mother, was baptized in Mt. Zion Church.[23]

In another account of being in church as a boy, Armstrong described a similar scene of impassioned worship and singing.

> My Mother used to take me to 'Church with her, and the Reverend ('Preacher that is') used to '*lead off* one' of those 'good *ol* good '*Hymns*. And before you realized it—the 'whole' Congregation would be "*Wailing*—'Singing like 'mad and 'sound so 'beautiful. 'I' being a little boy that would "Dig" 'Everything and 'everybody, I'd have myself a 'Ball in 'Church.[24]

We do not know exactly what songs Armstrong sang in church, only that his "heart went into every hymn."[25] But because we know it was a Baptist church, we do have an indication of the type of songs he is likely to have sung. R. Emmet Kennedy, who as an adult would transcribe New Orleans street songs, as a child began transcribing African American spirituals and hymns. Kennedy was of Irish descent and born on January 11, 1877, on 2nd Street in Gretna, Louisiana.[26] The family moved to 8th Street Corner shortly after Emmet's birth in the center of the East Green area of Gretna, a predominantly African American community.[27] At the back of the house was the New Hope Baptist Church on 7th Street, attended by the woman who cooked and cleaned for his family, known to Kennedy as Aunt Julie Sparks. Her two sons Sammy and Johnny were Kennedy's childhood playmates and his next-door neighbors. Kennedy remembered:

> Nothing could be more appropriate for the musical setting of my first heard Negro spirituals sung *ensemble* than Sunday morning at Putney Ward's New Hope Baptist Church in Gretna. The least important though most intrusive figure is a curious, impatient little boy standing on a high-chair in the kitchen door and looking out over a long stretch of back-yard, beyond which stands the little old church. The back window of the church is open, and through it the little boy is eagerly watching his playmates, Sammy and Johnny, who have gone to Sunday school with their mother. Aunt Julie is standing near the open window with her two sons, and their voices ring out with welling gladness as they sing the triumphant "shout" called, "Free At Last."[28]

Kennedy would attempt to sing along and began to write down the songs he heard. Living in daily contact with African Americans, his transcriptions provide a unique record of African American life in and around New Orleans when Louis Armstrong was a boy. Not only did Kennedy transcribe the songs: he also performed them. An early example of Kennedy singing the songs he had known since childhood was a concert of the Algiers Musical Society on Monday, November 12, 1906, where "Mr. R. Emmet Kennedy, Composer and Pianist, of Gretna, La.," would be accompanied by "Miss Elinor Hardy, Soprano, also of Gretna, La.," and the New Orleans tenor "Mr. M. Donellan" to perform "several genuine negro hymns."[29] According to the program, the event took place because "There has been much discussion in the music journals of late as to the influence that negro music (that is, the true melodies of the negro race in this country, as handed down from slavery times) will have on the 'classical' music of America."[30] A journal article that had been influential in this debate was "Negro Melodies" published in *Music* in 1892. It is likely that this was one of the sources that Dvořák consulted for his *New World Symphony* (1893).[31] In an article that appeared in the *New York Herald* on May 21, 1893, titled "The Real Value of Negro Melodies," Dvořák is attributed as saying:

> In the Negro melodies of America I discover all that is needed for a great and noble school of music. They are pathetic, tender, passionate, melancholy, solemn, religious, bold, merry, gay, or what you will. It is music that suits itself to any mood or purpose. There is nothing in the whole range of composition that cannot be supplied with themes from this source.[32]

This, in turn, generated much discussion about the merit of "Negro Melodies" as the basis for a new school of musical composition. At the time, Kennedy was one of the few white people who knew this music intimately and was able to transcribe what he heard. But Kennedy went further: he performed the songs in dialect as closely as he was able to the original versions. At the 1906 concert, he performed among some secular songs, the spirituals "Got a Home in De Rock," "Oh! Angel," and "His Trouble So Hard." At a later concert on April 30, 1907 of the Society he performed "Who Dat Callin' Me Yonder?" with full chorus.[33]

In 1910, Kennedy published two books using his Celtic name, Robard Emmet Ua Cinneidig. The first of these books was published in January: a small book of twelve Irish poems *The Songs of Aengus* that Kennedy had printed at Myers' Printing House Ltd., in New Orleans.[34] His second book of 1910, *Remnants of Noah's Ham (According to Genesis)*—privately printed with original photographs by the author—was intended to provide "little sketches of negro life meant to show the better side of negro nature, in contra-distinction to the rough, belligerent side which is familiar to many that have seen the portrayals of the minstrel platform, and to many more who have listened to the modern 'coon song' melodies that have taken so strong a hold on the general public."[35] In 1925 he published *Mellows: A Chronicle of Unknown Singers*. The book contained six "Folk-Songs"; of these four were fully harmonized; six "Street Cries of New Orleans," five "Work Songs," and twenty-eight spirituals of which twenty were harmonized.[36] Kennedy claimed:

> In making the settings of these songs and spirituals it is my desire to give faithful transcriptions as my memory recorded the singing of the Negroes in my native town. Some of them were taken down at first hearing, sometimes with slight variations if sung by more than one singer. I have tried to follow as closely as I know how the intuitive harmonies and instinctive rhythmic peculiarities of these musical people, and have tried to suggest in the accompaniments the primitive, rudimental element so marked in all their productions.[37]

One of the earliest songs that Kennedy heard was "Rock Mount Sinai." Kennedy remembered, "Aunt Julie's voice was a warm, colorful mezzo with the extraordinary range peculiar to her race. I have known passers-by to stop outside her gate and listen to her singing, so enthralled were they by its arresting sweetness and emotional depth."[38]

Very few transcriptions of African American song were made until well into the twentieth century. We know from reports of observers that African Americans sang in three- or four-part harmony in the nineteenth century.[39] An account from 1834 made reference to "the songs of Zion . . . caroled in tones of sweetest melody by many co-mingled voices, when native harmony outvies [sic] instructed skill."[40] These songs, we are told, were "barbarously harmonious" with "wild, strange, irregular harmony."[41] The earliest large-scale collection of *Slave Songs of the United States* (1867) only reproduced the melody. As William Allen conceded in the preface, "the intonation and variation of even one singer cannot be reproduced on paper. I despair of conveying any notion of the effect of a number singing together"; therefore, "we have thought it best to print only the melody; what appears only in some places as harmony is really variations in single notes."[42] Given the scarcity

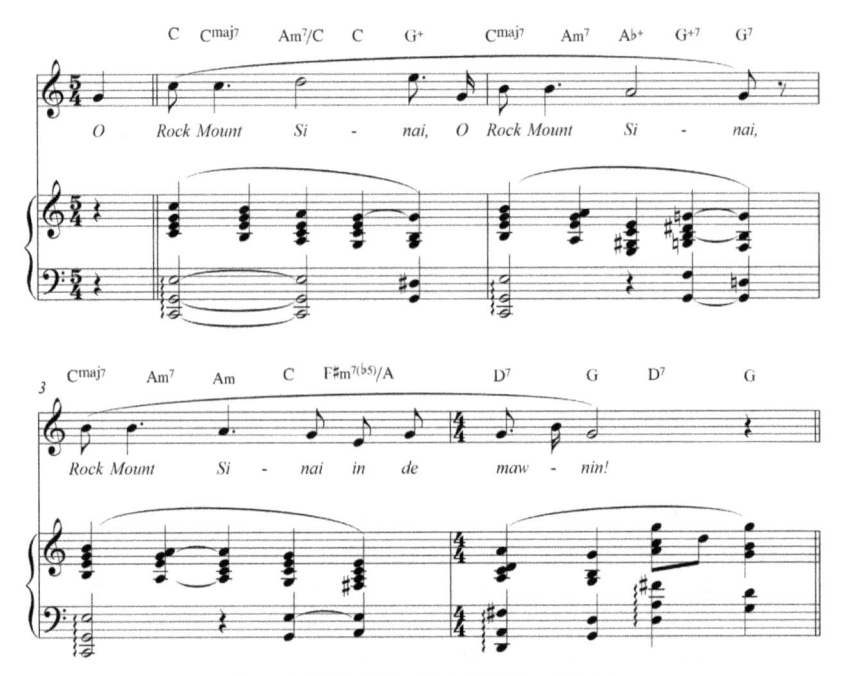

Example 8: "Rock Mount Sinai," *Mellows* (1925)

of reliable transcriptions of harmonized African American song, Kennedy's harmonized spirituals provide a rare, partial insight into nineteenth- and early twentieth-century African American harmonic practice.

The melody of "Rock Mount Sinai" (see Ex. 8) and many of the other spirituals Kennedy published had simple diatonic melodies. This was typical of the majority of spirituals that had been transcribed. Henry Edward Krehbiel published in 1914 an analysis of the melodies of 527 African American spirituals and folksongs that he and other folklorists had collected. Of this total, 331 were found to be in an "Ordinary Major" scale. The next largest group was 111 "Pentatonic" songs: these songs had just five notes of the diatonic scale. Then there were seventy-eight melodies that were "Major without seventh." Next in descending order were sixty-two "Ordinary Minor" melodies. A further forty-five melodies were described as "Major without fourth." Thirty-four were "Minor without sixth," and nineteen were in the harmonic minor scale: "Minor with raised seventh (leading-tone)."[43] What unites all of these melodies is that they are based on the same notes and scales that are found in European music making. If an arranger of spirituals was required to produce a piano accompaniment for any of these spirituals, European harmony could be employed. The only melodies that Krehbiel analyzed that were incompatible with European harmony were twenty-three described as "Mixed and vague," twenty were "Major with flatted seventh," and eight that were "Minor with raised sixth."[44] It follows from this that the vast majority of African American folksongs and spirituals could readily be harmonized using European conventions. What seems initially surprising is that so few of these melodies contained what we would today call blue notes. Just twenty-three were described as mix and vague and therefore could contain both the major and minor thirds; around the same number had the flatted seventh: a feature considered one of the hallmarks of African American song.

In "Rock Mount Sinai" (see Ex. 8), although the melody is in the key of C major and can be notated without the need for accidentals, the harmony contains a good number of accidentals and therefore has what music theorists describe as chromatic harmony. While some nineteenth-century European composers had experimented with chromatic harmony, they had done so based on a thorough grounding in European harmony and counterpoint. The question that Kennedy's transcriptions raise is, how could African Americans produce harmony of the complexity of "Rock Mount Sinai" with little or no musical training? How could the congregation of the New Hope Baptist Church produce three, four, or sometimes five-part harmonies without arrangements? One explanation that was advanced at the time was what could be described as the happy accident theory. An early twentieth-century observer, H. L. Mencken, displaying a prejudice that was extreme even by the standards of his own time, argued, "Savages know nothing of the modes—or keys—that white men use. They see nothing wrong about inserting a glaring B flat or C sharp into the key of C major. They did this in many of the spirituals, and sometimes the effect was extraordinarily brilliant and thrilling." Mencken believed that African Americans had used European religious songs and "improved the harmonies of the hymns for much the same reason. That is, they wandered into 'errors' because they knew no better—and the errors turned out to be lush and lovely."[45] The difficulty with this theory is that one would expect to find a variety of "errors" and all the chromatic intervals would appear with equal frequency. In fact, this is not the case. There is a particular tendency to sing the flatted third and the flatted seventh in African American song. To explain this, André Hodeir has suggested, "these blue notes resulted from the difficulty experienced by the Negro when the hymns taught him by the missionaries made him sing the third and seventh degrees of the scale used in European music, since these degrees do not occur in the primitive five-tone scale."[46] This explanation is also problematic. The melody of "Rock Mount Sinai" contains both the major third and the major seventh, and it is evident from this that singers at the New Hope Baptist church could sing these intervals with ease if they chose to do so. As is often the case in the spirituals that Kennedy transcribed, the melody is diatonic but there are both major and minor thirds in the harmony part. Other theorists have addressed this question and concluded that African Americans "probably saw little distinction between major and minor modes and used the major and minor thirds interchangeably."[47]

Whatever the merit of this analysis, the point remains: attempts to explain the tonality of African American music using European concepts of scales and modes are fraught with difficulties, and these difficulties have not been resolved after more than a century of analysis and scholarship. An understanding of barbershop harmony does, however, explain the appearance of both minor and major thirds in African American song. A comparison of the barbershop harmonization of "Swanee River" (see Ex. 3) with "Rock Mount Sinai" (see Ex. 8) is informative. There is a similar harmonic rhythm where chords change on each note of the melody; there is the same tendency for chords to include the tonic note of C; even some of the more unusual chords ($A^\flat$ augmented and $F^\sharp$ minor seventh with flatted fifth, for example) are found in both arrangements. The reason for this is that both barbershop harmony and the harmonization of African American spirituals and hymns—as they were actually performed—were rooted in the same musical practices and tradition. The relationship between melody and harmony in African American song was understood by some contemporaneous commentators. Alain Locke observed, "Over-emphasize the melodic elements of the spiritual, and you get a sentimental ballad à la Stephen Foster. Stress the harmony and you get a cloying glee or 'barber-shop' chorus. . . . It is only in a subtle fusion of these elements that the genuine folk spiritual exists or can be recaptured."[48]

It is clear that Armstrong was part of a culture where music was all around him. He heard street songs of the peddlers and became a coal seller himself; he sang with a street quartet—one among a number of informal quartets and spasm bands on the streets of New Orleans. He sang in church where he did "a whole lot of singing" and it was there that he claimed to have acquired his "singing tactics."[49] All of the music that he heard around him was rooted in an African American harmonic practice of which barbershop harmony is one manifestation. These harmonic practices were evident in spirituals, in the street songs of traders, in quartet singing, spasm bands, and increasingly applied in early jazz bands.

CHAPTER 5

"WHEN I WAS AT SCHOOL, I PLAYED ALL CLASSICAL MUSIC"

THE ABIJAH FISK SCHOOL THAT ARMSTRONG ATTENDED WAS SITUATED close to his home and the Mt. Zion Baptist Church. Abijah Fisk was a rich coffee merchant who had an interest in education and who donated six hundred volumes of books to the city library.[1] In Armstrong's time at the school, Arthur P. Williams was the principal. Born Norwich, Connecticut, in March 1846, Williams came to New Orleans in 1864. Music was an important part of the Fisk curriculum. Williams conducted and performed in concerts and taught "piano, organ, and voice."[2] In the years before Armstrong attended the school, two of its teachers were musicians who performed in New Orleans dance orchestras including the John Robichaux Orchestra: James Williams MacNeal (born New Orleans December 23, 1879), who was vice principal of Fisk School from 1900–1903; and his brother, Wendell Phillips MacNeal (born October 7, 1878), appointed a teacher at Fisk School in November 1898. Wendell toured with Prof. W. J. Nickerson's Orchestra in 1899, and he resigned from Fisk School in 1900.[3] Although the brothers had no direct influence on Armstrong, they instilled an institutional bias toward music education at the school.

We do not know when Louis Armstrong began his schooling, but we know from the 1910 census that he was at school in that year.[4] The census also records that at this time he could not read or write. The likelihood is that he was still in the first or second grade at this time. Although his recollection may be tinged with a little boastfulness, Armstrong remembered, "Before I knew it I was in the second grade, reading newspapers for the older folk that helped raise me in my neighborhood."[5] Certainly at some point after 1910 he became literate. Throughout his life, he was committed to "swinging a lot of type writing": sending countless letters to fans, world leaders, and jazz writers.[6]

These letters contain his own personalized style of punctuation—frequently using ellipses instead of periods—he also used capital letters to express emphasis. He did sometimes use phonetic spellings to express colloquial speech in his writing, but he was probably concerned to spell in a conventional way at other times. This may explain why he carried a dictionary with him when he was on tour.[7] Unconventional as his writing style was, it was far from the product of a poor education. The Abijah Fisk School, and likely the Waifs' Home too, gave him a good basic grounding in literacy. But in 1910 he was just beginning to learn to read and write, and this argues for Armstrong not starting school until around 1908, because, he recalled, "I went only to *Fifth* Grade because I had to *work* along with my schooling."[8] In 1909 a sixth grade was added in segregated public schools in New Orleans, and later in 1913 this was extended to include a seventh grade.[9] We can be sure that Armstrong's last possible term at Fisk School was the autumn of 1912, because he was sentenced to the Colored Waifs' home for eighteen months in January 1913. While it is possible that he had left school before the end of 1912, if he was in fifth grade at this time, and he had advanced a grade each year, he would have started his schooling in 1908.

Armstrong's other recollections of his school days give us more information about his education. Armstrong remembered, "Old Mrs. Martin was the caretaker of the Fisk School."[10] This was Carmelite Martin, who lived at 515 Franklin Street with her large family.[11] Armstrong continued, "Two of the boys turned out to be good and real popular musicians."[12] These were the drummer Henry Martin and his brother "Kootchy" [sic] who played piano and guitar.[13] Both musicians were somewhat older than Armstrong.[14] Henry Martin (born June 1892) was late to enter education.[15] He is listed among the 1904–1905 students of Fisk School to receive honors in the first grade.[16] Although Henry could not have been in the same grade as Armstrong, his sister Orleania very likely was in Armstrong's class. According to Armstrong, Carmelite also had three "beautiful daughters with light skin of the Creole type: Orleania, Alice and Wilhelmina."[17] Orleania, who was around the same age as Louis, would take his hand after school—the school day ended at 2:30 p.m.—"and they would go off together to look at the good things displayed in Segretta's window."[18] But Louis had a crush on her older sister Wilhelmina. A lack of confidence, and probably the fact that she was four years older than him, prevented Louis from ever letting her know that he was in love with her.[19] In later years he regretted his lack of courage. He reflected mournfully, "the poor child died before I got up the nerve to tell her."[20]

Armstrong did not give much indication of what he learned in school about music, but he did say: "When I was at school, I played all classical music. And when I was in the orphanage we played duets and that was their music. So that instills the soul in you, you know. Liszt, Bach, Rachmaninov, Gustav Mahler, and Haydn."[21] While it is clear from other accounts that he played music at the Waifs' Home, it is unlikely that he *played* anything while he was at Fisk because the music curriculum was entirely vocal. In 1902 the New Orleans Public School Board issued the *Manual of Music Work* for use in New Orleans public schools.[22] The manual advised teachers on what to teach and how to teach music through singing. There was no instrumental music in any of the grades.

First grade teachers were advised to ensure that a pupil's "mouth is well open, and the tones soft and true."[23] The manual continues, "Teach the scales as a song, using 'la' or 'loo.' Then teach the name of each tone—Do, Re, Mi, etc."[24] Using this system, each pitch of the major scale is ascribed a syllable. The advantage of this system is that the tonic note of any key is always called "Do"; the next note higher up the scale (the supertonic/major second) is always "Re"; the next note (the mediant/major third) is "Mi." This system is not concerned with absolute pitch, but rather with relative pitch: "Re" is always two semitones higher than "Do," "Mi" is always two semitones higher than "Re," the next note "Fa" is always a single semitone higher than "Mi," and so on. Using this system Armstrong would have learned to sing a major scale starting on any note. The manual was accompanied by charts that were used in the classroom; none of these are known to have survived. Once the children had mastered singing the major scale using this solfeggio system, the manual instructed, "Open the chart and show the representations on the scale of the staff."[25] Basic teaching in rhythm was also given in the first half term: "Teach the meaning of the bar, measure, beat and accent, and begin the practice of beating time. Allow the children to extend the right arm upon the desk, and use the index finger for marking time. . . . Call attention to the exercises that begin with the weak beat, and those that begin with the strong beat."[26]

In the second half-term solfeggio singing was again drilled into the students.

> Begin here a systematic study of the tones of the scale. Sing softly at first, dwelling on the tones to impress the effect on the mind. Apply this drill to other scales until the child can return with ease and accuracy from any tone of the scale to Do—(Tonic); to Si—(Leading Tone); to

Sol—(Dominant) and to Fa—(Sub-dominant). . . . The greater part of the work in this grade should be rote-singing. Songs with strong rhythm should be selected, to impress accent. Always prepare the class with songs appropriate to the seasons and special occasions. Insist upon soft singing.[27]

The second year of music education largely reinforced the first. Teachers were advised, "Scale practice cannot be over-estimated, so drill on the scales, first with the names of the tones—Do, Re, Mi, etc., then with "loo," "coo" or "mo," until the children can sing freely, lightly and softly in all the scale indicated in the chart."[28] At this early stage, "a few essential points in theory" were also taught, and written work was required that included the use of measures and clefs.[29] This was a basic preparation that every school child in the New Orleans school system could have expected to receive for at least half an hour every day while they were in their first two years of schooling.

In the third year of schooling pupils were introduced to the concept of keys and key signatures, and instructed that the "'Do' of any scale is the key-note, and that the position of 'Do' on the staff determines the number of sharps or flats used in the signature."[30] "The chart for the third year of music study also introduced "the first idea of the effect of the minor scale."[31] The teaching of minor scales in the third year required the study of chromatic notes including the "flat-seven." Teachers were advised to "drill carefully on this new idea."[32] It seems that Armstrong learned these lessons well. When he was performing with Zilner Randolph in the early 1930s, Randolph believed that Armstrong could not read music. "Randolph was astonished when he put a new and challenging arrangement in front of Armstrong, who promptly sang it, complete with solfège syllables, flawlessly and effortlessly."[33]

During the first spring and summer at school, Armstrong would probably have learned to sing "Welcome Little Robin" by Eleanor Smith; "The Day is Bright and Sunny" by C. A. Kern; "Singing" by R. T. Stevenson; and "The Little Horsemen" by Amalie Felsthensal and other seasonal songs.[34] Songs considered appropriate for the autumn were "Bye-lo Land" by Chas. E. Boyd, and "The Huntsman," arranged by J. A. Brahms.[35] In the winter "The Song of the Rain" by Walker and Jenks, "Why Bells for Christmas Ring" by Eugene Field, and "Fire Stories" by Emma Mundella would likely have been among the selections.[36]

With the publication of *The Eleanor Smith Music Course* in 1908, the New Orleans public school system was able to broaden the range of songs taught in the early years of schooling.[37] The intention of this book was to "present music that shall assist in the best technical and artistic training possible to young people."[38] The Orleans Parish School Board would have found the book in accord with its existing syllabus as the songs were "designed for rote singing ... which will help to improve the intonation and perfect the rhythmic sense of the children, besides serving as material for reading and writing music."[39] The collected songs were in three sections. The first section consisted of songs that were sung in unison and unaccompanied. These songs were sung with the words on the down beat with very little rhythmic variation. The second part consisted of "rote songs for study and practice." These songs were also sung in unison and unaccompanied, but they were rhythmically slightly more varied. Part three were the "rote songs with accompaniment." Again, there was no part singing: all were sung in unison. With only a handful of exceptions, they had diatonic melodies and accompaniments. Some of the songs were composed by Eleanor Smith or adapted from songs by other composers. There were also a good number of nursery rhymes, cradle songs, and folksongs from around the world. There was a Chinese nursery rhyme, a Silesian folksong, a Russian and a Swedish tune, Bavarian cradle songs, a Norwegian nursery rhyme and a folksong, a Bohemian folksong, French folksongs and nursery songs, and English folksongs. Well represented among this international selection of songs were those adapted from German composers, and along with German folksongs, nursery songs, and cradle songs was "He Who Would a Soldier Be." Long after Armstrong left school, and as war ended in Europe, it was the German selections that brought to an end the use of the *Eleanor Smith Music Course: Book 1*, in the New Orleans public school system.[40]

Louis Armstrong received, as far as we can tell, the type of school musical education that was typical for his contemporaries. This was a music education based entirely on singing. He was taught to sing in unison using the solfeggio system of note identification. This system develops a strong sense of relative pitch, and this method can be used as a way to find suitable harmony notes—if Armstrong wanted to find the major third note above the melody note (as he would do singing tenor with a barbershop quartet), all he had to do was to think of the melody note as "Do" and sing the appropriate "Mi." It is possible that he may have learned a little of European part singing. It is claimed that in the third and fourth grades students were introduced to two-part singing, and then three-part singing in the fifth grade.[41] What his musical education would probably not have done was to prepare him in any way to play a musical instrument. As was typical at the time, the ability to sing music was considered a prerequisite for the ability to play music on an instrument. This was a lesson that Armstrong learned well. As fellow New

Orleans trumpeter Mutt Carey observed, "Louis sings like he plays. I think Louis proves the idea and theory which holds if you can't sing it, you can't play it. When I'm improvising, I'm singing in my mind. I sing what I feel and then try to reproduce it on the horn."[42]

CHAPTER 6

"MY BRAZILIAN BEAUTY"

ARMSTRONG SPENT HIS EARLY LIFE NOT ONLY SINGING IN CHURCH AND attending school but also getting into trouble on the streets. Unless there were earlier incidents, his first brush with the New Orleans Police Department is recorded in a newspaper article in the *New Orleans Daily Item* July 19, 1906, reporting that Louis Armstrong appeared before Judge A. M. Ancoin in the Second City Criminal Court charged with petty larceny. It is likely that his age at the time and the fact that the charge was not that serious were contributing factors to his discharge.[1] In 1910 he was in trouble again, arrested between Gravier Street and Tulane Avenue on October 21 among a number of boys "for being dangerous and suspicious characters."[2] The charge of being "dangerous and suspicious" was legislation that enabled the New Orleans Police Department to arrest anyone regardless of whether or not an actual crime had been committed. A brief article appeared the following day describing a "Juvenile Round-Up" of "quite a number of boys. No less than eight being brought to Juvenile Court."[3] These included:

> Clarence Roberts, of no. 941 St. Mary Street, and John Centilivere, of St. Ferdinand and Chartres Street by patrolman Mike Sansovich, while Detectives Charles Mellon, William Kennedy, John Dantonio, and Patrolman Anthony Sabrier arrested Henry Smith, of Lafayette and Fulton; James Kent, of 338 Saratoga Street; Archie Anderson, of 631 Dryades Street; Willie Telfry, of 416 S. Franklin Street; Louis Armstrong, of Perdido, between Liberty and Franklin Streets, and Eddie Moore, of Liberty, between Gravier and Perdido Streets.[4]

The court was not as lenient on Armstrong as it had been at his previous appearance, and on this occasion, he was remanded to the Waifs' Home. In recently found notes from the Waifs' Home of October 21, 1910, Armstrong is recorded as being 9 years old and among the new arrivals. He was subsequently discharged on November 8, 1910, to an aunt pending trial.[5] Armstrong made no mention of this brief period of detention in the Waifs' Home in any of his autobiographies, saying he had "no idea what a Waifs' Home was" when he was sentenced in 1913.[6]

One incident that went unreported in the press was a fight that Armstrong was involved in that was broken up by Patrolman Harry Gregson. The officer recognized Armstrong as someone who sang in a street quartet. Gregson had sung with Stale Bread's Spasm Band. In his youth, Gregson had "crooned the popular songs of the day through a piece of gas pipe, since he couldn't afford a proper megaphone."[7] These songs were performed by Gregson either solo or in chorus with the other members of the Spasm Band.[8] One song Gregson remembered as enticing tips from the prostitutes of Storyville was "I've Got a Girl in the White Folks' Garden."[9] Armstrong told him that he knew this song, and Gregson complimented Armstrong that "the song of 1895 was still being performed by the youth."[10]

Researchers have long suspected that Armstrong had been in trouble from an early age because the report of his arrest on New Year's Eve in 1913 referred to him as "an old offender." As part of its reporting on the New Year festivities, the January 2, 1913, edition of the *New Orleans Times-Democrat* carried a story "Few Juveniles Arrested." The paper reported, "Very few arrests of minors were made Tuesday, and the bookings in the Juvenile Court are not more than the average. . . . The most serious case was that of Louis Armstrong, a twelve-year-old negro, who discharged a revolver at Rampart and Perdido Streets. Being an old offender, he was sent to the negro Waifs' Home. The other boys were paroled."[11] Armstrong was not as unfamiliar with the Juvenile Court or the Waifs' Home in 1913 as he would claim throughout his life.

On many occasions, Louis Armstrong told the story of what happened to him on New Year's Eve of 1913, and, as was often the case with Armstrong, through the telling and re-telling, his accounts became standardized into a kind of routine. For this reason, it is reasonable to question Armstrong's accounts of this event and others. Once he had told a story in a particular way, he was apt to continue to repeat the story time and again even if it was a romanticized version of events. Within these stories he often repeated apparently inconsequential detail. One piece of detail he repeated on a number of occasions was that he had been singing "My Brazilian Beauty" with his quartet at the time of his arrest. In a Heritage TV program of August 2, 1960, Robert McCully and Adam Lynch interviewed Armstrong. In the interview, Armstrong reiterated the important role that the church had played in developing his singing talent: "At the age of twelve, I was singing in a quartet; I always could sing, and my mother always took my sister and I to church."[12] He then went on to talk about singing in the quartet saying, "So quite naturally, I always could sing, and I was singing tenor at the time... and we'd go around the gamblers and the hustlers and pass our hat, you know, and sing."[13] Armstrong was proud that he could contribute to his family through singing. He told his interviewers he could "bring a dollar and a half of his take home that was divided up. That was a lot of money. I could help my sister and my mother, and myself, to pay rent and have a new shirt, a new pair of shoes, you know."[14] Armstrong was asked, "Did the kids you played with think that you were about the best that they'd heard?" Armstrong replied, "Well, you know, we weren't thinking about who was the best at anything in those days, we was just glad we could sing together and sound so good."[15] The discussion then turned to the events of New Year's Eve 1913. Armstrong continued:

> So when I got to the age where I noticed everybody celebrating, Christmas and New Year's Eve with pistols, Roman candles, shot guns, cannons, anything they got in their possession. They shoot it up in the air, but I didn't know that there was a law against it. See, you could get away with it alright, see. When I came on and fired my stepfather's old [musket?] 38 gun—it only had blanks in it—mama kept on hiding it, but I'd find it, I had this in my bosom one night and we was going down Rampart Street singing,
>
> *My Brazilian Beauty,*
>
> And that was an early tune.
>
> [sings] *Over the Amazon,*
> *That's where my lover's gone, gone, gone.*
>
> You know, that bass would make that run there [on the words "gone, gone, gone"]; that was something... It was New Year's Eve, coming into 1913. See?[16]

Researchers had been unable to identify "My Brazilian Beauty" as there is no record of the song at the Copyright Office of the Library of Congress. Lynn Abbott, after much searching, eventually located a "professional copy" in the sheet music collection at UCLA. The song that Armstrong remembered as

"My Brazilian Beauty" was actually titled "Down on the Amazon" and composed by Billy Johnson in 1903.[17] The *New York Clipper* claimed it "a howling success" featured by "TOPLINERS everywhere."[18]

Armstrong remembered the events of New Year's Eve 1913 in another interview: "I was out singing with my quartet. . . . We were going up Rampart Street singing 'My Brazilian Beauty,' and a little old cat across the street pulls out a kid's cap pistol and shot it at us—Dy! Dy! Dy! Dy! Dy! The cats in my quartet say, 'Get him Dipper!' (they used to call me Dippermouth) and so I shot [with his stepfather's .38 pistol] *Zoom, Zoom!* And all of a sudden two white arms hugged me, and I looked up and there was a big tall policeman. Boy, I thought the world was coming to an end."[19]

> Why it was that Louis and his friends were particularly attracted to the song "My Brazilian Beauty" Armstrong did not reveal, but it was not because of the exotic location. As he said later in an interview, "At the time I didn't even know there was a place called Brazil. And years later, when I went to Brazil on tour—then it dawned on me."[20] On one occasion he referred to this song as the quartet's "theme song" and it went: "My Brazilian Beauty down on the Amazon / that's where my baby's / gone, gone, gone (we had a guy who could bass that). Every night I'm dreaming of 'my Brazilian beauty down on the Amazon.'"[21]

One possible reason for the popularity of the song with the quartet was the harmony of the chorus. It was based on a chord sequence that would become common in jazz tunes. The original sheet music is in the key of B♭. For ease of comparison with earlier tunes discussed it is transposed to the key of C.[22] The chord sequence of Example 9 [is based upon a series of dominant seventh chords. A dominant seventh chord is a major chord (as it has a major third), a perfect fifth, and a flatted seventh. This is therefore a four note chord. Dominant seventh chords are so fundamental to barbershop singing that the "barbershop seventh" has been described as the "meat 'n' taters" chord. Commercial arrangers of barbershop, it is claimed, strive to achieve between 35 and 60 percent of these chords.[23] However, the most desired seventh chord is the "super seventh": this is a chord in barbershop harmony that makes the "nerve ends tingle."[24] When sung using particular mathematical ratios between the notes, these chords have a ringing effect. As Deac Martin argues, "Because of their 'coincidence of harmonics,' so termed by physicists, the harmonic tones are in the ratio which in combination best produce the 'ring' of overtones characteristic of well-sung barbershop harmony."[25]

Example 9: Billy Johnson "Down on the Amazon" (New York: Dowling Sutton Music Publishing Co.,1903)

The notes of our chord have the exact frequency ratios 4–5–6–7. With these ratios, overtones reinforce overtones. There's a minimum of dissonance and a distinctive ringing sound. How can you detect this chord? It's easy. You can't mistake it, for the signs are clear; the overtones will ring in your ears; you'll experience a spinal shiver; bumps will stand out on your arms; you'll rise a trifle in your seat.[26]

Maurice Reagan, who did much to explain the theory of barbershop singing to revivalists in the 1940s, went into some detail of the mathematics of the super seventh. Reagan was also raised in a musical culture where solfeggio singing was commonly understood, and he wrote in terms with which Armstrong would probably have been familiar: "The seventh chord is one of the most satisfying chords in harmony. It consists of Do-Mi-Sol-Ti-Do. In terms of vibrations or cycles Do may be 100—and if so—Mi is 125—Sol is 150—Ti is 175 and the upper octave Do is 200."[27]

In European harmonic practice, there is only one dominant seventh chord in each key. For example, in the key of C major the dominant chord is a chord of G seventh. This is a four note chord that includes the root of the chord (G), the major third of the chord (B), the perfect fifth (D), and the flatted seventh (F). Using only the notes of the C major scale (the white notes on a piano), these are the only notes that will produce a chord with a major third and a flatted seventh. When other dominant seventh chords are used in a sequence or cycle of fifths, as is the case with "Down on the Amazon," these chords are described as secondary dominants. Donald Johns describes a cycle of dominant chords as "funnel tonality."

> Simply put, "funnel tonality" is a convenient term for pieces that begin away from the tonic, out of key, or in an otherwise unstable tonal state. It is a dynamic process in which the composer seeks to *achieve* a tonality, to reach an ultimate arrival point that is appropriate, that sounds right, but is not always obvious from the beginning.[28]

In the case of "My Brazilian Beauty," the chorus opens with a chord of A seventh (A, C♯, E, G). It is evident from the inclusion of the C♯ in the chord that this chord is not in the key of C major. The following chord is a chord of D seventh (D, F♯, A, C). F♯ is not in the key of C. Then a chord of G seventh (G, B, D, F): the dominant chord in the key of C major. As is the case with funnel tonality, the chorus of "My Brazilian Beauty" begins in a remote key, technically D major, passing through G major, before resolving to C major. This type of harmony had become commonplace by the early twentieth century in ragtime and popular music of the period, and by the time of the barbershop revival that began just before WWII, Martin argued, "The outstanding characteristic of barbershop harmony is the dominance of the resolving dominant (barbershop seventh) chords as recognized by musicians. In sequences, they are resolved on the circle of fifths attributed to Bach."[29] The question this raises is, can funnel tonality be attributed to Bach (or the European classical tradition more broadly), or is funnel tonality the product of barbershop principles? Resolving this question has far-reaching consequences. This harmonic cycle has been fundamental to jazz and blues tonality. The dominant view is that the harmony of jazz is of European origin. Winthrop Sargeant in his groundbreaking book *Jazz Hot and Hybrid* (1938) did much to explore the tonality of jazz, but, he concluded, "Harmony, as the jazz musician employs it, is a purely European structural principle."[30] Another writer Leroy Ostransky, in *Understanding Jazz* (1977), believed, "The harmonies of early jazz are much the same as those found in a large number of eighteenth-century dances and nineteenth-century evangelical hymns. The early jazz player accepted the harmonies of his musical environment and went on to develop what he was mainly concerned with: melody and rhythm."[31] If funnel tonality is the product of the European musical tradition, then it would be justified to agree with the prevailing view. It is apparent that barbershop harmony substantially influenced the harmonic development of jazz and blues. The question is, how fundamental was this influence? If funnel tonality had its origins in barbershop harmony, this would give rise to a complete rethink regarding the role that barbershop harmony has had on twentieth-century music making.

One argument that has been advanced to suggest that the secondary dominant chord cycle has its origin in European music points out that Romantic composers used secondary dominant chords on the second degree of the scale (D seventh rather than D minor seventh in the key of C major). What is less common is the use of a secondary dominant on the sixth degree (A seventh) as found in "My Brazilian Beauty." One example that Peter Van de Merwe cites is the beginning if Liszt's "Liebestraum" no. III (1850) with the chord progression E seventh, A seventh, D seventh, G seventh, and C major.[32] He goes on to say that this "harmonic pattern (often without the first chord) was to become a great favorite in popular music of about half a century later, not only in the popular style but in ragtime as well." The association with this harmonic pattern and ragtime was such that "it has even been called the 'ragtime progression.'"[33] However, we should be wary of assuming that coincidence implies causality. Romantic composers were actively engaged in exploring the use of chromatic harmony. It is possible that Liszt and others may have coincidentally use the same chromatic chords that ragtime composers employed half a century later. It may also be that ragtime composers may have learned these same harmonic progressions from a source unrelated to European romantic composition. It takes a considerable leap of faith to suggest that a few fleeting measures of Liszt could have spurred the consistent use of this harmonic formulation and led, as Van de Merwe argues, to "these later examples: as for instance in 'Sweet Georgia Brown,' composed just three-quarters of a century after 'Liebestraum.'"[34] While ragtime composers may or may not have been familiar with "Liebestraum," given that quartet singing was ubiquitous by the late nineteenth century, no ragtime composer would have been ignorant of barbershop harmony. Some, like Scott Joplin, performed with a quartet. His first composition is credited to "Scott Joplin of the Texas Medley Quartet."[35] The origins of the dominant cycle of chords that gives rise to funnel tonality is not a discussion that can be resolved at this point, but it is an issue that will be returned to with regard to Armstrong's recordings, as this chord cycle appears in many of his recordings in the 1920s.

CHAPTER 7

"ME AND MUSIC GOT MARRIED IN THE HOME"

LOUIS ARMSTRONG EXPLAINED THE CIRCUMSTANCES AROUND HIS committal to the Waifs' Home many times. On New Year's Eve 1913, Armstrong and his friends had hoped to earn a little money singing on the streets. He recalled, "Our quartet was standing on the corner of Perdido and Rampart Streets singing, a boy passed us shooting off his little old six-shooter."[1] In an effort to go one better, Armstrong let off his parents "38" that he had secretly obtained and was arrested. While his arrest and committal to the Waifs' Home took him away from his friends and the street life of New Orleans, it did not thwart his musical ambitions—quite the reverse. It was in the Waifs' Home, according to Armstrong, that he and music "got married."[2] His natural ability as a singer and a comedian ensured that he quickly made new friends. He also used this opportunity to form a new vocal quartet. As he explained, "It was a shot from my daddy's old '38' on New Year's Eve down in good ole [sic] New Orleans that really started my career."[3]

During World War II, Robert Goffin was in New Orleans and took the opportunity to interview Joseph Jones, who ran the Colored Waifs' Home. Jones became the supervisor of the Waifs' Home in 1906 after retiring from serving in the Spanish American War.[4] He told Goffin that it was his habit to take Fridays off, and one Friday he visited a cigar maker, Viéjas Ose. The cigar maker had some old instruments in his attic, and Jones decided to take a look.[5] Jones was persuaded to buy the instruments that included two horns, a piccolo, a baritone, a drum, and a bugle. He paid seven dollars for the lot. It was around 1911 that the first Waifs' Home Orchestra was formed. By this time, Jones had also acquired a tuba, a clarinet, and a bass drum to supplement his earlier purchases.[6] To get support to form a Waifs' Home Orchestra, Jones spoke with Judge John J. Fogarty (born New Orleans 1865).[7] It seems that Fogarty was not impressed with the idea. Undeterred, Jones contacted Peter Davis, who had developed a reputation as a musical director for marching bands.[8] In March 1912, Peter Davis began work at the Waifs' Home where he "taught instrumental music and directed the band, choir, and singing quartet."[9] In the original band, Henry René played the clarinet.[10] He would later learn the cornet and Anglicize his name, becoming better known as Kid Rena.[11] The other members of the original orchestra were Jeffrie [sic] Harris (baritone), Gus Van Zan (viola), Isaac Smooth (bass drum), James Brown (snare drum), and Peter Davis played the horn.[12]

Jones kept a daily log of the boys in his care, and he showed Goffin the log for January 1, 1913. On this date, there were in total seventy boys in the home; one had been discharged, and one—Louis Armstrong, born "July 4, 1900"—had been admitted. This brought the total back to seventy inmates.[13]

There has been some controversy about whether Armstrong could already play the cornet before he entered the Waifs' Home. Jones was adamant he had "never touched an instrument" before he became a pupil of Peter Davis.[14] This is confirmed by Armstrong: "Mr. Davis had them [the Waifs' Orchestra] playing a little of every kind of music . . . I'd never tried to play a cornet before . . . But hearing Joe Oliver—Bolden and Bunk Johnson, I had an awful urge to try to learn the cornet."[15] Armstrong remembered: "Now, at the Home they had a little orchestra made up of the older boys—but I had no idea I'd ever be in it. I liked to sing but I didn't take music seriously so I could play an instrument."[16] Although he respected Peter Davis's musical ability, Armstrong said Davis would whip him whenever he had the chance. He claimed Davis would say, "You're one of those bad boys from Liberty and Perdido Streets and I don't like you."[17] Davis did however notice that "Louis had one strong voice, for sure."[18] In time, Davis relented and introduced Armstrong into the band. According to Jones, Louis first played tambourine and then the snare drum in the Waifs' Orchestra before being introduced to the bugle, but he also played bass drum and viola to fill positions as people came and went from the Home.[19] This is consistent with Armstrong's recollection: "He [Peter Davis] kept insisting in giving me a tamborine [sic]. So I fool with that for a while. Then he give me a snare drum . . . Then he gave me an alto horn."[20] James Lincoln Collier has observed that Armstrong quickly learned to play the alto horn: "With his great ear, [Armstrong] had no difficulty working out appropriate parts to the song that the band played." As Collier says, this was "a considerable feat for a beginner. Clearly, through some combination of natural talent and his early singing experience, Armstrong already possessed a feeling for harmony beyond the usual."[21] In fact, Armstrong explained how his early singing experience with his street quartet enabled him to play the alto horn. In the original typescript for *Satchmo*, Armstrong wrote of how Peter Davis approached him about playing the alto horn.

> But I am very [in] need of an alto player, how 'bout trying your luck at it? . . . I said, anything you say Mr Davis (with all the confidence in the world) . . . So he gives me this alto . . . I being a singer all my life, my better judgement told me that *an Alto is an instrument that sings a duet in a brass band the same as the baritone or the tenor would do in a quartet.*[22]

From this it is clear that Armstrong was aware that he converted the lines that he sang in a quartet to brass instruments, and that he conceived of the notes that he would play as the notes sung by the baritone and tenor voices in quartet. It is through an understanding of the principles of barbershop quartet practice that we can begin to understand Armstrong's approach to playing a brass instrument. The songs that Jones remembered Louis playing included "Swanee River" and a "dance number that he had learned with the quartet."[23] Given that "Swanee River" was staple of the barbershop quartet repertoire and could be harmonized in many different ways, Louis was able to transfer the actual lines that he sang directly to his horn.

Peter Davis is quoted as having remembered, "Less than a year after he went to the home, Armstrong was the bugler. 'He would pester me so much, all the time, that I had to go ahead and let him try,' said Davis."[24] According to Armstrong, "Finally the little cornet player went home and Mr. Davis taught me how to play *Home Sweet Home* on that."[25] According to Jones, this was one of the instruments that came from the attic of Viéjas Ose.[26]

Drummer Paul Barbarin first saw Armstrong when he played in the Waif's Band: "I admired him when I first heard him," said Barbarin: "He stood out from the others. His tone was kind of powerful even as a kid. He was a natural."[27] Zutty Singleton said that shortly after Louis was committed to the Waifs' Home, "Then I saw Louis playing in a band at a picnic." He was playing with the Waifs' Band: "We got up real close to him to see if he was actually playing those notes. We didn't believe he could learn to play in that short a time. I can still remember, he was playing 'Maryland, My Maryland.' And he sure was swinging out that melody."[28]

It is clear that Louis learned very quickly, but could he have been leading the band on cornet within just five months if he had no previous experience of playing an instrument before entering the Waifs' Home? The question arises because on May 31, 1913, the *New Orleans Daily Picayune* ran the story

"Juvenile Band." The story described "little black imps, sixteen of them, in honor of Federal Decoration Day, each bearing a criminal record, equipped with every wrinkle that goes to making up a brass band, [that] paraded the streets of New Orleans." This was the band of the "colored department of the Society for the Prevention of Cruelty to Children's Waifs' Home" under the supervision of Joseph Jones and Peter Davis. They were "Marching proudly through the streets with drum and fife, [as] they rendered several selections, patriotic mostly, and were loudly encored from the sidewalks." Listed as "leader" of the band is "Louis Armstrong," but his name is followed by "Sam Johnson, solo cornet," and "Henry Rene, second cornet," and all the other musicians including the flag boy are named.[29] Given that Sam Johnson played solo cornet, it is unlikely that Armstrong was the lead cornet player in the band at this time. It would have been a remarkable achievement if Armstrong was the lead instrumentalist after just five months. One possibility is that he was leader in the sense that the grand marshal leads a parade band.[30] It could be that at this time Armstrong was the lead bugler, as it is claimed that "Little Armstrong was a sight to behold as he marched in the band's lead, in his blue uniform, twirling his bugle and making it flash in the sun before gluing it to his lips."[31] What does seem likely is that by Labor Day 1913, Louis was playing cornet with the Waifs' Home Brass Band. Kid Ory's band had been engaged for the event that would march through the Rampart and Perdido Street neighborhood. Ory's band was taking a break when they noticed a young cornet player with Captain Jones's Colored Waif's Home Brass Band.[32] It was Louis Armstrong.

By the end of 1913, Armstrong was definitely leading the band on cornet. An article in the *New Orleans Times-Democrat* lists Armstrong as "Louis Armstrong, leader, cornet." By this time there were three cornet players in the band: Armstrong, Peter Davis, and Sam Johnson. "Henry Rainey" now playing alto is likely to be Kid Rena, who had previously played the other cornet.[33] Among the tunes that were played at this event were "'Little Bunch of Shamrock,' 'Dixie,' 'Maryland, My Maryland,' 'America' and other selections."[34]

The transition from "old offender" to leader of the band in just five months, and then playing cornet within a year, does indicate the profound impact that the Waifs' Home had on Armstrong—an impact that Armstrong confirmed: "I do believe that my whole success goes back to that time I was arrested as a wayward boy at the age of thirteen. Because then I *had* to quit running around and began to learn something. Most of all, I began to learn music."[35] In his eighteen months in the Waifs' Home, Armstrong would have not only have continued his quartet activities and learned to play the cornet, he would have continued his schooling in singing and the basics of musical notation and theory. Armstrong recalled two singing teachers at the Home: "Miss Spriggins" and "Miss Vignes, who taught the higher grades." "Miss Spriggins" was probably Naomi Spriggins, who graduated from Straight University in 1912, before she became a public-school teacher assigned to the Waifs' Home.[36]

Although from a time after Armstrong left the Home, a 1918 *New Orleans Times-Picayune* feature highlighted the singing groups at the Home and identified Peter Davis as the director. Although Davis probably directed the choirs and quartets, Spriggins and Vignes taught voice culture, and as part of the New Orleans public school system they probably would have used the same syllabus: the *Eleanor Smith* songbooks, as used in other New Orleans schools.[37] These songs, as noted earlier, were all sung in unison or with accompaniment. The songs that the choirs and quartets sang under Davis's direction had, by 1918, developed a different repertoire from that taught by Spriggins and Vignes. The 1918 *Times-Picayune* article listed among the songs "Swing Low Sweet Chariot," "Shall We Meet Beyond the River," "Jesus Washed My Sins Away," "Onward, Christian Soldiers," and "Good-bye Broadway, Hello France."[38] This repertoire was suited to harmony singing.

Louis also continued to sing in a quartet in the Waifs' Home. With Armstrong at the Home was Louis "Kid Shots" Madison. Madison was born in New Orleans, February 19, 1899, and although a little older than Armstrong, he did not progress as quickly in music.[39] He played drums in the Waifs' Band and only later took up the cornet. He went on to record in the 1920s with the Original Tuxedo Orchestra.[40] After Madison and Armstrong were released from the Home, they worked together loading coal in Poydras Market and continued their musical association.[41] Madison sometimes sang baritone with Armstrong in his quartet on amateur nights at the Crescent Theater.[42] Another inmate when Armstrong was in the Waifs' Home was Kid Rena (born August 30, 1898).[43] Although Rena played with his own band in New Orleans in the 1920s and made several trips to Chicago, he only recorded late in his career in 1940 when he was no longer considered at his best.[44] Red "Happy" Bolton who sang with Louis in his street quartet was also at the Waifs' Home.[45] James William Bolton was a little older than Armstrong. He was born in New Orleans, March 25, 1900. At the time of his registration for military service in 1917, he was living at 1326 Gravier Street, New Orleans, and working as a "drum player" and "musicianer" at West End Tavern.[46] Bolton was known to entertain audiences with "a scat number as a comic interlude"; he was also reputedly "a good buck dancer," and it has been claimed that Bolton shaped "Armstrong's own singing style."[47]

It is understandable why Armstrong in retrospect acknowledged the important role that the Waifs' Home played in his musical development. He was still able to sing in a quartet, and probably sang in the choirs and quartets that Peter Davis organized; he received a musical education from Spriggins and Vignes; and he learned to play an instrument.

Some writers have questioned whether Louis was re-committed to the Waif's Home after his release in 1914. According to Jones, Armstrong was discharged from the home on June 16, 1914, and did not return until he was an invited and honored guest on June 17, 1931.[48] This is very likely correct, because the records that Jones showed to Goffin back in 1943 have now been found.[49] On the other hand, it is possible that Armstrong may have continued to play with the Waifs' Band from time to time after his release. Evidence for this comes from Preston Jackson: "I had heard Louis play before in 1915 at a playground dedication when the Jones Waif Band featured Louis and Henry Rena. Louis was terrific even then. I was going to the school where the playground was. That's how I happened to hear him."[50] He identified the playground as Thomy Lafon Playground and one of the tunes they played was "Maryland My Maryland."[51] Thomy Lafon was born a free man of color, who could easily have passed as white but never did so. A successful businessman, he donated money to the Lafon Orphan Boys' Asylum and to the Home for Aged Colored Men and Women.[52] The Thomy Lafon School was burned down by a white mob in 1900, and the orphanage at the Thomy Lafon Annex of the House of the Good Shepherd experienced an unexplained fire in 1906. Preston Jackson, born 1902, was a pupil of the Thomy Lafon School a little after this. Preston Jackson wrote a brief unpublished autobiography and a photocopy of the manuscript survives. Jackson wrote:

> There was a four cornered lot adjacent to Thomy Lafon School. The city decided to convert the lot into a public playground. That lot was full of debris and full of foul, green water. We students agreed to help the men employed by the city to clean that lot. That lot finally was cleared of all the debris, and the holes were dry that formally held that foul, green water. Swings were installed and a tennis court, checker boards and a swimming pool. The Jones Waifs Home Band was invited to the opening of the park. That was when I first saw Louis Armstrong.[53]

The playground opened at the corner of Sixth and Magnolia Streets in 1915—the first playground for African American children in New Orleans.[54] The *New Orleans Times-Picayune* of August 29, 1915, reported:

Under the chairmanship of J. Madison Vance, negro attorney, who delivered the opening address, dedication services of the Thomy Lafon Playground, the first public playground to be opened in the South for negroes, were held Saturday afternoon at Magnolia and Sixth Streets. Speeches lauding efforts to uplift the negro race by properly training the young; a flag raising, patriotic songs, music and dancing featured [in] the ceremony.[55]

The evening edition of the *New Orleans Item* of August 28, 1915, reported on the program for that day's events, but it went to press too early to report on the event itself. It noted that "Leading negroes of the city will participate in the dedication," and reported that "Flag-raising and patriotic songs" would be conducted" under the leadership of Ella S. Boyd, supervisor of the playground.[56] This was a lengthy program including all the dignitaries who were involved in the event. It seems likely that if the Waifs' Band had participated that they would have been mentioned, and they were not. It seems Jackson probably confused this occasion with some other appearance of the Waifs' Home Band.

Example 10: Chorus, "Maryland My Maryland" (1906), stock arrangement

What is beyond doubt is that "Maryland My Maryland" was part of the band's repertoire. There are two other reports of the Waifs' Band playing this tune; one is a newspaper report.[57] Armstrong made a recording of "Maryland My Maryland" in 1946 as part of the film *New Orleans* with musicians he had known since childhood: Kid Ory on trombone, Barney Bigard, clarinet, and Zutty Singleton on drums.[58] Although the film falls well short of a historically accurate attempt to depict the emergence of New Orleans jazz, Armstrong's rendition of "Maryland My Maryland" is much as he would have played it with the Waifs' Band three decades before. It is usual in a New Orleans ensemble for the cornet to take the melody and the trombone to play a harmony part. However, by comparing the stock arrangement of 1906 with their recording, it becomes apparent why Ory on trombone played the melody and Armstrong played a militaristic counterpoint on cornet: they played it this way because this is how it was written in the stock arrangement.[59]

We will probably never be certain whether Armstrong was playing by ear or if he played from written arrangements in the Waifs' Band. Peter Davis reputedly would not permit the band to "jazz up a number," and photographs of the band show them with music stands.[60] On the other hand, John Casimir (born 1898) sang some snatches of a tune he called "Come on Nancy, Put Your Glad Rags On" in an oral history interview, relaying how in the Waifs' Band, "There were five or six fellas there playing cornet and they would give Louis all the breaks."[61] The opening lyric of "Sailing Down the Chesapeake" is "Come on Nancy, put your best dress on." The song received copyright in 1913, so it could have been part of the repertoire when Armstrong was in the band. The *Remick Orchestra Folio No. 14* contained "the season's most popular" dance pieces of 1913, and was arranged for two violins, viola, cello, bass flute, clarinet, two cornets, trombone, drums, and piano. It included a written cornet break between the verse and chorus.[62] Although we cannot be sure if Armstrong played this break as written, we can be sure that a break was a part of the stock arrangement. The balance of probability is that he had a rudimentary grasp of music notation, the ability to "spell" (work out his part, in the vernacular of early New Orleans musicians) but not at this stage able to "read" (sight-read) notation. But given his remarkable musical memory he could, with practice, learn to play his part once he had heard it. The evidence of the 1946 recording of "Maryland My Maryland" suggests that once he had learned a piece he would never forget it.

CHAPTER 8

"I WAS SINGING SELLING COAL"

TOWARD THE END OF HIS LIFE, LYING SICK IN A HOSPITAL BED AT THE Beth Israel Hospital on March 31, 1969, Louis Armstrong began to write what he intended to be his final autobiography.[1] In this account he told the "Real life story and experiences at the age of seven years old with the Karnofsky (Jewish) Family, the year of 1907."[2] Throughout his life, Armstrong felt indebted to the Karnofsky family. When he was young he worked on their junk wagon, and later on their coal round, and Mrs. Karnofsky regularly provided him with meals. He wrote:

> When I would be on the *junk* wagon with *Alex* Karnofsky (one of their sons), I had a little *Tin Horn*—the kind the people *celebrates* with.—I would *blow* this long tin *horn* without the *Top* on it, *Just*—hold my *fingers close* together. Blow it, as a *Call* for old Rags—*Bones*—Bottles or *Anything* that the people and the kids had to *sell.* The *kids* would bring us *bottles* and receives *pennies* from *Alex.* The *Kids* loved the *sounds* of my tin horn. The Karnofskys lived on the corner of *Girod* and *Franklin* Streets. One block away from Girod Street Cemetery.[3]

He continued, "After *blowing* the *tin* horn—so long—I *wondered* how would I do *blowing a real horn,*—a *cornet* was what I had in *mind.* Sure enough, I saw a *cornet* in a pawn shop *window—Five dollars*—my *luck* was just *right.* With the *Karnofskys* loaning me on my *Salary—I saved* fifty cents a *week* and *bought* the *horn.* All dirty—but was soon *pretty* to me."[4]

Not only was the Karnofsky family responsible for Louis's first cornet, in this new account they were responsible for his passion for singing, too: "Speaking of the wonderful Karnofsky *family.* Just before I began to grow up and Singing with Papa and Mama Karnofsky, Morris and Alex—we would

55

all sing this special tune, while Mama Karnofsky would have the baby in her arms—Rocking him until he would go to sleep."[5] The song, identified as "Russian Lullaby" by Armstrong, had by the time he was eleven years old instilled in him "singing from the heart."[6] Armstrong remembered, "I was real relaxed *Singing* the *song* called 'Russian Lullaby' with the *Karnofsky* family . . . When Mrs *Karnofsky* would start singing these words to 'Russian Lullaby' we all would get our *places* and sing it."[7] The family encouraged his efforts: "The Karnofsky Family kept reminding me that I had Talent—perfect Tonation when I would Sing."[8]

In this account, Armstrong substantially rewrote his musical history. If this account is true, we have to add *child protégé* to the list of Armstrong's other impressive achievements.[9] Moreover, if it were true, then we would need to completely disregard everything that Armstrong had previously said about first learning the cornet at the Waifs' Home. In this new version of his early years, Armstrong claimed, "After *blowing* into it a while I realized that I could play '*Home* Sweet Home' then *here* come the *Blues*. From *then* on, I was a *mess* and *Tootin* away. I *kept* that *horn* for a *long* time. I *played* it *all through* the *days* of the *Honky* Tonk. People thought that my *first horn* was *given* me at the *Colored Waifs' Home for Boys* (the orphanage). But it *wasn't*."[10] So had Armstrong spent a lifetime misleading researchers, publishers, and fans about his early years, to finally put the record straight at the end of his life? Had he actually been playing cornet since 1907?

Armstrong's earliest reference to the Karnofsky (spelled "Konowski") family is found in *Horn of Plenty* (1947). Because the notebooks that Armstrong supplied to Goffin are missing for the early part of his life (if they ever existed), it is difficult to know how much of what Goffin reported can be relied upon. Given that Goffin was a poet and a lawyer, it is likely that that the literary flourishes are Goffin's creation whereas the basic chronology was supplied by Armstrong. Goffin wrote, "Going back gloomily toward Perdido, he [Armstrong] stopped at the employment agency on Rampart Street. Redhead Happy was selling papers in the vicinity." Armstrong was told that there was a job available at "Konowski's, the coal man."[11] He enquired, was offered the job, and began the next day. If this account is correct, given that Konowski should read Karnofsky (as Maurice Konowski is mentioned a little later on in the narrative), then Armstrong was first working for the family around 1909 or 1910.[12] However, in his subsequent autobiography, *Satchmo* (1955), he wrote that he worked with the Karnofskys *after* working at Andrews Coal Yard. This was in stark contrast to his claim in his hospital bed manuscript that the Karnofsky job was his first job, "So I was very *glad* over it."[13] Is it possible to reconcile this apparent contradiction?

The available evidence suggests that Armstrong did not begin working in Andrews Coal Yard until after leaving the Waifs' Home and it probably wasn't his first job either. In a 1945 interview, he said, "I left the home to help make a living for my mother and sister. Between following parades and selling newspapers, I practiced on my horn."[14] This is consistent with his recollections in his first autobiography, where he said that after leaving the Waifs' Home, "I couldn't find any real job, so I started selling newspapers. I got that through a little white kid named Paul," whose brother had a newsstand.[15] A similar claim was repeated in *Horn of Plenty*: "At this time Louis tried earnestly but vainly to earn a living in a steady job. He went back to Charlie and sold Newspapers . . . He tried his hand as odd man in a dairy . . . One morning driven to desperation, he stopped at Morris Konowsky's [sic]."[16] In this account he was told that he was too big to be a helper and too young to be the driver and he was turned down for a job.[17] Armstrong's mother tried to persuade him to go and work with his "stepfather" on a coal wagon. By the time of his release from Waifs' Home his mother had taken up with a man called "Mr. Gabe" who worked at the Andrews Coal Yard.[18] At some point after leaving the Waifs' Home, Armstrong worked at "Henry Ponce's place" in the evenings. Armstrong said, "I got another job driving a coal cart during the day." This was at "C. A. Andrews Coal Company at Ferret [sic] and Perdido Streets two blocks from the honky-tonk."[19] The Andrews Coal Company was incorporated in 1899, and it was based at 1061 South Rampart Street through to 1910.[20] In late 1910 or 1911, C. A. Andrews Coal Company relocated to the corner of Perdido and Freret Streets at the address Armstrong remembered.[21]

We can be sure that Armstrong was working for Andrews in the fall of 1915 because he was still working for Andrews when his cousin Flora Miles gave birth to a son named Clarence. Armstrong would later adopt Clarence after he had a fall and received brain damage. He remembered that the night that Clarence was born there was "a terrible storm, one of the worst New Orleans had ever had."[22] He described how people and animals were killed and there were many people made homeless. The September 30, 1915, edition of the *New York Times* broke the news: "Hurricane Sweeps Over New Orleans: Kills Ten Persons and Causes Property Loss of Millions of Dollars."[23] In fact, 275 people died in the hurricane, and the property loss ran to thirteen million dollars.

In one version of events, Armstrong was still working for Andrews when America entered World War I on April 2, 1917. Armstrong remembered how everybody was required to either enlist or to work and Armstrong had "the coal cart to fall back on, thanks to my good stepfather Gabe" who worked for Andrews."[24] He goes on to say, "I was fifteen years old, and I felt like a real man."[25] Armstrong said that he continued to work for Andrews until he "found something better," meaning it was "something that was easier."[26] This easier job was the job that he took with Morris Karnofsky, and for this reason Armstrong said, "I stayed with him a long time . . . selling stone coal at a nickel a bucket."[27] Turning to the typescript for *Satchmo*, we learn in a section dated "1916–17": "While shoveling coal, an sitting behind LADY (my mule) all day, I was offered several jobs . . . None of them paid very much money . . . But they were much more easier . . . First I worked for Morris Karnoffsky [sic] . . . He had a stone coal (that's what we called hard coal) wagon which went all through the red light district (storryville [sic]) selling stone coal a nickel a water bucket . . . Or, five cents a bucket."[28] However, working with Morris at this time does not preclude the possibility that he had worked on the junk wagon at an earlier date.

It is doubtful that Armstrong worked for the Karnofsky family in 1907 selling coal, as Morris Karnofsky would have been thirteen years old and his brother Alex ten. In the chapter on the Karnofsky Family written in his sickbed in 1969, Armstrong wrote, "Their *two* sons, their ages *19* or *20* years old—went into *business*. I *alternated* with the *two sons. One* went out in the street, buying Old *Rags—Bones—Iron—Bottles—Any* kind of Old *Junk.* Go *back* to the *house* with the *big* yard—*empty* the *wagon—pile* up the old *Rags* in *one* place, the *bottles—Bones* and the *rest* of the *Junk,* all in *separate places.*"[29] The ages of Morris and Alex are recorded in the 1910 New Orleans census. The head of the Karnofsky family, Louis, is aged forty-two, married for sixteen years, born in Russia, and his occupation is difficult to read but it is probably "Junk Seller." His wife, Tillie, is thirty-eight years old. She too was born in Russia, and together they had ten children. The older children, including Morris, age sixteen, and Alex, age thirteen, were born in New York and this is where their parents married. Morris's age is consistent with his WWI Draft Registration Card that records he was born March 19 1894 or 1895. The registering officer had crossed out the five and overwritten four.[30]

The family is not in New Orleans in the 1900 census.[31] According to the 1910 census, the first child born in Louisiana is "Dave," aged seven. His older sibling Lillie, aged eight, was born in New York. It seems likely that the Karnofsky family came to New Orleans around 1903.[32]

One significant detail that Armstrong provided in the hospital manuscript explained how "Mother Karnofsky would rock the Baby David to Sleep" singing the "Russian Lullaby" at a time when Armstrong claimed he was seven years old.[33] The Karnofsky family had two daughters that were younger than David, but David was the youngest son.[34] When David was registered for service in WWII he gave his date of birth as September 20, 1904.[35] Much after 1907 he would not have been a baby, and this does seem to confirm that Armstrong knew the family from this time. A further reason to believe that Armstrong knew the Karnofsky family from an early age is that he said that after work he had supper with the Jewish family. His own family would wait up for him to come home.[36] He goes on to say, "Then my Step Father Tom, May Ann, Mama Lucy and me will go to bed." His stepfather could be "Thomas Lea" [Lee?] who was living with the family in 1910 at 1303 Perdido Street.[37]

A further reason to think that Armstrong knew the Karnofsky family from before his time in the Waifs' Home is where they lived. In the period 1907 through to 1914 the family lived at 1304 Girod in the area that Armstrong remembered. By 1914 the business address remained the same but their residential address was at "427 S Rampart."[38] It seems likely from the entries in *Soards'* that there was another branch of the Karnofsky family had for some years been living in the South Rampart Street area and this is perhaps the original reason for Louis Karnofsky bringing his family to New Orleans.

Armstrong stayed in contact with the family in later years as he commented that by the time he had become "one of the popular cornet players of the area . . . David the youngest of the family had grown into a fine young man and had a business of his own."[39] David, age sixteen, was still living with his parents at 427 Rampart Street and working as a clerk in the tailor's shop that his brother "Alec" owned in 1920.[40] By this time Louis Karnofsky owned a clothing store, and Morris worked as a chauffeur.[41]

What are we to make of these conflicting accounts? The balance of probability is that Armstrong did know the Karnofsky family from around 1907 when David was still a baby. At that time, he could well have worked with the family collecting junk. Louis Karnofsky is listed as a junk dealer in *Soards' New Orleans City Directories*, throughout this period. It is possible that by the time of Armstrong's release from the Waifs' Home, in the summer of 1914, Morris Karnofsky had established a coal round, and Armstrong applied for a job. On this occasion, he was turned down because he was too young to drive the wagon and too old to be a helper. With help from his "stepfather Gabe," Armstrong was successful in subsequently getting a job with Andrews. Finally, after a few years, and in an effort to find something that was a little easier than working for Andrews, Armstrong worked for Morris Karnofsky selling coal. If this is the correct version of events, then the likelihood is that it was not until he was working on the coal round with Morris that he was advanced the money to buy his first cornet.

Laurence Bergreen makes an interesting observation about Armstrong's time working for Andrews. He notes that Armstrong "rarely got a chance to play cornet these days, and when he did, he seems to have made little impression, for the glowing reminiscences of his musicianship that mark other periods of his life are absent from this one."[42] One account of Armstrong playing with a band directly after leaving the Waifs' Home comes from the guitarist Louis Keppard. He claims that Joe Oliver let Louis play with their band when they were playing at "Buddy Bottlers" place on Franklin Street.[43] This is supported by the string bass player George "Pops" Foster (born 1892) who said "Louis played Saturday nights at Buddy Bartlett's tonk and didn't have no regular job."[44] Buddy Bartlett (Bottler, Bodly, Bottley, and other variants) is a legendary figure in the folklore of New Orleans jazz. There are many accounts of a balloonist who ascended from Lincoln Park in the early years of the twentieth century. The park was "run strictly by colored people, [and was] one of the best equipped parks of its kind in the South."[45] Because Buddy Bolden played in neighboring Johnson Park, these balloon ascents have become a part of the Buddy Bolden legend. Some informants believed that it was Bolden himself that used to go up in the balloon. There may have been more than one balloonist in Lincoln Park at different times, but the one who worked in the saloon where Armstrong sat in with Oliver was Joseph Haywood. The *Indianapolis Freeman*, an African American owned newspaper that gave regular reports from the travelling shows, reported from Lincoln Park in September 1907: "The world's greatest and most daring colored aeronaut, Jos. Haywood, will make his 'death defying' ascension in his balloon each week."[46] In a later report, Joseph Haywood is given as the treasurer and superintendent of the committee that ran Lincoln Park. A report in the *Chicago Defender* of June 5, 1915, said the Park was pleased to "congratulate Mr. James for his continued good ready shows from start to finish. And Mr. Joseph Haywood (Budy Bodly [sic]), the manager, makes it pleasant for all."[47] This confirms Joseph Haywood and the balloonist recalled as Buddy Bottlers/Bartlett/Bodly are one and the same. A search of *Soards' New Orleans City Directory* confirms that Joseph Haywood had a saloon at 1301 Gravier Street on the corner with Franklin.[48] Keppard recalled that Louis would "come there [Joseph Haywood's saloon] with his little short pants on, and Joe [Oliver] knowed [sic] that he could play cornet a little bit, you know, so Joe said 'Come on Louis and play.' Well of course I was playing guitar with him, so, well he let him play, but Louis couldn't hardly play nothing but the blues, and I couldn't keep time with Louis at that time. You know he wasn't like what he is today."[49] Although Manuel Manetta, who was playing with Oliver and Keppard at this time, believed Armstrong's first horn had been a "lead" horn given him by "Old Man" Jones from the Waifs' Home, Armstrong probably did not have a cornet of his own at this time.[50] In one account, he did not play the cornet for around eighteen months after leaving the Waifs' Home.[51] Another thing that mitigates against Armstrong having been given a cornet on his release from the orphanage is that Sotheby's in New York auctioned what was believed to be the cornet that Armstrong learned to play on in the Waif's Home in 2002. The cornet had been on display in the Louisiana State Museum in New Orleans after it had been purchased from Peter Davis. From this we can assume that Davis had no knowledge of Armstrong having been given his cornet on his release. It is also doubtful that this is Armstrong's first instrument. The cornet had the maker's mark "Marceau." This was a trade name used by the mail order company Sears Roebuck from 1920 onward for its cheapest instruments.[52]

Armstrong confirmed that when he came out the Waifs' Home he "couldn't get enough money together to even talk about a horn of my own," so he rented one when he had an opportunity to play.[53] Then he saw a Tonk Brothers nickel plate cornet in Uncle Jake's Pawn Shop. Charles J. Tonk and his brother William established Tonk Brothers as an importer and distributor of musical instruments in Chicago around 1894.[54] The cornet that Armstrong wanted was bent and had holes in the bell, but Armstrong persuaded Charlie, the white man who supplied him with newspapers, to advance him the ten dollars he needed to buy the horn.[55]

Despite not owning a cornet of his own to begin with, Armstrong began to make an impression on older New Orleans musicians. Another of Andrews's employees was Black Benny, who was the bass drummer with Kid Ory's parade band. Louis, throughout his life, sought the company of people who could protect him and he was attracted to Benny because he "was a kind of rowdy fellow" with a reputation of being able to look after himself.[56] Like so many New Orleans musicians, Benny sang in a barroom quartet. Remembering Benny's quartet, Armstrong said, "You should have heard his old barroom tenor sing 'Sweet Adeline,' or 'Mr Jefferson Lord—Play that Barber-Shop Chord.'"[57] It was Benny who introduced Armstrong to Kid Ory's band: "The first time I remember seeing Louis Armstrong," Ory recalled, "he was a little boy playing cornet in the Waifs' Home band in a street parade. Even then he stood out. One evening, Benny brought Louis, who had just been released from the Waifs' Home, to National Park, where I was playing a picnic. Benny asked me if I would let Louis sit in with my band. I remembered the kid from the street parade and gladly agreed."[58] Ory thought that Louis first sat in with his band "back before the first war," and that Louis was about twelve or thirteen at the time. If Ory's estimate of Armstrong's age is correct, this could have been the summer of 1914.[59] This would also be consistent with his recollection that "Louis was quite a youngster so Benny picked him up and set him on the bandstand which was built quite high off the floor, and after I heard him play one number, I told him I thought he was going to be a great trumpet player, and I wasn't mistaken in thinking so."[60] The number that Armstrong played was probably a blues. Ory said, "I remember how Benny, the drummer, said how about letting my boy play the blues."[61] On another occasion, recalling the same event, Ory said, "Louis came up and played 'Ole Miss' and the blues, and everyone in the park went wild over this boy in knee trousers who could play so great."[62] Mutt Carey was the trumpet player in Ory's band and thought of himself as the "Blues King of New Orleans." As he remembered this event, "When Louis played that day he played more blues than I have ever heard in my life. It never did strike my mind that blues could be interpreted in so many different ways. Every time he played a chorus it was different and you knew it was the blues, yes, it was all blues."[63] Pops Foster remembered what could have been the same occasion:

> About 1914 I was playing with Ory's band doing advertising for an affair the Turtles were putting on at National Park . . . After we went a few blocks, I saw Louis Armstrong standing on a corner watching, and said, "Hey, there's little Louis over there!" We got him in the wagon and he went on to play the advertising with us, and then we carried him out to the park to play. The only thing Louis could play then was blues, so we played them all day long. Louis played them good too. As far as I know, that was the first time Louis played with a big time band. Before that Louis just played with kid bands.[64]

Ory was impressed: "I liked Louis' playing so much that I asked him to come and sit in with my band any time he could."[65] Louis gladly accepted and "He always came accompanied by Benny, the drummer. In the crowded places, Benny would handcuff Louis to himself with a handkerchief so Louis wouldn't get lost."[66] Pops Foster also claims to have got Armstrong his first music jobs while his repertoire was still limited to the blues: "In those days, every man had his own style, and you hired the one whose style fit what you wanted.

Well, with Louis we had to play the blues all night, because that's about all he could play. But Louis could sure play some blues."[67]

Around the time that Armstrong sat in with Ory's band, the violinist Emile Bigard (born 1890) led the band musically. Emile's nephew, the clarinetist Barney Bigard, remembered:

> Ory's band was a soft playing band at that time. They had Mutt Carey (trumpet), Johnny Dodds (clarinet), Kid Ory (trombone), Wilhelmina Bart (piano), George "Pops" Foster (bass) and Henry Zeno (drums). They played nice and soft which was just what the people wanted to hear at that time. Like schottisches, waltzes and even some Scott Joplin pieces. [68]

Although Ory was the business manager of the band, Emile was the musical leader, as Barney explained:

> You see what made my uncle leader was that most of the guys in the band couldn't read worth beans. A couple of them could "spell" a little and so when a new tune would come out usually the violinist, who had more musical knowledge than most of the others, would go and buy the sheet music and call a rehearsal. The violin would play the straight lead for them and keep on until the trumpet player got it. When the trumpet had it down then the rest of them would fall in with their parts.[69]

This is much as Armstrong had described of his own rehearsal methods. First the melody must be mastered by Mutt Carey, and then the other harmony instruments, Kid Ory on trombone, and Johnny Dodds on clarinet would find their parts. And just as with Armstrong, we find the same background in barbershop singing for these musicians.

Kid Ory was born on Christmas Day 1886 on Woodland Plantation, La-Place, Louisiana, about thirty miles upriver from New Orleans.[70] As a child he and other youngsters from the area formed a "humming group." First, they would learn a melody; then, he remembered, "We hummed, and when we knowed [sic] the tune itself, the melody, one of us would take the melody, three-part, four-part harmony . . . Sometimes we couldn't get the correct chord, you know, four-part harmony, we couldn't get it all the way through, we'd double up, you see."[71] Ory recalled how they would gather on a bridge on the plantation at night and "In the dark, just couldn't see anyone, no one could see us, could hear us, you know, singing on the bridge."[72] At the time they didn't use instruments. Ory recalled, "My first instrument was a cigar-box banjo that I made myself. When I was a little better than ten years old, my father bought me a real banjo from New Orleans."[73] Later other homemade instruments were added and they would "try to sing along with it."[74] Although by the time Armstrong was sitting in with his band Ory was working professionally with a store-bought instrument, the method his band employed to find their harmony parts were the same as he had employed since childhood. Once someone in the band knew the melody, Ory could then harmonize using principles he had learned in the humming group, and he would apply these principles to his instrument.

The clarinetist in Ory's band, Johnny Dodds (born April 12, 1892), came from a musical family and also had a background in singing harmony.[75] His younger brother Warren "Baby" Dodds said of his mother, "I don't recall that she played any musical instruments but she used to sing religious songs with the rest of the family,"[76] and his father was "very religious and he only played and sang hymns and sacred music."[77] His father and his brother played violin, and one of his sisters played the melodeon. His father and sister also used to play harmonicas. He explained, "My sister used to play some blues and I tried to pick it up."[78] What united all of the members of the family is that they would sing together. As Baby Dodds clarified, "Everybody in the family used to sing. It was the most beautiful quartet you ever heard, to hear that outfit sing. I could sing soprano or tenor and my brother john used to sing real high tenor."[79] The Dodds brothers also started out on homemade instruments. Baby Dodds aspired to play the drums: "So I finally got an idea," he said, "I took a lard can and I put holes in the bottom and turned it over and took nails and put holes in the top of it. Then I took some rounds out of my mother's chairs and made drum sticks out of them. Sometimes we used to go in the back yard, to our back place. There was a baseboard and I used to kick my heels against the baseboard and make it sound like a bass drum, using the can as a snare drum."[80] Johnny's first instrument was a toy flute that may have originally belonged to his brother.[81] With Baby Dodds playing his homemade drum, "it sounded so good that all the kids in the neighborhood came around to get in on the fun."[82] Johnny Dodds began playing in Ory's band around 1910.[83] According to Pops Foster, Ory liked the way Dodds played, "so he hired him." And "Ory's band was the only one Johnny played with until he left New Orleans."[84]

It seems likely that Armstrong sat in with Ory's band as often as he could after his release from the Waifs' Home, and that he had quite a limited repertoire at this time. According to Manuel Manetta, Armstrong could only play three tunes. These were "Sister Kate" (which Manetta said Armstrong wrote in 1917), "Wind and Grind," and "just an old blues," a version of which was recorded by Manetta on piano for the Hogan Jazz Archive in New Orleans. He remembered that Armstrong would play this blues "day and night."[85] At this time he remembered Armstrong was living at Perdido and Liberty Streets directly behind Joe [John] Segretto's saloon at 1132 Perdido.[86] The saloon had a piano player and drummer and Armstrong could be heard playing along in his backyard. Manetta remembered Armstrong sitting in with Ory's band. At this time, he was playing a brass "C. G. Conn horn given to him by Joe Oliver."[87] Armstrong did confirm that Oliver had given him a cornet during the time he was playing at "Henry Matranga's honky-tonk." Oliver reputedly told Armstrong, "I'm sick of looking at that beat-up cornet. I'm going to give you a horn."[88] Armstrong said, "I prized that horn and guarded it with my life, I blew it for a long, long time before I was fortunate enough to get another one."[89] According to Armstrong it was a cornet made by York that he was given by Oliver rather than a Conn. Either way it would have been an improvement of the Tonk Brothers cornet Armstrong had played before this time.

The balance of probability is that Armstrong did not have a cornet after leaving the Waifs' Home, and he borrowed money from either Charlie the newspaper seller or the Karnofskys to buy the Tonk Brothers cornet. There is no reason to doubt that Joe Oliver gave Armstrong a Conn or a York cornet sometime before the end of 1917. The reason we can date this is that Armstrong said he did not buy his first new cornet until after the closure of Storyville on November 12, 1917. As Armstrong remembered it, "I got my first brand new cornet on an installment plan with 'a little bit down' and a 'little bit' now and then."[90] This enabled Louis to get his first regular gig in New Orleans. Armstrong said, his "first [music] job in New Orleans" was "playing in a honky-tonk-Matranga's at Franklin and Perdido" and that he was seventeen years old at the time, playing with Boogus on piano and Sonny Garbie on drums.[91] At this time he still had a job "at the coal yard loading carts." This was confirmed by Manetta, who said that Armstrong could often be seen loading coal at Poydras Market at the time. According to one account, Armstrong found work at Henry Matranga's bar because Bunk Johnson did not turn up to play one night.[92] Armstrong said he was hesitant about playing because he had not "touched a cornet for the last two years."[93] Armstrong explained that he did not have a cornet, and Matranga said, "I'll go with you right now to Jack Fink's. I'll buy you a cornet and it'll belong to you after two months if you don't miss a single night."[94] Because he hadn't played for a period and his lip was not in good shape he reputedly fell back on singing popular songs.[95]

One tune that Armstrong is attributed as playing during the period he worked for Matranga is "Swanee River."[96] In *Horn of Plenty* it is recorded that Oliver came to hear Armstrong when he was playing at Matranga's.[97] Oliver then asked Louis to sit in for him at Pete Lala's for three nights because Oliver was due to work in Mobile.[98]

It is possible that Armstrong was working on and off selling milk, selling coal, and playing at Matranga's through the flu epidemic of 1918 and up to the end of World War I. In one account, he quit the coal cart on Armistice Day and began his career as a full-time musician.[99] The likelihood, however, is that he had probably given up selling coal before the end of the war. Armstrong was required to register for the draft and gave his occupation as "Musician" and his employer as "Pete Lala." If he had been working on a coal round (and working as a musician at night), he would have had good reason to give his occupation as "coal seller" and his employer as Andrews or the Karnofskys. Selling coal was a restricted occupation.

It has become part of the legend of New Orleans jazz that with the closure of Storyville the New Orleans musicians were unable to make a living and went to Chicago and elsewhere. This is a legend that Armstrong played a part in disseminating.[100] Although many musicians had left New Orleans long before the closure of Storyville (and many more would stay on afterward), one musician who did appear to fit this narrative was Joe Oliver. As Armstrong told of these events, "In 1917 they closed down the district and all the honky-tonks and in 1918, when Joe Oliver left New Orleans with Jimmy Noone to play in Chicago, they put me in his place in Kid Ory's band playing at Tom Anderson's restaurant."[101] However the circumstances around Joe Oliver leaving for Chicago were not actually related to the closure of Storyville. According to Ory, "In my dance band at that time—around 1917—Joe (King) Oliver was my trumpet player. I received an offer to take my band to Chicago, but I was doing too well in New Orleans to leave. Joe, however, along with Jimmie Noone, who was my clarinetist, decided to go up to Chicago."[102] According to Stella, Oliver's wife, Joe left New Orleans because he had been arrested when he was playing at the Stable on Poydras Street with Kid Ory's band.[103] According to Stella, "one night, the place was raided and everyone was taken to jail; Joe thought it was awful that a man who was making an honest living could be taken to jail like that, so he went to Chicago."[104] This appears to have resulted from a dispute between the owners of the Stable and the Roof Garden. Oliver had by this time become a big attraction. According to Ory, "The owners of the Roof Garden 'got jealous' and turned them in. It was during prohibition. The musicians, over by the band stand, were surprised when they were taken away with the customers" and fined $2.50 each.[105] It was this, rather than the closure of Storyville, that persuaded Oliver to leave New Orleans and go to Chicago.

Before he left New Orleans, Oliver offered Ory some advice on how to fill his place in the band. But Ory said he had "already picked out his replacement."[106] Both Ory and Oliver had Louis Armstrong in mind. According to Ory, "There were many good, experienced trumpet players in town, but none of them had young Louis' possibilities. I went to see him and told him that if he got a pair of long trousers I'd give him a job. Within two hours, Louis came to my house and said, 'Here I am. I'll be glad when eight o'clock comes. I'm ready to go.'"[107] Armstrong told a slightly more romanticized version of the same event:

> The minute the train [carrying Oliver to Chicago] started to pull out I was on my way out of the Illinois Central Station to my [coal] cart—when Kid Ory called to me. "You still blowin' that cornet?" he hollered. I ran back. He said he'd heard a lot of talk about Little Louis. "Hmmm..." I pricked up my ears. He said that when the boys in the band found out for sure that Joe Oliver was leaving, they told him to get Little Louis to take Joe's place. He was a little in doubt at first, but after he'd looked round the town he decided I was the right one to have a try at taking that great man's place. So he told me to go wash up and then come play a gig with him that very same night. What a thrill that was! To think that I was considered up to taking Joe Oliver's place in the best band in town.[108]

Whether Armstrong actually owned a cornet at this time is open to question. Ory said he had to buy him one to enable him to play with the band.[109] This piece of detail is omitted from Armstrong's recollection.

> The first night I played with Kid Ory's band, the boys were so surprised they could hardly play their instruments for listening to me blowing up a storm . . . I was doing everything exactly the way I heard Joe Oliver do it. At least I tried to. I even put a big towel around my neck when the band played a ball down at Economy Hall. That was the first thing Joe always did—he'd put a bath towel around his neck and open up his collar underneath so's he could blow free and easy. And because I'd listened to Joe all the time he was with Kid Ory, I knew almost everything the band played, by ear anyway. I could catch on real fast.[110]

Ory tempers his recollection of these events to reflect on Louis's improvement over time: "After he joined me, Louis improved so fast it was amazing. He had a wonderful ear and a wonderful memory. All you had to do was to hum or whistle a new tune for him and he'd know it right away. And if he played a tune once, he never forgot it. Within six months, everybody in New Orleans knew about him."[111] As a result, according to Armstrong, "Kid Ory really did get a lot of gigs. He even started giving his own dances, Monday nights downtown at Economy Hall. Monday night was a slow night in New Orleans at that time, and we didn't get much work done in other places. But Kid Ory did so well at Economy Hall that he kept it up for months and made a lot of dough for himself. He paid us well too."[112]

Another early band that Armstrong played with casually was the Tuxedo Orchestra, run by the trombone player William "Baba" Ridgley, who said that Armstrong "jobbed around" with them: "He was young, very young; he hadn't started playing with no bands hardly yet."[113]

Baba Ridgley (born 1882) began his musical education playing string bass.[114] Every Sunday morning, "Professor" Jim Humphrey would visit Jefferson Parish where Ridgley lived and give him lessons.[115] Humphrey encouraged Ridgley to try the trombone, and after a year and a half, Ridgley started playing trombone with the Silver Leaf Orchestra.[116] His musical education was probably still quite elementary as he remembered that the first tune he played was "Harmony Rag," which was easy with "just a few whole notes and vamp."[117] He also played by "head" on trombone and learned to play the blues.[118] According to Ridgley, Humphrey's arrangements for the brass band that he taught in Jefferson Parish were "simple things they were already familiar with: songs, hymns . . . The tunes would already be in their heads, but at the same time, they were learning to play their instruments."[119]

Although Humphrey would have provided some knowledge of reading music, Ridgley relied substantially on playing by ear. Ridgley was asked "what he was thinking about when he played Dixieland trombone in the old days," and he explained that "most of the old-time trombone players either didn't read music or read music very little, and they made up their parts, playing bass notes mostly, or a 'slide' [i.e., glissando], with an occasional small solo; they faked their parts, relying on their ears to tell them what to play."[120] In a similar way to Armstrong, Ridgley explained the importance of at least one musician in an ensemble being able to read music well enough to play the melody from sheet music. He explained that if one of the "musicians could figure out the melody from an orchestration, they would make up the other parts."[121] Another way that the Tuxedo Orchestra would learn a new tune was from a recording. The clarinetist Zeb Leneries could pick off the melody from a recording and had the "ability to help other musicians in the band to make up their own parts."[122] Morris French thought that when Armstrong "first started, he and others would get tunes from phonograph records."[123] According to Ridgley, Armstrong "had a wonderful ear and was good at playing harmony parts."[124] Learning a new tune was a time-consuming process; it could take from "two to five hours," but, once a tune was learned, they "always played it the same way."[125] Through this rehearsal method, "the band members grew to know what to expect from the other members; they knew they could depend on one another to play the same way every time."[126]

Although Ridgley was the business manager of the Tuxedo Orchestra, as was usual in a New Orleans ensemble the orchestra was led musically by a cornet player: Papa Celestin.[127] Papa Celestin ran the Tuxedo Brass Band, too, and the musicians were much the same in both organizations.[128] When Armstrong joined the Tuxedo Brass Band, Joe Howard "was playing second" and according to Ridgely, "Louis was playing first with Celestin."[129] If this is true, then maybe he doubled on the melody.

Armstrong's first opportunity to play with the Tuxedo Orchestra was when they were hired to play a social club event at Milneburg on the southern shore of Lake Pontchartrain. Armstrong and the Tuxedo Orchestra were "to meet the members at their club in the 300 block of North Dupre on Saturday morning and march the three blocks to Canal Street, where they would board the train to take them to Spanish Fort."[130] Celestin could not make the engagement and Joe Oliver was not available either. Oliver offered to send "a good scholar" as his replacement.[131] Armstrong reported to the band wearing a police cap that was too big for him, a little blue coat, and his cornet under his arm in a dirty bag.[132] Although Ridgley had concerns about whether Armstrong would be able to play with the orchestra, as they would need to play requests, Armstrong knew all of the dance music and songs including "Old Kentucky" that Ridgley mentioned.[133] It transpired that "Louis could play more of them than the rest of the band."[134] In his time with the Tuxedo Orchestra, Louis was remembered as "a devilish little boy . . . if they were playing a funeral or something like that in the rough part of town the bad boys would follow Louis up, get right by him, call him everything you could think of, tell him 'cause you're playing with the Tuxedo Band you think you're somebody.'" The showman in him was also developing at this time. With the Tuxedo he would "dance, shadow-box, [and] everything."[135]

With the exception of his final autobiography that never got beyond a handwritten manuscript, Armstrong had given a fairly consistent account throughout his life of his musical development. He thought of himself primarily as a singer, and he had learned to play the cornet in the Waifs' Home. He had borrowed instruments after his release from the Home up to the time that he bought a Tonk Brothers cornet; he had been given a better cornet by Joe Oliver, and by 1918 was ready to begin his career as a professional musician. All of the bands that he worked with played predominantly by ear, although the leader of the band would learn the melody of new tunes from sheet music. Once the melody was mastered, the other band members would find their parts using their internalized knowledge of singing harmony in quartets and in church. Much of this narrative is supported by those who knew him, and some of these events can be dated through their connection to historical events; however, these accounts suggest that Armstrong was, with the exception of his time at the Waifs' Home, largely self-taught. This narrative also omits any significant mention of Bunk Johnson—the man who claimed to have taught Louis Armstrong and the man that Armstrong would claim was "my musical insparation [sic] all my life—'yea man.'"[136]

CHAPTER 9

DID BUNK TEACH LOUIS?

BUNK JOHNSON HAS LONG POSED A CREDIBILITY PROBLEM FOR JAZZ scholars. He made a significant contribution to the writing of *Jazzmen* (1939), the first book to place New Orleans at the center of the development of jazz, but he very often got his dates wrong. He claimed to have played with Buddy Bolden, the legendary first man of jazz, before 1895. This is probably before Bolden took cornet lessons. He claimed that he and Bolden started New Orleans jazz, but by the best estimates of researchers he was believed to have still been a child when Bolden was at the peak of his powers in the early years of the twentieth century. Thomas Brothers wrote in 1999, "Johnson made many claims about his historic role that were later shown to be false."[1] Since that time some of Bunk's claims have been reexamined and the historical evidence indicates that he was born earlier than many jazz scholars believed. It is also clear from interview notes of Bolden's trombone player, Willie Cornish, that Bunk did play regularly with Bolden.[2] But there is another contentious point: Bunk claimed that he taught Louis Armstrong to play the cornet. On this subject Brothers argues, "Since Johnson's contradictory claims have appeared in biographies (as recently as 1997), it is worth printing Armstrong's clear statement, which appeared in an article titled 'Bunk Didn't Teach Me,' with byline 'as told by Louis Armstrong,' from *The Record Changer* in 1950," and this was a flat denial that Johnson taught him anything.[3] There is, however, still grounds for doubt. There are other articles written by Armstrong that suggest that Bunk did teach him. So, did Bunk teach Louis?

The news that "Bunk Taught Louis" first appeared in *Down Beat* in June of 1939:

> So many articles have been written by phonies who claim they started jazz that I hesitate to reveal the truth . . . The facts have been checked

and re-checked and are as close to the truth as will ever be known ... Willie "Bunk" Johnson, the cornetist who taught Louis Armstrong his first music, tells the story.[4]

The article went on to quote a letter from Bunk to Bill Russell. Bunk claimed he was with "King Bolden's Band" in 1895 and 1896, and this was long before there was any "Dixieland Jazz Band." At the time, this was a considerable revelation. The white "Original Dixieland Jazz Band" claimed to be the creators of jazz, having first recorded as a "Jass" or "Jazz" band in 1917. If Bunk's claims were true, and there were many who came to doubt it, then Johnson was not only the sole surviving jazz musician who played with Buddy Bolden, but through his tutelage of Louis Armstrong, he provided a link back to the origins of jazz. *Down Beat* enthused: "There were three great cornetists, they say—Buddy, Bunk, and Louis. Their music was passed from one to the other. Bolden played a real 'stomp trumpet,' and Bunk added fast fingering, runs and high notes with a sweet tone. Then Louis combined the two styles with his own ideas to become the man who is recognized today as the greatest hot musician of all time."[5] In a section subtitled "Satchmo Agrees It's True," the article claimed they were presenting "facts which Louis himself has corroborated."[6] However, as time went on, Armstrong tried to distance himself from Bunk's claims, saying that Bunk had not taught him anything.

Bunk Johnson had much to gain from promoting himself as the teacher of Louis Armstrong. When the article was written, he was working on a rice plantation driving a truck. His earnings and health were not in good shape, whereas Armstrong was at the height of his fame. Bunk's testimony must therefore be treated with some caution especially in the light of Armstrong's strong denial. But there are some areas of agreement that neither Armstrong nor Johnson dispute. Armstrong did concede that he followed Johnson around in his younger years, and said: "I used to hear him in Frankie Duson's Eagle Band in 1911. Did that band swing! ... He could play funeral marches that made me cry."[7] Although following Bunk on parades and taking lessons from him do not amount to the same thing, there is no doubt that Armstrong was influenced and inspired by him.[8] Armstrong remembered, "When I was a kid in New Orleans, Bunk had a better tone than anybody, I think. A genius—played a lot of beautiful blues."[9] It is also claimed that "Louis learned his style from Bunk," specifically his tendency "of getting behind and catching up later."[10] But there were aspects of the *Down Beat* article that Armstrong may have found troubling.

Louis Armstrong is giving his old teacher a trumpet, and promises of jobs for Bunk have come from many sources. Perhaps soon we will all have the opportunity to hear the man to whom we owe an unpayable debt of gratitude—the man who taught Louis Armstrong and thereby influenced the whole scope of modern swing music—Bunk Johnson.[11]

Despite Armstrong's apparently unassailable place in the history of jazz as the first great soloist, perhaps he feared he could be upstaged by Bunk. This could have made the rediscovery of his alleged onetime teacher problematic.

One person who should have known whether Bunk taught Louis was Sidney Bechet, as he had known both Bunk and Louis in New Orleans. He cannot, however, be presented as a neutral observer, because he had a long-running professional rivalry with Armstrong. In part this was because, as the banjo player Danny Barker explained, in a New Orleans band, "Everybody acknowledged the cornet player as the leader because he carried the lead, and everybody improvised around him."[12] New Orleans clarinetist Barney Bigard, however, suggested that one exception to this was Sidney Bechet.

> Sidney was murder on trumpet players. Now he and Louis Armstrong couldn't get along so you know the rest of those horn blowers were going to catch hell. See Sidney and Louis were both "The King" on their instrument. They didn't record too much together because of the friction. One would want top billing and so forth and that would be a humbug right there, before they got to the music. They both wanted to play lead. Naturally if you're from New Orleans, that's the old way. Trumpet always has the lead and everything else works round it.[13]

Born May 14, 1897, Sidney Bechet was a few years older than Armstrong.[14] Bechet also had the advantage of coming from a Creole family who valued music as a pastime if not as a profession. Bechet's father played flute and could play a little on the trumpet. All his brothers played: Homer played bass; Albert, violin; and Leonard the trombone.[15]

Sidney had a memory of hearing "syncopated music" that went back to the spring of 1903.[16] Leonard, Sidney's older brother, also remembered hearing a vocal group called the Singing Creoles who toured the cafés of New Orleans who "expressed in their refrains, the elementary traces of syncopation."[17] Together the brothers heard street musicians close to Hope's Hall: an "accordion, a mandolin, bass and a clarinet," and as children they danced on the sidewalk to these musicians.[18] Leonard remembered the transition between popular music and ragtime and said it circulated through the sections of New Orleans as "monotonous chants": a blend of Creole song and the blues accompanied on guitar.[19]

Sidney's first instrument was a tin flute that he would play in the evenings with two neighbors: Elizabeth Landreaux (she would be better known in later years as the singer Lizzie Miles) and Wilhelmina Barth. Lizzie remembered, "As kids we'd play together in the evenings when work was done." Lizzie would sing, Wilhelmina would play piano, and Sidney "owned a little nickel-tin flute, that's what he'd play."[20] Around 1908, the Bechet family formed the nucleus of the Silver Bell Band. According to Goffin, "Sidney who was eleven years old became the clarinetist," brother Leonard played the trombone, "while Joseph Bechet played the banjo, Sidney Desvigne the trumpet, Simon Morero [sic] bass, and Alfred Demaselière the drums."[21]

Bechet knew both Bunk Johnson and Louis Armstrong from around 1911 when Armstrong began to follow Bunk around in the parades. As Bechet wrote in his autobiography, "I started playing with Bunk Johnson in the Eagle Orchestra. That used to be Buddy Bolden's band, and Buddy made such an impression around there that people never did stop thinking of it as his band, even long after he got taken."[22] At the time, he said, "I was living at home, and Bunk Johnson came and promised my mother that he would watch out for me: he'd come by for me when he was to play and he'd take me back."[23] What distinguished the Eagle Orchestra from the other bands, at the time, was their ability to play the blues. According to Bechet, other bands could play ragtime but, "when it came to the blues, you couldn't beat Bunk or the Eagle Orchestra."[24]

Bechet reflected on how "It was Bunk Johnson who was first to make me acquainted with Louis Armstrong. Bunk told me about this quartet Louis was singing in. 'Sidney,' he said, 'I want you to go hear a little quartet, how they sing and harmonize.' He knew I was crazy about singing harmony."[25] Bechet and Bunk would also go to shows together: "He'd take me out to those circuses whenever they came into town and they had any singing in them, and he'd take me to vaudeville and all. Whenever there was some quartet or opera, or some harmony, or some big band somewhere, we'd always go."[26] At the time, according to Bechet, "Louis was living over on Perdido Street and then, like I said, he was singing in this quartet. They were real good . . . they had a way. There was a fellow singing there, Little Mack was his name, he was the lead; he became a hell of a good drummer later. And Louis, he sang tenor then."[27] Bechet went many times to listen to Louis and his friends sing, and said, "I got to like Louis a whole lot, he was damn' nice. I was a little older than him. At that time, he sort of looked up to me, me playing in bands and being with the big men."[28] On one occasion Bechet ran into Louis on the street and asked him home for dinner because he wanted Louis and the quartet to come to his house so that his family could hear them sing. But "Louis, he sort of hemmed around, and said he couldn't make it. I could see there was something troubling him and finally he let it out. 'Look, Sidney,' he says, 'I don't have any shoes . . . these I got won't take me there.'"[29] Sidney gave him fifty cents to fix the shoes, but Louis never did turn up. It is likely that these events took place before Louis went into the Waifs' Home in 1913, because Bechet made the observation, "Of course, Louis was playing the cornet a bit before he went into that Jones school, but it was, you know, how kids play."[30] If Louis was taking his first tentative steps to play the cornet with Bunk Johnson before 1913, this would be consistent with Bunk's recollection: "When I would be playing with brass bands in the uptown section (of New Orleans), Louis would steal off from home and follow me. During that time Louis started after me to show him how to blow my cornet. When the band would not be playing, I would let him carry it to please him."[31] Armstrong did confirm, "Whenever ol' Bunk came by, I'd leave my corner [where he was selling newspapers] and follow the wagon . . . He'd let me carry his horn when he wasn't playin,' and it was a big thing for me."[32] Johnson also dated these events: "It was the later part of 1911, as close as I can think. Louis was about eleven years old," and that he started playing the cornet "by head."[33]

Bunk gave quite a bit of detail about how he taught Louis while he was working for "Dago Tony" on Perdido and Franklin Street: "Louis used to slip in there and get on the music stand behind the piano. He would fool around with my cornet every chance he got. I showed him how to hold it and place it to his mouth, and he did so, and it wasn't long before he began to get a good tone out of my horn. Then I began showing him just how to start the blues, and little by little he began to understand."[34] This is corroborated by Louis, who in a 1945 interview said that he used to follow the parades and get as close as he could to Bunk Johnson: "that grand old man of cornet. Whatta man! He used to let me hide behind the piano when he worked for Dago Tony, and I fooled around with his horn every chance I'd get, till I got a sound out of it, Bunk showed me how to play the blues."[35] According to Bunk, "music became easy to him—by head, by ear. And Louis could play anything that he could whistle."[36] If Bunk's recollection is correct, then this must surely date from before Armstrong went into the Waifs' Home.[37] By the time of his release, he already knew how to hold a horn and how to place it in his mouth. Allowing

Armstrong to carry his horn on marches, and showing him basic technique, does not amount to teaching Louis to play cornet—particularly as Bechet said he went into the Waifs' Home still playing in a childlike way. If Bunk did teach Louis in a more formal way, it seems likely that it was after he was released from the Waifs' Home in June 1914. After Armstrong was released from the Home, Bechet said he hired Louis to play an advertising job at the Ivory Theater.[38] Louis was to play cornet and Little Mack was on drums. Bechet said, "That was the first time I ever heard Louis play the cornet."[39]

Not long after this, Louis began to hang around "Buddy Bartelot's" (another spelling for the stage name of the balloonist Joseph Haywood) place where Bunk and Bechet played with the Eagle Orchestra. According to Bechet, "This would be around 1913. Louis used to try to play like Bunk a little, and Bunk would give him lessons too."[40] This is significant, in that Bechet independently verified that Bunk did teach Louis. But the one time that it cannot have been was 1913; Louis was detained for all of that year and for the first half of 1914. Armstrong was still listening to Bechet play after his release from the Waifs' Home because he said, "While I was working at the coal-yard [which was after his release from the Waifs' Home] Sidney Bechet, a youngster from the creole [sic] quarter, came uptown to play at Kid Brown's, the famous parachute jumper who ran a honky-tonk at Gravier and Franklin."[41] Bechet, it seems, does confirm that Bunk taught Louis at some time after he left the Waifs' Home. In another recollection, Bechet remembered how Black Benny—who he came to know through working at Andrews Coal Yard—had told him about a young cornet player who could play "High Society" on his cornet better than Bechet could on his clarinet. Bechet said, "'Well I'd like to see that boy.' He said 'All right, come over with me.' And we went, and it was Louis. And I'll be doggone if he didn't play 'High Society' on the cornet."[42]

In 1941 Armstrong wrote a short article for *Down Beat* in which he says he "had a big surprise in New Iberia, Louisiana, when my 60 year old former teacher, Bunk Johnson, sat in and went to town on a solo with the band."[43] However, later in his career Armstrong was adamant: Bunk "never would tolerate us kids. That story, that he used to teach me and I used to play with his horn, ain't true. He never had time for us kids."[44] Furthermore, "Bunk didn't actually teach me anything; he didn't show me *one* thing."[45] He recalled, "There was a honky-tonk at Gravier and Franklin Streets [Joseph Haywood's] ... At night I'd put on long pants—I was about 17—and I'd hang around this honky-tonk where Bunk was playing," and "Bunk didn't show me nothing."[46] He even went as far as to claim, "Bunk didn't even know me."[47]

One way to date when Armstrong was taught by Bunk—if indeed he was—is by looking at the repertoire that Bunk says he taught Louis. Bunk recalled that Louis wanted to learn to play a tune that Bunk called "Take It Away." This is an alternative title to "Buddy Bolden's Blues," a tune that became popular around 1904 in New Orleans, and "Salty Dog," another song that had been in circulation in New Orleans from early in the twentieth century.[48] Among the published tunes Bunk recalled Armstrong wanted to play was "Didn't He Ramble." This became a staple of the funeral bands in New Orleans and was published in 1902.[49] "Circus Day" is likely to be "Oh, You Circus Day" (1912), which was available for "Band and Orchestra."[50] One of the tunes Bunk remembered Armstrong wanting to learn was "Ball the Jack," which was published in 1913.[51] On another occasion Bunk wrote to Bill Russell: "On Saturday the Eagle Band use to play at the Masonic Hall for Smith and the dances used to last until four O'clock and then they would go over to the tunk my crowd would be waiting for me. I had a piano player, and a drummer. They would play until knock off at the Masonic Hall with the Eagle Band. Then I would go there and play the blues and nothing but the blues and Louis favorite piece was 'Balling the Jack.'"[52] If Bunk's recollection is correct regarding "Ballin' the Jack," Louis was following Bunk after 1913, and it is at this time that he most likely to have given Armstrong lessons—if he actually did.

But there is some testimony that suggests that Bunk was not in New Orleans after 1910. According to Pops Foster:

> Bunk played a beautiful horn and nobody else around New Orleans played the same style Bunk did. He played the most beautiful tones. After a while Bunk got to drinking so bad they fired him and then he went with Frankie Dusen's band . . . Bunk would show up to play so drunk he'd be draggin' his coat across the floor and couldn't find the bandstand . . . He'd drink til he passed out and then sleep it off on a pool table, get up, and start drinking again . . . He got to drinking so bad that even the Eagle Band fired him about 1910 and no one else would hire him. He left town with a minstrel show and I didn't see him again until 1937 when I was playing with Louis Armstrong's band in New Iberia, Louisiana."[53]

Foster went on to say that at the time when Armstrong started playing on the riverboats in 1919, "Bunk wasn't even around New Orleans when Johnny Dodds and Peter Bocage got Louis the job with Fate Marable on the riverboats."[54] If Bunk was not in New Orleans in the period 1910 to 1919 then this would seem to rule out the possibility that Bunk taught Louis. Bunk probably did leave New Orleans to work in the travelling shows and may well have been away for periods, but other musicians, including Armstrong, recall Bunk being in town after Armstrong's release from the Waifs' Home.[55] "William Johnson" is an extremely common name, however an entry in *Soards' New Orleans City Directory* of 1913 of a "musician" by this name at 1408 Perdido could well be Bunk.

The most compelling evidence that Johnson did teach Armstrong comes from a casual and somewhat drunken conversation that was overheard many years after these events. Jerry Blumberg, who played trumpet with Bunk on his last tour up north in 1947, remembered, "Harold Drob and I one day found Bunk at the end of one of his drinking cycles" in the Automat in Manhattan.[56] Bunk was in a disheveled condition and had gone to order some eggs. According to Blumberg, "He probably hadn't been to bed in a couple of days. That suit he wore was all creased up."[57] Bechet came in and sat at the same table. When Bunk joined them, he was hardly able to hold his fork "and was getting eggs all over."[58] First Bunk mentioned Freckle Face Mary, a girlfriend of his back in New Orleans, and he reminded Bechet of how "when I was leaving out, the front door, you were coming in the back Sidley [sic]."[59] This made Bechet uncomfortable and he responded, "Please Bunk. That was years ago. How come you never mentioned that to me before?"[60] Bunk's mood became serious: "Sidley, [sic] Why is Louis saying those things about me that I never taught him? You were there. You know I taught Louis. I used to teach you both in the same place." Bechet's response does seem to confirm that Bunk taught Louis: "Bunk, you know Louis. You can't change him. There's not a thing you can do about it. Just try not to be bothered by it."[61] While it is possible that Bechet simply went along with what Johnson was saying to avoid getting into an argument, given that he had independently confirmed that Bunk taught Louis on another occasion, and he had written in his autobiography, "Louis, he was like a son to Bunk. He'd taught Louis some, and Louis used to practice with Bunk," the balance of probability is that Johnson did teach Armstrong.[62] If this is true, then it raises the question of why, even after Johnson's death, when he was no longer a challenge to Armstrong (if ever he was), he still adamantly denied that Johnson taught him anything?

If Bunk did teach Louis, there is perhaps another reason why Louis wanted to downplay this suggestion. The answer may lie as much with Joe Oliver as with Bunk Johnson. The *Down Beat* article that announced "This Isn't Bunk: Bunk Taught Louis" made the observation that with the rediscovery of Bunk

Johnson "The influence of King Oliver upon Louis has been exaggerated, but through no fault of those who claim that Oliver taught him."[63] Armstrong would concede that "Bunk was my idol," but he would go on to say "but Oliver used to come over to the honky tonk where I played and sit in. He'd show me things you know. He had some ideas. I think he was a little more alive musically than Bunk. Everything I did, I tried to do it like Oliver."[64] Armstrong would consistently claim that it was Oliver who was his mentor and not Johnson. Joe Oliver had died in impoverished conditions a year before the *Down Beat* story appeared, and Armstrong was aggrieved that "Joe never got the break Bunk Johnson did."[65] Plagued by bad health, rotting teeth, and high blood pressure, Oliver was compelled to retire from music making. In 1937 Louis Armstrong took a band to Savannah, Georgia, where Oliver was then living. Armstrong remembered, "He's got so bad off and broke, he's got himself a little vegetable stand selling tomatoes and potatoes . . . I gave him about $150 I had in my pocket."[66] Joe "King" Oliver died on April 10, 1938, in Savannah.

Armstrong remembered how Oliver "took such a liking to me he started giving me lessons and answered anything I wanted to know. He taught me the modern way of phrasing on the cornet and trumpet."[67] Joe Oliver was "never was too busy to help the youngsters, you know. He did a lot for me. It broke my heart to lose him."[68]

> To me Joe King Oliver was the greatest of them all. He certainly didn't get his right place in the mentionings of Jazz History as he so rightfully deserved. He was a creator with unlimited ideas. And he had a heart as big as a whale when it came to helping the underdog in music such as me. I was just a kid, Joe saw, I had possibilities and he'd go out of his way to help me or any other ambitious kid who were interested in their instrument as I was.[69]

Armstrong mused:

> I was very young when I first heard Joe Oliver. He was with the Onward Band, a brass band they had down there in New Orleans—a good brass band. About twelve pieces: with three trumpets and three cornets. Joe was playing cornet at the time. Two of them would play lead; there was Joe and Manny Perez. I used to second line behind them. When Joe would get through playing I'd carry his horn. I guess I was about 14. Joe gave me cornet lessons, and when I was a kid I ran errands for his wife.[70]

Armstrong also was able to listen to Oliver while he was on his coal round, as he recalled:

> How he [Joe Oliver] used to blow that cornet down on Storyville for Pete Lala . . . I was just a youngster who loved that horn of King Oliver's . . . I would delight delivering an order of stone coal to the prostitutes who used to hustle in her crib right next to Pete Lala's cabaret . . . Just so's I could hear King Oliver play . . . I was too young to go into Pete Lala's at the time . . . And I'd just stand there in that lady's crib listening to King Oliver . . . And I'm in a daze . . . I'd stand there listening to King Oliver beat out one of those good ol good-ones like "Panama" or "High Society."[71]

Joe Oliver became a father figure to Armstrong, and it would be Oliver who would persuade Armstrong to leave New Orleans and embark on a career that would make him a household name. Armstrong owed a lot to Oliver. He possibly also felt somewhat guilty: he could have done more for "Papa" Joe in his final years and possibly regretted that he had not done so. Instead Bunk seemed poised to eclipse Oliver, and maybe this is really why Armstrong tried to downplay Bunk's formative influence.

CHAPTER 10

"GOING TO THE CONSERVATORY"

BY THE TIME ARMSTRONG WAS EIGHTEEN YEARS OLD, HE HAD SUNG AT amateur nights with his quartet, performed with the Waifs' Home Orchestra, played with Kid Ory's Orchestra, had jobbed with the Tuxedo Orchestra, and had impressed older New Orleans musicians with his ability to learn melodies by ear and to make up harmony parts. However, his reading skills were less developed, or as veteran New Orleans music educator Willie E. Humphrey put it, when Armstrong went to work on the riverboats, "Louis couldn't do much, but he could play."[1] During the time that Armstrong worked with Fate Marable's Orchestra on the Streckfus paddle steamers, Armstrong began to improve his reading of music and, critically, he would continue to play by ear and do so on an expanded repertoire.

The Acme Packet Company was founded by Captain John Streckfus Sr. in 1884, shipping freight from Rock Island, Illinois.[2] In response to the expanded railroad network that was increasingly taking trade away from the river, the company launched the first riverboat built expressly for excursions in New Orleans in 1901.[3] Named using the founder's initials, the *J.S.* worked the upper Mississippi and the Ohio River during the summer.[4] The first musicians employed by Streckfus on the *J.S.* were a trio of black musicians playing mandolin, guitar, and banjo, out of Des Moines, Iowa.[5] Around 1903 the company ran excursions between New Orleans and St. Paul, and hired Charlie Mills—a black piano and calliope player—who led three white musicians who played trumpet, violin, and drums.[6] It seems that the presence of a mixed race band on the boat was not an issue for the company or its customers. The next musician to take over from Mills leading the musicians on the *J. S.* was Fate Marable, a black musician who hired white musicians to play in his ensembles. Initially Marable led a duo. He reflected on how in 1907 the *J. S.* "sailed to New Orleans that year with me at the piano, and a white fellow playing the violin. That's all we had." Later on, "we added one more piece until we had what we thought was a great big band. Four pieces—piano, violin, trumpet and drums. All of them white boys but me, and playing strictly ragtime."[7] Marable's instrumental quartet was playing on the *J.S.* in 1910 when the boat caught fire. The fire started while people were dancing and initially the band paid little attention to the commotion. The violinist, Red Robinson, said, "I am going to see what is wrong."[8] When he had not returned to the bandstand after a few minutes the cornet player, Ollie Ferguson, said to Marable, "I am going out to see what is the matter and find out where our violin player Red has gone."[9] He did not return either. Finally, Marable left the bandstand leaving the drummer on his own. The band was not reunited until the boat had moored up and musicians and passengers had been taken off. The boat did not survive the fire and sank.[10] The loss of the *J.S.* prompted the company to reorganize. The following year the newly titled Streckfus Steamboat Line bought the entire fleet of the Diamond Jo Packet Line and adapted the boats for use as excursion steamers. The modified steamers were overseen by the four sons of John Streckfus Sr.: Joe (the oldest), Roy, John Jr., and Verne (in descending ages).[11] Up to 1917, Marable had used musicians who predominantly came from his home town of Paducah, Kentucky. He explained, "We were going in and out of New Orleans all the time . . . and I began to notice the type of music they were playing there. It just got under my skin."[12] Marable had come to realize his Kentucky band although they played "real nice, they could not compete with the New Orleans boys."[13] Marable's decision to form a band of New Orleans musicians, that would come to be known as the New Orleans Cotton Pickers, may not have been entirely based on musical aesthetics. The Streckfus Steamboat Line faced competition from the larger Eagle Packet Company that ran excursion boats out of St. Louis; however, in 1918 the Eagle's fleet was destroyed by ice and this led the Streckfus Line to concentrate its efforts on dominating the St. Louis excursion trade.[14] It could be that the decision to form the New Orleans Cotton Pickers was part of a corporate strategy to provide something up to date. It may not be a coincidence that the first recording by a "jazz" or "jass" band a year earlier, "Livery Stable Blues," had been a sensation for the Original Dixieland Jazz Band who hailed from New Orleans. Given that music played a prominent role on the excursion steamers, and emphasis was placed on keeping abreast of the changes in musical tastes, it is likely that the Streckfus family supported and may even have guided Marable toward this decision. The Streckfus family had a musical background and took an active part in the musical management on the boats. Captain John Streckfus Sr. played the violin and ensured that his sons were provided a musical education.[15] His sons Roy and Verne played violin and Joe and John Jr. played piano.[16] Marable was well suited to provide what the Streckfuses wanted as they demanded a high standard from their musicians. New Orleans drummer Zutty Singleton explained, "There was a saying in New Orleans. When some musician would get a job on the riverboats with Fate Marable, they'd say, 'Well you're going to the conservatory.' That's because Fate was such a fine musician and the men who worked with him had to be really good."[17] Armstrong also held Fate Marable in high regard: "Every musician in New Orleans respected him."[18] He had developed a reputation among the piano players of New Orleans. Armstrong recalled, "He had fine jam sessions with the piano greats of those days . . . He always won the greatest honors with them."[19]

It is claimed that Marable offered to personally teach Armstrong to read music. Marable said, "'Now, Louis, you are a special trumpeter but you must learn to read. I will teach you every morning at 10:00.' He needed the discipline, needed to learn it. I told him if he didn't take my lessons, I would fire him. Louis didn't show up for his lessons. He had agreed to them. He had said 'Yes,' but he didn't show."[20] Given that Armstrong seemed keen throughout his life to take every opportunity to improve his musicianship, and considering his regard for Marable, avoiding these lessons seems out of character.

According to Verne Streckfus, "Louis Armstrong couldn't read at all when he first joined the band, however, he could learn a piece by hearing it played through once."[21] There were other musicians in the orchestra who could not read music; this raises the question of how they survived in such a demanding situation. The answer is found in the way that Marable conducted rehearsals. Although Marable had benefited from a good musical education—his mother was a piano teacher in Paducah, Kentucky, and he had studied at Straight University in New Orleans—it was not essential for the musicians in the band to read fluently because he would play to them at the piano and they would learn new music by ear.[22] It is not clear if Marable played just the melody to his musicians or if he played the musicians their parts. Given that there was a tradition in New Orleans of the reading musicians playing the melody to enable non-readers to find suitable harmony parts, it is possible that this is how Marable organized rehearsal. Marable acknowledged, "Lots of those jazz musicians couldn't read music—never mind an arrangement . . . Sometimes, there was only one man in a jazz band who could read."[23] Marable took a pragmatic approach, saying, "I have played ragtime, jazz-time and swing and I believe that the Dixieland style of jazz gives a man the best chance to play what's in him. A real jazz musician doesn't require the other man's thought through arrangements. He plays as a solid musician of his own making."[24] Although some of the band could not read music, all the musicians would have sheet music in front of them when they performed. According to Verne, although they turned the pages at the start of a new number, "it didn't mean anything."[25]

Accounts differ as to who it was that got Armstrong a job on the riverboats. Baby Dodds and Pops Foster were working on the boats in 1918. Foster had been playing on the riverboats at the outbreak of the influenza epidemic and he remembered that "we had to lay off for a couple of months" before finishing out the summer season. He worked as a longshoreman loading and unloading boats and then rejoined Marable.[26] According to Dodds, it was Foster who wanted Armstrong to join the band. Baby Dodds's brother, John, was then working with Armstrong in Kid Ory's Orchestra, and John didn't want Armstrong to leave the band. According to Baby Dodds, "Finally, I won out. It was a big job but I made it and we had Louis with us on the boat. Louis and I stayed on the boats from the fall of 1918 until September of 1921."[27] Foster had been influential in getting Dodds onto the riverboats. As Foster remembered things, Peter Bocage (born 1887) who organized and played in many of the New Orleans ragtime bands, and Johnny Streckfus (probably the father) had approached him about working on the riverboats.[28] They tried out three or four drummers before accepting Dodds, who got the job because of his reading skills. "I went down to St. Catherine's [sic, Katherine's] Hall where he was playing every night with Willie Hightower's band and finally got him to come with us."[29] Bocage continued:

> Fate and I were friends when he first came down here, see . . . Fate was the onliest colored boy in the band; all the rest was white boys . . . They only had about four or five of them in the band, see. But when they got ready to put a New Orleans band on there, well, I got—Fate asked me to get the men for him, see? Well I, I got a ten-piece band for him, see, and I was playing trumpet.[30]

Bocage also said that he had been responsible for getting Armstrong the job on the riverboats with Marable. In May 1918 the boat was due to go upriver for the summer season, and Bocage didn't want to go. Instead he took a job with Armand J. Piron at Spanish Fort.[31] Bocage recalled that Armstrong was playing with Ory at the time: "they were playing on Claiborne St.—they had a dance place back there. So, I took Fate back there and—to see him, you know? And he decided to go."[32] Foster did confirm, "We got Louis Armstrong out of the Ory Band to play with us [on the boats]. Louis was the only one out of Ory's band who could read at all, and Louis couldn't read so good."[33]

There are, however, a number of different accounts of how Armstrong came to work on the riverboats. In another account, Louis Armstrong had come to the attention of the Streckfus brothers when he was working with Kid Ory and Joe Oliver at Economy Hall.[34] Usually Marable was responsible for getting the musicians for his orchestra, but according to Verne Streckfus, Louis was an exception. Verne remembered that he and his brother had to apply for a permit to attend a function where Ory, Oliver, and Armstrong were playing. According to Verne, Louis was so shy that later they had to go over to South Rampart Street (where Armstrong lived) to persuade him to join the *Capitol*.[35] Finally there is Armstrong's own account. In this version, the Ory band met another band on the corner of Rampart and Perdido and got into a contest. Armstrong remembered "a man was standing on the corner listening to the 'fight.'"[36] This was Fate Marable, who wanted Armstrong to come and join his band. The constant running through all these accounts is that Armstrong was with Ory's band at the time before starting on the riverboats.

When Armstrong played in Ory's band, Verne said that Armstrong played a cornet that had been loaned to him by Ory, and when Armstrong joined the band on the *Capitol* he used a cornet that belonged to the boat.[37] This is confirmed by Dodds.[38]

> I remember when he [Louis Armstrong] first came on the boat, he didn't have a horn. And in Davenport, Iowa, Bix Beiderbecke and some of the other white musicians came on the boat to listen and talk to the different musicians. Louis told Bix he didn't have a horn, so Bix said, "Well, meet me when I go out and I'll see if I can get you a horn." And Bix took him out afterwards and helped him pick out a horn.[39]

Armstrong did later say that each spring the boat would go to Davenport, Iowa, and that was where he first met Beiderbecke. He remembered Bix as "a nice ofay kid the young musicians wanted to introduce me to."[40] However the first time he heard him play was when he heard Beiderbecke's recording of "Singing the Blues" in 1927. Thereafter they would jam together after finishing their gigs when they were both working in Chicago.[41]

Baba Ridgley, who Louis had known from the Tuxedo Orchestra, was with Louis for the first year that he was on the boat. At the time, the band consisted of Louis Armstrong (cornet), Baba Ridgley (trombone), Pops Foster (string bass), Joe Howard (cornet), Baby Dodds (drums), Davy Jones (mellophone), and Johnny St. Cyr (banjo).[42] Some of these musicians, and others who later joined Marable's orchestra, were good readers, and they were particularly influential in helping Armstrong with his musical studies. According to Dodds, "There were some other wonderful musicians in the river boat band beside Fate Marable. There was Joe Howard who was a very even-tempered nice-going fellow. He would try to tell you everything right if he possibly could and would show us anything that he could to improve the group. But he would get angry with himself sometimes and we could see the different expressions on his face. He would never bother anybody though. He helped Louis a great deal with the mastering of musical ability."[43] Dodds remembered, "Louis learned a lot about music from Joe Howard on the boats."[44] As Foster remembered it, "Joe Howard, one of the old trumpet players in Fate's band, gave Louis a lot of help. Louis should give Joe a whole lot of credit."[45] Howard helped Louis in other ways too. Peter Bocage remembered that Marable used stock arrangements and was asked how Armstrong, who was a poor reader, could manage. Bocage remembered that Joe Howard was in the band and that he was "pretty fair as a musician," and he was the lead trumpet.[46] He explained that Louis "had to have a lead man with him, you see? Louis, Louis would get in there if it was the last thing he did, you understand? He was just talented like that."[47] At this stage in his career, Louis was unable to play the lead on new arrangements because he was a poor reader; however, what he could do was play second by finding an appropriate harmony part to Howard's lead.

Another musician to help Armstrong was Norman Mason. He was born in Miami, Florida, and at a young age his family moved to the Bahamas where his father, a trumpet player, played in the Episcopal Church. When Norman was eight years old his father began to give him lessons. He studied both classical and church music and became an expert reader.[48] At around the age of eighteen, he joined the Rabbit's Foot Minstrels.[49] In November 1914 the Rabbit's Foot Minstrels were in Helena, Arkansas. The *Indianapolis Freeman* reported, "Our superb Gold Band and Orchestra under Prof. E. B. Blake is still featuring the latest publications . . . Norman Mason, our brilliant cornet player is still featuring high ones."[50] Mason was still with the Rabbit's Foot in January 1918 now playing in the "Imperial Jazz Orchestra." It was when that band was in New Orleans that Mason was recommended to Marable.[51]

Mason was interviewed in 1952 about his time with Armstrong on the riverboats and how they worked together. He remembered Louis as being an easygoing fellow who greeted him the first time they met with "Hello,

Gate; let's play something."[52] Mason explained how the two musicians could work together. Mason would "take the lead, play a chorus, Louis would listen, and then give out his own version."[53] Mason believed, because Louis could not read music "this forced him to improvise his own style."[54] According to Mason, Armstrong's style was much the same then as it was later in his career. The only difference he detected was that on the riverboats Louis had more "vibrance."[55]

The person who probably had more influence on Louis than anyone on the riverboats was another veteran of the Rabbit's Foot Minstrels, David Jones.[56] Armstrong remembered meeting Jones on his first trip. This he remembered as being on the "*Sidney*, with a big wheel in the back."[57]

> Before I reached Natchez I had made friends with a member of the band who was to do a great deal for me—almost more than anyone else besides "King" Oliver. His name was David Jones and of course everybody called him "Davey." He played a very unusual instrument called a "melophone."[sic] . . . He was a trained musician, too, and it was Davey who really taught me to read music.[58]

Jones was born around 1888, in Lutcher, Louisiana, less than fifty miles upriver from New Orleans.[59] Armstrong remembered, "between trips on the boat I'd go up on the top deck with the mellophone player, David Jones, and he'd teach me about reading music—how to divide, like two four time, six eight time, had me count different exercises."[60] According to Dodds, Jones was an "easy-tempered fellow who didn't drink at all. His musical ability was also very high and he would show anyone all he knew."[61] Foster also commented on the influence that Jones had on Armstrong: "Dave Jones, the mellophone player in the band, helped Louis too. Dave played as much music on mellophone as Louis did on trumpet."[62] But Armstrong also had what he described as "that voody voody to play jazz there" on the riverboats with Jones, and said, "We'd just go to a department store and get one of them copies [of sheet music]. The man who could read take the lead, and we had it from there."[63] Although this is somewhat cryptic, again Armstrong appears to be describing the practice of New Orleans musicians to have one musician who could read the melody line while other musicians would make up their own harmony parts and countermelodies. According to Armstrong, "Davey Jones cared so much about me being trained better that he taught me for half an hour every afternoon through the six months we were on the river that summer."[64] He remembered, "We would find a quiet place on deck and he'd work with me. He would show me a passage written down and explain it to me and tell me what I should do with it, and then he would carry the melody on his melophone [sic] and I would follow him with the trumpet."[65] Jones recognized that Louis could blow and swing and that music was natural to him. But he told Armstrong that he would never be "able to swing any better . . . until you learn to read. Then you will swing in ways you never thought of before."[66] It is perhaps this realization that was fundamental to Armstrong's development during these years. The ability to read music would supplement what he already knew, broaden his horizons, and open up new possibilities.

Working on the riverboats provided Armstrong with his first steady income from music. The musicians were paid fifty dollars a week and five dollars a week bonus. The bonus was not paid until the end of the summer to ensure the musicians completed the season. Food and lodgings on the boat were supplied free of charge.[67] The musicians were fed at a separate table. According to Dodds, "Some of the fellows thought the food was good but I didn't think so."[68] Working on the Streckfus excursion boats gave Armstrong his first opportunity to play regularly before a white audience. According to Verne, "He was shy and bashful and he had never played for white audiences before."[69] Armstrong was also able to sing with Marable's orchestra. Dodds remembered, "Louis and I used to take vocals on the riverboats."[70] Armstrong may also have used his time on the riverboats to develop his showmanship. The Streckfus brothers bought a sliding whistle for Dodds to play but he "didn't even look at it."[71] Armstrong, on the other hand, did and played it as he had done with his street quartet in New Orleans. He would later record with the instrument on "Sobbin' Blues" with Joe Oliver.[72] Tantalizingly for researchers in jazz trivia, the riverboats may also have been the occasion for Armstrong's first appearance in a film: "In 1919 the band made a short while playing on the top deck."[73] This was, of course, a silent film and Dodds remembered seeing it screened.

The repertoire of Marable's orchestra consisted of popular dance tunes and what Dodds described as "semi-classics and numbers like that."[74] According to Dodds, they "didn't play many blues on the boat":[75]

> The white people didn't go for the blues like they do now. They try them now but they don't know the blues. They think any slow number is a blues type. That's wrong. Blues is blues. In New Orleans we used to play the blues and the very lowest type of dancers used to love such things. They were played very slow and fellows and their girlfriends would stand almost still and just make movements. It was rowdy music, and

yet it wasn't rowdy in a way, either. They often expressed some tragedy, just like "Frankie and Johnny." "Frankie and Johnny" was one of this style of blues they used to sing a long time ago.[76]

Musical tastes were changing. Dance bands increasingly played the blues. Fate Marable would go on to record "Frankie and Johnny" in 1924.[77] But some blues were played when Armstrong was working on the riverboats. Marable remembered, when Armstrong first joined him, one tune that went down well with the audiences was "St. Louis Blues" (1914). Marable relayed how "the power of Armstrong's trumpet sent the famous W. C. Handy composition bouncing off the boat to the shores in both directions."[78] As Marable explained it, "It was an entirely different kind [of] music." It differed from "ragtime which preceded it or the swing which followed."[79]

One way that the new music differed was in its rhythm. During this period, there was a transition from the two-beat syncopations of ragtime to the steady four beats per measure of jazz. The Streckfus brothers took an active interest in the repertoire of the bands on their boats and also the way that the music was played. Dodds said it was because of the way that the Streckfus family wanted their bands to play that led them to leave Marable.

> Streckfus wanted us to play differently and he told Marable so ... The Streckfuses were musicians and they knew what they wanted and they wanted us to beat a different time than we had been using. Some of the older people on the boat couldn't dance to our music and Streckfus wanted to introduce what he called toddle time. It was really two-four time but he wanted four beats to the measure. It's what they are doing today. To me, four beats was all wrong ... Louis was also to play differently from what he had been used to. And I just couldn't do this toddle time on my drums.[80]

Part of the problem was that Dodds thought of himself and Armstrong as the "the stars on the boat," and as he saw it: "if we were the stars, why monkey with us. We had already made a reputation with our music and the people were satisfied. So finally Louis and I left the boat together after handing in written resignations. That was about the first of September, 1921."[81]

Although Dodds seems to have had great difficulty adapting to what the Streckfuses wanted, it seems that Armstrong was more adaptable. Joseph Streckfus said, "I recall the fall of one season when Fate Marable, Louis Armstrong, and fellow musicians in the band that completed the summer season on the *SS 'St. Paul'* at St. Louis, and were transferred to the excursion Str. *'Capitol'* at St. Louis ... This band, while at St. Louis on the SS *'St. Paul,'* was the talk of St. Louis—all were good musicians for dancing. Had good rhythm, tempo," and critically, Streckfus recognized that they "played jazz that was different."[82] It seems likely that their repertoire was somewhat limited, because Joseph went on to say, "Personally, I believe that if this band played more variety, they could become the best band in New Orleans."[83] The *Capitol* was returning to New Orleans for the winter season with the band on board, and Joseph thought that this would provide an opportunity for the band to rehearse each day and expand their repertoire.[84] The boat's first stop was in Chester, Illinois, and a rehearsal was called with the intent to give the band "some ideas that were somewhat different from the music as played at St. Louis."[85] This rehearsal did not go well; the band seemed unable to understand how Streckfus wanted them to play. Streckfus had been particularly impressed with the recordings of Art Hickman's Orchestra.[86] At Cape Girardeau, Joe Streckfus and his wife passed a shop in the high street with a Victrola in the window. They decided to enquire if the shop had the Art Hickman recordings they had at home to "demonstrate to our orchestra what we are driving at."[87] The Streckfuses purchased a recording of Hickman's Orchestra playing "Avalon." In fact, Hickman's version of "Avalon" (a song first recorded by Al Jolson in the same year) was a medley of two tunes: "Avalon" and "Japanese Sandman" (1920).[88] The sheet music for both of these tunes is notated in cut-time. The difference between common time (4/4) and cut-time (2/2) is subtle. Ragtime had usually been notated in 2/4 with two quarter-note beats to the measure. Cut-time has what can be interpreted as four quarter notes per measure where each pair is effectively tied together to produce two half measure notes. Both these time signatures stress two down beats per measure. A march could therefore be notated in either 2/4 or 2/2 time with the foot falling on the two beats of each measure.

Joe Streckfus bought two other Hickman recordings: "Love Nest" and "Young Man's Fancy," along with "Avalon," "and all were delivered to the *SS Capitol*."[89] These titles were recorded during the summer of 1920, the last, "Avalon," in October of that year.[90] What all three of these recordings have in common is that they are heard as being in 4/4 time. Art Hickman's Orchestra interpreted the cut-time of the sheet music as 4/4 with the four-beat walking feel that would become typical of later jazz. This was in part due to Art Hickman on piano who consistently played four chords to the measure. It was also in part due to the recordings and sheet music being marked as "Fox Trots." The Fox Trot had started to become popular around

1914—pioneered by husband and wife Vernon and Irene Castle. Their book *Modern Dance* attempted to "uplift" and "purify" dancing to "place it before the public in its proper light."[91] Published at the height of the ragtime craze, the Castles advised, "The One Step is the dance for rag-time music."[92] They would assure their readers, "The One Step, as taught by the Vernons at Castle House, New York, bears no relation or resemblance to the once popular Turkey Trot, Bunny Hug, or Grizzly Bear."[93] These dances had developed alongside ragtime with its syncopated rhythms based on two beats to the measure. The Castles had been influential in introducing the Fox Trot: a smoother flowing dance that was better suited to four beats to the measure and slower tempos than the One Step.[94] The difference between the older ragtime rhythms and the newer 4/4 feel can be seen in the sheet music of "Avalon." Example 11 is the opening three measures from the lyric of "Avalon."[95] Because the bass part—as written—emphasizes beat one and beat three of each measure, this piece could be played with this emphasis throughout and have the feel of a slow march. On the other hand, because the right hand of the piano part has notes on all four beats of the measure it is possible to play this piece with four even beats to the measure as Hickman did. This had the effect of converting the tune to 4/4, or as the Streckfus's described it, playing it in *toodle time*.[96] A second interesting feature are the solfeggio symbols that appear above the melody. Given that solfeggio singing was so widely used, the publisher provided the singer with the "Do" "Re" "Me" initials to assist the vocalist.[97] The third feature of note is the observation that Joseph Streckfus made about the tendency of "Avalon" to change from key to key. He remembered in the Hickman recording of "Avalon" there was "one chorus in one key, then a few bars of modulation and into another key, and played [a] second chorus in that key." Then there was a few "bars of chord modulation and into another key."[98] This he believed was "the first record of its kind."[99] The Hickman recording of "Avalon" is in the key of G, and the only modulation of key is at the segue into "Japanese Sandman" where the key modulates to C before returning to G for the reprise of "Avalon." So, why did Streckfus interpret "Avalon" as having a series of modulations every few measures? One possibility is that there is a subtler type of modulation that is apparent from the sheet music. The sheet music for "Avalon" is notated in the key of F major and this is indicated with the single flat (B♭) in the key signature throughout. The opening chord (see Ex. 11) is F major and this chord is the first chord that can be constructed from the notes of the F major scale. Chords are constructed by the vertical stacking of thirds (alternate notes) from a root note; F major has the notes F, A, and C. The

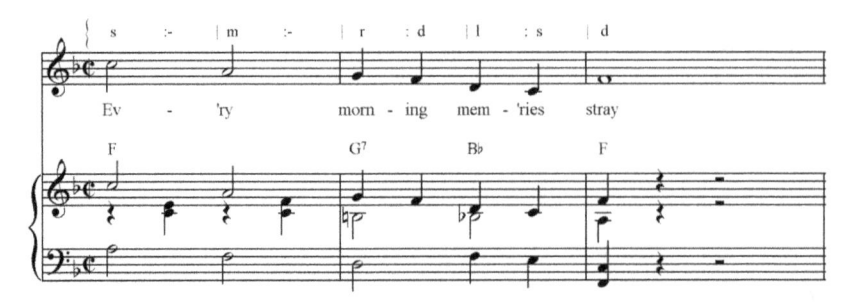

Example 11: Al Jolson and Vincent Rose, "Avalon" (Fox Trot Song, 1920)

chord that can be constructed from the second degree of the scale of F major is G minor. This chord contains G, B♭, and D. In "Avalon" the second chord is G major (G, B♮, and D). This chord is not in the key of F major because B♮ is not a note found in this key: there is a B♭ in the key signature. The chord that follows is a chord of B♭. This chord is in the key of F major and is on the fourth degree (or subdominant) of the scale (B♭, D, and F). The harmonic progression with the major chord on the second degree of the scale has its origins in barbershop harmony, as the African American ethnomusicologist John Work III observed in *American Negro Songs and Spirituals* (1940): "A chord progression which is peculiar to them [barbershop quartets] is the progression from the two-seven chord with a sharp [or a natural where the note is already flattened in the key signature] to the subdominant chord with a sfortzando effect."[100] This progression results from the voice leading of the baritone voice. The baritone voice starts from its traditional place on the fifth of the chord (C in the key of F major) on the last beat of the first measure represented as the lowest note in the piano player's right hand (see Ex. 11). The next note is B♮ and this is the major third of the G-seventh chord (see Ex.11, m. 2).[101] This voice then descends a semitone further to B♭ providing the root of the B♭ chord before arriving on A♮ in the third measure. The baritone voice is now on the major third of the chord of F major and is occupying the position usually held by the tenor voice. In these few measures, we find some of the evolutionary processes of ragtime developing into jazz: the change in rhythm from 2/4 to 4/4 (notated as cut-time) and the distinctive harmonic formulations of barbershop harmony.

According to Joseph Streckfus, "It wasn't long before we were in rehearsal of these pieces by ear. Louis Armstrong, with his trumpet in his hand, came down alongside the Victrola and would pick up on his trumpet the notes in the several chords in the modulations, giving the saxophone section their chords, likewise the brass their changes in chords, and by repeating over and over again, all chords were down pat."[102] Given that the chord changes of "Avalon" were "peculiar" to barbershop harmonic practice, according to John Work III, Armstrong had an advantage over the members of the band who had a traditional training in harmony when it came to picking off the harmony. That evening Marable and his orchestra played "Avalon" to the twelve hundred dancers that were on board and "they stopped the show. Folks crowded around the orchestra stand and applauded and applauded. They never had heard music like that."[103]

The rhythm and tempo of Marable's orchestra became central to its success, and this was commented on by trombonist Robert Carter, who said, "That was the reason they hired Fate and those bands, because they had a different kind of beat . . . They always had a good bouncey [sic] sort of feeling."[104] Marable and his orchestra seem to have learned this lesson well. Listening to Marable's 1924 recording of "Frankie and Johnny," Gunther Schuller has observed that the band "played consistently with a rhythmic drive and energy somewhat akin to swing."[105] By the swing era the 4/4 walking rhythmic feel dominated. But it was not only the change from 2/4 to 4/4 time that was different with the Fox Trot; the Streckfus brothers thought that the tempo that the band played at also needed to be slowed down. While in New Orleans in the fall of 1920, Joseph Streckfus made a visit to the Orpheum Theater on St. Charles to listen to the pit orchestra led by Johnny DeDroit.[106] Later that evening DeDroit played in the Grunewald Hotel for a dance that Streckfus also attended.[107] He recalled, "I could hear and feel that band had the tempo, syncopation and rhythm, and played the right pieces for dancers. The beat was so prominent that I caught myself keeping time with my foot."[108] Using his pocket watch, he counted the beats per minute of DeDroit's band for the various pieces they played. At the following day's rehearsal, Joseph Streckfus asked Marable's orchestra to play the same pieces "just like they played them" for the dances on the boats.[109] Consistently Marable's orchestra played twenty beats per minute faster than DeDroit. Streckfus spent two weeks trying to persuade Marable to play these pieces at a slower tempo until finally Marable played one piece in the final set at the slower speed. Streckfus was on the bridge at the time and recalled hearing "loud hollering," and he thought that something had happened. The dancers were getting off the boat and Streckfus saw Louis Armstrong heading toward him, cornet in hand, and with a smile on his face, saying, "We's got it . . . We played it slow like you wanted it, and I's put in a little swing, and did they like it!"[110] In Streckfus's view, slowing down the tempo made it possible for the band to syncopate the music; whereas, at a faster tempo, this was not possible.

Playing dance music at specific tempos became standardized in the Streckfus steamers. Clarence W. Elder, a musician who began working on the Streckfus riverboats in 1922, remembered John Streckfus Sr. attending rehearsals "with his watch in his hand, and if the band failed to keep the proper tempo (70 beats a minute for fox trots and 90 for one steps) somebody got hell. If it happened too often then there were new faces on the bandstand."[111] Joe Streckfus also attended rehearsals and he would set the tempo. According to Leon King, a musician who worked on the *St. Paul*, Joe Streckfus was a "big fella and he'd get out there and bounce" at the tempo he wanted. He wanted a "bouncing" tempo: "Nothing too fast, nothing too slow." It was easy for the musicians to know when they had the tempo just right. When they saw him "bouncing and laughing" they knew they had it.[112]

It is likely that it was during the return trip to New Orleans in 1920 that Armstrong began to develop as a soloist. Up to this point, he had played second to Joe Howard and Norman Mason. A few days after introducing the Hickman recordings to the band's repertoire, a decision was made that Joseph Streckfus believed "started the success of Louis Armstrong and Fate Marable": Armstrong made his first solo performance.[113] From Streckfus's recollection, the piece he played was "LaVeda." "Louis Armstrong stood up alone and played his first trumpet [*sic*, cornet] solo accompanied with the piano. This was the first time. The applause and requests were so outstanding, they repeated the number."[114] In Verne's account of this evening, he said, "He hadn't ever taken a solo until one night at Caruthersville, Missouri, when the lights were turned down low, he was told to step forward and play a solo; he was elated afterwards, so that he wanted to do it more."[115]

Armstrong's reason for leaving the riverboats probably had nothing to do with how the musicians were asked to play, as according to Joseph Streckfus, "Armstrong was always ready and willing to try out anything for the good of the band"; he was simply ready for something different.[116] He expressed a high regard for the musical taste and judgement of the Streckfus family: "They were real *Groove* people. And Loved music, the way that *I did*."[117] Armstrong's own explanation for leaving was "I was getting tired of the routine on the boat and ready for a change, so I decided to join the orchestra at Tom Anderson's cabaret. They featured me on trumpet solo. On the side, I joined up with the 'Tuxedo' marching brass band."[118]

Whether Armstrong went straight to work for Anderson is unclear. On another occasion he said that after leaving the riverboats, "two seasons later I went to work at the Orchard cabaret for twenty-one dollars a week! Tom

Anderson tempted me with more money and I moved over to The Real Thing, where I worked with Luis Russell, Barney Bigard and Albert Nicholas."[119]

By the time Armstrong left the riverboats, he had been to the Marable "conservatory" and come out of it a more technical musician. He had additional reading skills that could supplement his extraordinary ability to learn melodies, countermelodies, and harmony parts by ear playing second to Joe Howard and Norman Mason. Along with learning to read music, Armstrong was continuing to do what he had done from his early years both with the quartet and with instrumentalists: he was finding harmony parts and countermelodies to someone else's lead. With the New Orleans bands, this would have been a repertoire made up of blues and New Orleans standards. With Marable, Armstrong was applying the same principle to popular songs and, to use Baby Dodds's description, semi-classics. It was not that Armstrong had to choose at this time whether to play from notation *or* to play by ear; he could play from notation *and* play by ear, and increasingly he would do this on an expanding repertoire. He was not alone in playing by ear when necessary on the riverboats. Baba Ridgley never considered himself a good music reader. The trombonist Preston Jackson told of how he played second trombone on the riverboats. He could not read music, and this went undiscovered until the first trombonist went sick.[120] The bass player Pops Foster was not a good reader either. By the time he was working on the riverboats he said he could "read a little, but not much."[121] His own explanation of how he constructed his bass lines was "Hell, I just play any old-go-to-hell note, as long as it swings!"[122] It is interesting that the jazz writer Rudi Blesh observed in Foster's playing a departure from functional harmony that outlined the chords, and found instead evidence of him constructing countermelodies: "Pops often did more than simply 'run changes' . . . frequently, (especially if the tune or chords inspired him) he would build countermelodies to what one or another of the horns was doing. There are not many examples of this, unfortunately, on record, but I have seen him do so many times."[123] Blesh continued, "On some such occasions, his bass countermelodies would be projected pizzicato, but frequently—especially in the blues—they would be arco." More research is needed, but this does raise an interesting question: given that there is little evidence that early New Orleans musicians, inclusive of bass players, thought in terms of vertical harmony, how did they develop their bass parts? It would seem possible, from Blesh's observation, that bass players, like the other pitched instruments in a jazz ensemble, may have constructed countermelodies.[124]

Having played on the riverboats for three years, and having returned briefly to New Orleans, Armstrong remembered, "In 1922, Joe Oliver sent me a telegram in New Orleans saying, 'I want you to come up and join me.'"[125] On August 8, 1922, Armstrong left New Orleans by train telling the porter, "I'm goin' to Chicago, man. I'm goin' to Chicago to play for my idol, Papa Joe."[126] Armstrong was about to embark on what he remembered as "thrilling days" that he would "never forget."[127]

CHAPTER 11

"DIPPERMOUTH BLUES"

THERE IS VERY LITTLE INFORMATION ABOUT JOE OLIVER'S EARLY YEARS. It is thought that he was born in Abend, a few miles from Donaldsonville, Louisiana, on December 19, 1885; no birth certificate has been found to confirm this.[1] We are told that Oliver's mother died sometime around 1900, and Joe subsequently came to New Orleans, where he lived and worked at Levy & Gonsenheim, a shirt-making factory at 2502 Magazine Street.[2] Stella Dominique worked just around the corner on Second Street. Joe and Stella were married on July 13, 1911.[3]

Information about his development as a musician is contradictory. On one hand, there are reports of Oliver leading a band soon after arriving in New Orleans, but other accounts place his maturing as a musician much later.[4] He started on trombone and switched to cornet. Although he had been playing with bands earlier, Preston Jackson remembered, "About 1914 I should say, Joe began to improve a lot. He used to practice very hard. I remember he once told me that it took him ten years to get his tone on his instrument."[5] The piano player Richard M. Jones thought, "Practically overnight, he woke up and started playing. He was a good reader and a good technician. Anything you'd stick up, he'd wipe it right off."[6]

Oliver, as a cornet player and musical leader, needed to be a good reader. It was essential for at least one member of the band to be able to play the melody of new tunes from the sheet music. While in the early dance bands the violinist or the piano player performed this function, by the 1920s the stock arrangements of the period assigned the lead to the cornet player. Oliver from early on had tried to instill in Armstrong the importance of playing lead. Armstrong recalled, "When I was a kid in New Orleans, I used to do a whole lot of figuration. Man I was crazy on that. Joe Oliver tell me, play the lead, boy, play the lead so people can know what you're doing."[7] When Armstrong was around fifteen years old, he remembered, "He'd hang around and he'd listen to me play a while. He'd tell me, 'Listen boy, play some more lead. Stop so much of that variation. Play some lead.'"[8] Armstrong admitted that at that time, "I'd play eight bars and I was gone . . . clarinet things; nothing but figuration and things like that, like what the cats called bop later; that was just figuration to us in the early days. Running all over the horn."[9] Oliver used the term "snakes" to describe these elaborations, advising Armstrong and trombonist Clyde Bernhardt, to get rid of them because "All them snakes you makin' loses the flavor."[10] It is interesting that Oliver used a term associated with black barbershop singing. A "snake" is an African American term for a "swipe" in barbershop slang.[11] It is possible that by the time Armstrong arrived in Chicago he had not completely absorbed all that Oliver had been trying to teach him, or maybe it was because Oliver was leading the band and did not want a rival; either way, Armstrong complained, "Joe held me back for a while, and the boys didn't understand it at first, but I guess the King knew what he was doing." But he conceded, "I learned a lot playing second to my idol."[12] Armstrong was in essence performing the role that he had with Joe Howard and Norman Mason on the riverboats: playing second to someone else's lead. Armstrong confirmed, "I love the man and his work so much until we made the most fabulous 'cornet team' one ever heard of. No matter where he'd turn while we were playing, whatever note he made I always had a 2nd note to match his lead."[13]

Brass bands often had more than one cornet player, but it was not common in dance bands before this time. The white bandleader Paul Whiteman was among the first to introduce a second cornet to his dance band in 1922.[14] Having two cornet players in the band opened up new possibilities. Given Armstrong's ability to find a suitable harmony part to Oliver's lead, the two became a sensation. Preston Jackson recalled, "Louis never knew what Joe was going to play, but he would always follow him perfectly. Louis was, and still is, as good a second trumpet as he is first; he never missed."[15] As Armstrong remembered it, "The musicians who hadn't heard anything like it would go absolutely *wild*."[16] One feature of Oliver and Armstrong, when they played together, were the breaks they employed, as Armstrong explained:

> During the first night on the job, while things were going down in order, King and I stumbled upon a little something that no two other trumpeters ever thought of. While the band was just swinging, the King would lean over to me, moving the valves on his trumpet, make notes,

the notes he was going to make when the break in the tune came. I'd listen, and at the same time, I'd be figuring out my second to his lead. When the break would come, I'd have my part to blend right along with his. The crowd would go mad over it!"[17]

Baby Dodds, who witnessed this from the bandstand, said, "Louis was so versatile that Joe would blow just a couple of notes while we were playing and tell Louis where the breaks would come, and they worked them right in the number."[18] The clarinet and trombone would sometimes "come along with the counterpoint or harmony to correspond. But otherwise Joe and Louis worked those things out alone."[19] Although Armstrong suggested that it was by watching Oliver's valve positions that he knew what break Oliver would make, the clarinetist Buster Bailey had a different explanation.

> King Oliver and Louis were the greatest two trumpeters I ever heard together. You want to know how they'd get those unison breaks to go together that went over so well with the crowd? Well, the tunes always break in the middle. What Joe was going to make in the middle break, he'd make in the first ending. Louis would listen and remember; then when the middle came, Oliver and Louis would both take the same break together.[20]

Lil Hardin, on piano, also had an opportunity to witness these breaks on a nightly basis. She had a further explanation for how the two men organized these breaks.

> Those double cornet breaks, the reason they got them so perfectly was that Oliver would sing a soft riff between the choruses, so when [Johnny] Dodds would be playing a chorus, Oliver would sing the first few notes of the break they would use the next time and when the time came for it, they would come right out with the break. No one else knew about that.[21]

This is close to one of the explanations that Armstrong gave for how he and Oliver played their breaks. In a radio interview in 1951, he was asked how they arranged the two-cornet breaks: "Yeah, it's no secret he'd make the break he was gonna make while the band was playing and we wouldn't even look at each other."[22] If this is correct then rather than Oliver singing the break to Armstrong, as Hardin suggests, he would play it on his cornet so that

Armstrong would know what was coming. But these differing insights are not necessarily mutually exclusive. "Dippermouth Blues" has an introductory break, and it is a tune specifically composed for, and in part by, Louis Armstrong. Dippermouth was one of Armstrong's nicknames during this period. Preston Jackson enthused:

> Oh Boy! Did those two men team together? When you saw Joe lean over towards Louis at the first ending you would know they were going to make a break in the middle of the next chorus. And what breaks they made . . . They played together for three or four years and wrote some numbers together. One of them was "Dippermouth Blues," later called "Sugar Foot Stomp."[23]

According to Baby Dodds, "'Dippermouth Blues' was a number that the whole band worked out. Each member of the outfit contributed his own part . . . everyone had his part in composing the thing."[24] Dodds also revealed something of the way that the band would compose and rehearse: "When we worked a number out and rehearsed it we always played it that way."[25] "Dippermouth Blues" was no exception, as he went on to say: "The only time that 'Dippermouth' was changed was when Louis went with Fletcher Henderson and they called the number 'Sugarfoot Stomp.' But it was 'Dippermouth' just the same."[26] Joe Oliver's Creole Jazz Band made two recordings of "Dippermouth Blues": the first version recorded for Gennett Records on April 6, 1923, and a version for OKeh in June of the same year.[27]

There is a thematic unity to "Dippermouth Blues" that is apparent when Armstrong's background in singing in a barbershop quartet is considered. The piece is based on simple barbershop cadences. Sigmund Spaeth in his 1925 book *Barber Shop Ballads* gave examples of the seven simplest barbershop endings or cadences.[28] All of the cadences in Example 12 have one thing in common: all of these chords contain the tonic note of C; the lead voice sings this note throughout.[29] The voices that change their note are the tenor and baritone voices. In these simple cadences, the tenor voice only changes note by a semitone either side of its start note of E♮ as the baritone voice changes its note by no more than a tone ascending from G to A, or alternatively by descending a semitone to F♯. The bass voice in all cases either doubles the lead voice or doubles a note that the tenor or baritone would otherwise sing. The first and second of these cadences has already been discussed in relation to "Swanee River" (see Ex. 1). The A♭ chord is what would become known as "That Barbershop Chord."[30] The chord forms because the tenor voice descends

[Musical notation]

Example 12: Spaeth's fundamental barbershop cadences (1925)

by a semitone to E♭ as the baritone ascends to A♭, and the lead voice stays on a note of C. If instead of ascending the baritone voice descends by a semitone, the resulting chord is C diminished, as given in cadence three (see Ex. 12). In European music theory, the flatted fifth is called the "diminished" fifth. The resulting triad (as it only has three notes) is formed from two successive minor third intervals: C to E♭ and E♭ to F♯. The addition of a further minor third interval, F♯ to A♮, would form a diminished-seventh chord. This is Spaeth's cadence number 6 (see Ex. 12). If we apply this insight to the introduction of "Dippermouth Blues," we can see how Oliver and Armstrong used their shared and internalized knowledge of barbershop harmony to unconsciously produce the harmony of the opening break.[31]

Oliver's copyright deposit for "Dippermouth Blues" shows that Oliver conceived of the top line of this break as the lead line, and therefore, if Oliver took the opening E♭, he then descended down the arpeggio of the C-diminished chord playing C, A, and F♯, as Armstrong, playing a minor third below Oliver, played C, A, F♯, and D♯ (the enharmonic equivalent of E♭).[32] This opening break is therefore the arpeggio (playing the chord tones sequentially) of the barbershop cadence 6 (see Ex. 13).

In 1927 the Melrose Music Company issued *Louis Armstrong's 50 Hot Choruses for Cornet*. The book contained forty-four transcribed solos by Armstrong and 125 two-bar breaks in all keys. Armstrong's interest in the project seems to have been entirely practical. He explained, "I sold a book of trumpet exercises to Melrose and bought a cute little Hupmobile."[33] Melrose's

[Musical notation]

Example 13: Joe Oliver and Louis Armstrong, introduction, "Dippermouth Blues" (April 6, 1923)

intention was educational, and the breaks were written for major, minor, dominant, and diminished harmony, to enable aspiring jazz musicians to play appropriate breaks. According to the piano player Elmer Schoebel:

> [Walter] Melrose said he was going to publish a set of Louis Armstrong breaks, but there was a technical problem of getting the Armstrong "hot" breaks down on paper. Finally, Melrose and I hit on the idea of having Armstrong record his breaks. We bought a $15 Edison cylinder phonograph and 50 wax cylinders, gave them to Louis and told him to play. The cylinders were duly filled up by Armstrong and the "breaks" were copied into written form. I transcribed the "breaks," which were published. These were not orchestrated at any time and were not made for that purpose.[34]

The recordings do not survive, but the published transcriptions consistently show how Armstrong appears to have conceived of these breaks in terms of barbershop voice leading.[35] Or to put this another way, he conceived of these breaks as the linearization of the possible note choices of the lead, baritone, and tenor voices in a barbershop quartet. In these examples, there is the often-repeated use of the D♯ to E♮ appoggiatura confirming the tenor voice on the major third. There is also the use of the notes A and G in the baritone voice (left unresolved at the end of the third break). As would be expected, the lead voice on C is present throughout. Applying a similar analytical approach to the head or melody as in the copyright deposit that Joe Oliver played on "Dippermouth Blues" (see Ex. 15), we find similar note choices.[36] Theorists have tried to understand the tonality of the blues and the flatted notes associated with this music. One approach has been to take blues melodies or

Example 14: Louis Armstrong, C major breaks (*50 Hot Choruses*, 1927)

Example 15: Joe Oliver's lead, "Dippermouth Blues" (copyright deposit)

solos and construct blues scales from the notes that are used. The head of "Dippermouth Blues" has, as Oliver conceived it, the following notes: C, D, E♭/D♯, E♮, F, G, A♭, A, B♭, B.[37]

This is strikingly similar to the blues scale that Winthrop Sargeant identified. Sargeant transcribed a number of blues and jazz recordings and wrote: "In the process of these observations and computations a definable scale began to take shape, and certain definable traits of melodic movement began to establish themselves as universally characteristic." He would go on to say, "For convenience, and because it is associated with the performance of the blues as well as with hot jazz proper, we will call it the blues scale."[38] The only note in the head of "Dippermouth Blues" that is not found in Sargeant's blues scale is A♭. Other theorists have included this note in their blues scales—for example, the classical composer Lou Harrison.[39] Had Sargeant included the flatted sixth in his blues scale this would have upset the symmetry that he believed he detected in the notes of the scale. Sargeant believed that there were two tetrachords (a tetrachord being a group of notes that span a perfect fourth) that underpinned the structure of the blues scale. These tetrachords he believed revealed the voice leading of the blues. He would go on to say, "If we arrange the most important tones of the scale according to tendencies of melodic movement instead of in the conventional extension from tonic to tonic, the relationship of the two tetrachordal melodic groupings becomes clearer." He observed, "Each of these groupings show the same arrangements of relative pitches; each centers around a 'tonic' of its own toward which the other tones tend to move."[40] What Sargeant believed was that the "blue notes, in each case, have a downward tendency, while the lower note of

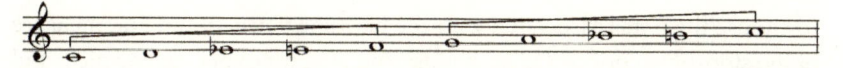

Example 16: Sargeant's blues scale

Example 17: Sargeant's tetrachordal melodic groupings

each grouping tends upward toward the [tetrachordal] 'tonic.'"[41] Sargeant's understanding is completely compatible with barbershop practice in relation to the upper blue note (B♭). In a minor third swipe in the baritone voice, the voice returns to the fifth (G) via the major sixth (Spaeth's "Blues Progression," Ex. 5). But as was also noted, the baritone voice can pass through the flatted sixth, and this justifies Harrison's inclusion of this note in his blues scale. Sargeant was also correct that the note of C is a cardinal note in the lead voice in barbershop. What he did not realize was that there is also a tendency for the tenor voice to return to the major third. There are, in fact, three cardinal notes C, E, and G that other notes return to as demonstrated in Spaeth's barbershop cadences (see Ex. 12). If these insights are brought together to analyze "Dippermouth Blues," it becomes apparent how close Sargeant came to understanding the nature of blues tonality and its relationship to barbershop harmony.

The head is followed by a clarinet solo that was similar on the two different recordings.[42] As Porter, Ullman, and Hazell point out, in the earlier Gennett version, Johnny Dodds "played two different choruses, building from the first into the second. At the June recording, Dodds plays a first chorus similar to that of the early version—and then repeats the statement verbatim!"[43] As they go on to argue, in the 1920s "a different esthetic prevailed . . . musicians tried to perfect their statements beforehand, and if they found something they liked they repeated it . . . the evidence suggests that the repetition of one's best ideas was not frowned upon as it would be in later jazz history."[44] Johnny Dodds's solo on "Dippermouth Blues" is on both recordings played against a stop-time chorus where the other instruments just play the first three beats of each measure for the first ten measures of each solo chorus.[45] Oliver included the stop-time chorus in his copyright deposit of "Dippermouth Blues," and it confirms that these choruses were conceived in terms of barbershop voice leading. The notes that Oliver assigned to the instruments backing Dodds are notes that are for the most part associated with the lead and tenor voice in Spaeth's cadences (see Ex. 12). This in turn makes it possible for Dodds to choose the notes associated with the baritone voice. In the first measure of the stop-time chorus, Oliver has assigned the notes of C (lead voice) and E♮ (tenor voice) to the backing instruments. Dodds plays a G (associated

Example 18: Backing on Dodds's solo, "Dippermouth Blues" (April 6, 1923, combined with Oliver's copyright deposit)

with the tenor voice) to complete the C major triad. In the second measure, the instrument representing the tenor voice descends to E♭ as Dodds plays an F♯. This results in a chord of C diminished. In the third measure both Dodds and the instrument representing the tenor voice return to G♮ and E♮ respectively. A comparison with cadence 3 of Example 12 will confirm that this is a common barbershop cadential formula as identified by Spaeth. In measure 5 there would have been some doubling if the parts from the copyright deposit were combined with the notes that Dodds actually played on the recording. In practice, this did not occur because the copyright deposit and the actual recordings are not quite the same. The difference becomes apparent in measure 6, where Oliver has written three notes in the backing of the copyright deposit. As before, the instruments representing the lead and tenor voices play C and E♭. To provide a root for the F seventh harmony, the baritone voice would need to descend a tone from its usual position on the G to F♮. This produces an incomplete F seventh chord, as there is no third. To play or sing a major third the baritone voice (or the instrument taking this role) would need to ascend a tone to A♮. Alternatively, to sound an F minor seventh chord, the baritone voice would need to ascend a semitone to A♭. Again referencing Example 12, it will be seen that all these chord combinations are possible using Spaeth's simplest barbershop cadences; however, full four-note chords are only possible once the bass voice leaves the tonic to take a note that would otherwise be sung by one of the other voices. This explains one of Sargeant's observations regarding blues tonality: "The Negro musician shows, for example, a distinct preference for the plagal cadence, for pseudo-dominant seventh-chords on the subdominant, for the type of close harmony loosely termed 'barber-shop,' and so on."[46] While less sophisticated theorists of blues tonality have tried to reduce blues harmony to simple three-chord triads, the reality is that in jazz counterpoint the harmony is far more complex, and, as Sargeant observed, "In 'barbershop' harmony the voices tend to stick together and move in parallel formations. As often as possible the movement is by chromatic half-steps. Seventh and ninth chords are as common as, if not more common than triads—especially seventh and ninth-chords of the 'dominant' formation."[47] The same argument holds true for the blues as actually performed by New Orleans jazz bands. As Oliver's copyright deposit makes explicit, the voice leading of the stop-time chorus in "Dippermouth Blues" was achieved by transferring the harmonic practices of a barbershop quartet directly to the instrumentation of a jazz band.

Measure 6 of the stop-time chorus of "Dippermouth Blues" (see Ex. 18) is also of interest because it demonstrates one of the features of the blues and jazz that is little understood: chord substitution. In measure 6, Oliver has written an F♮ in the top part of the backing, whereas Dodds actually plays an F♯. It is clearly not possible for one instrument to play both notes simultaneously: Dodds had to choose. Had Dodds played the F♮ this would have implied a chord of F seventh that is commonly found in this measure of a twelve-bar blues. But playing an F♯ converted the chord to C diminished. This too (or one of its inversions) is commonly found in this measure of the blues. If on the other hand Dodds had decided to ascend to A♭, this would have implied F minor seventh harmony: another common chord found in this measure of the blues as actually performed by New Orleans jazz bands. All of these chord substitutions are possible variations of Spaeth's cadences (see Ex. 12).

One other issue that the analysis of "Dippermouth Blues" raises is whether blues melodies (or blues scales or modes) are related to blues harmony. The prevailing view, which has persisted since the 1930s, is that the harmony of the blues and jazz is of European origin whereas the blue notes are derived from African American practice. The idea that blues melody and harmony are not related does not bear scrutiny when considered in relation to New Orleans counterpoint. It is simply not possible for the voices in a Bach chorale, or a barbershop quartet, to sing their melodies and countermelodies and not give rise to the harmony—no more than it is possible for the notes played by cornets, clarinets, and trombones when playing jazz counterpoint to be independent of the harmony that results. The co-incidence of these notes *is the harmony.*

One other issue that the stop-time chorus of "Dippermouth Blues" raises relates to the presence of the F♯ (or G♭, its enharmonic equivalent). This is not a note that Sargeant or Harrison included in their blues scales. F♯ is the augmented fourth or diminished fifth with reference to the tonic C. The flatted or "blues fifth" has been the subject of some debate among theorists. Sargeant argued that he had "heard the theory of a 'blues fifth' advanced, though I have never been able to find any consistent evidence to support such a theory."[48] In fairness to Sargeant, he did his research at a time when recordings were difficult to find, and he had limited access to reliable transcriptions. Gunther Schuller, in his extensive survey of early jazz recordings in 1986, concluded "that the flattened fifth exists in numerous recordings as early as the twenties."[49] Consequently, the flatted fifth is today widely accepted as a blue note.

Of all of the features in "Dippermouth Blues," it is Joe "King" Oliver's solo that has received the greatest attention from jazz scholars. This "justly famous" solo has been praised by many writers for its simplicity, structural cohesion, and execution.[50] Oliver's solo has become an integral part of the piece, or, as Armstrong put it, "There's your 'Dippermouth'; all your trumpet players just aren't going to sound good unless they put that solo of his in it."[51] But Armstrong acknowledged that, however hard other trumpeters may try, "no one living today could express themselves while playing that tune like Joe Oliver did."[52] In this solo, Oliver does not resolve the E♭ where it would be expected using conventional music theory. For the first chorus (see Ex. 19, mm. 1–12), Oliver consistently plays E♭ rather than E♮.[53] The note of E♮ does not appear until the first two measures of the second chorus of the solo, only to be replaced by E♭ which continues up to measure 31 of Example 19. What Oliver can be interpreted as doing is prolonging a simple barbershop cadence in the tenor voice. At the start of the third chorus (see Ex. 19, m. 25) he plays repeated notes of A♮, suggesting a brief reference to the baritone voice that is resolved with a return to G in the following measure. By repeatedly playing the minor third, he succeeds in maintaining tension that is not fully resolved until the closing measures with a final return of the tenor voice to the major third.

One aspect that ensured that Armstrong and Oliver worked well together was that they had two different, although complementary, ways of playing. Peter Bocage remembered, "Joe was very good . . . Joe was powerful; he didn't [have] too much of a tone, but he was good for jazz, because he could make all that ah—he could make it go like a dog, and all that, you understand—all

Example 19: Oliver's solo, "Dippermouth Blues" (April 6, 1923)

that 'wa-wa' stuff, and that he'd make all that on his horn, you know."[54] Mutt Carey said of Oliver's use of mutes: "Joe could make his horn sound like a holy-roller meeting; God, what that man could do with his horn."[55] Preston Jackson remembered Oliver "imitating a rooster and a baby" on his horn, and, he went on to say, "He was a riot in those days."[56] According to Tommy

Brookins, "Oliver took the majority of the solos. He had a real 'gutbucket tone' and really moved."[57] At this time Armstrong was rarely heard to solo in live performance. But Brookins remembered one evening when Oliver was not well: "On that evening when he was sick, Oliver played as a member of the ensemble but let Louis solo and, believe me, Louis really played, showing everyone present all he knew, all his tricks, and he received after each song tremendous acclamation."[58] But Armstrong's style was different: he preferred to play without a mute.

It seems that the repertoire that Oliver and the band played at the Lincoln Garden was much the same as the tunes that they recorded. Guitarist Eddie Condon remembered hearing Oliver's band perform "Froggie Moore," "Chimes Blues," "Sweet Baby Doll," "Jazzin' Babies Blues," "Mabel's Dream," "Rent Room Blues," "High Society Rag," "Where Did You Stay Last Night?," and "Working Man Blues."[59] On his recordings with Oliver, Armstrong had few opportunities to play a solo, and it is likely that this was true of the live performances, too. Armstrong said of his first evening with Oliver that he didn't take a solo until "the evening was almost over" because he wanted Oliver to get all the praise.[60]

On the riverboats and with Oliver, Armstrong's role had been mainly to play second. His role was to find harmony parts to melodies and breaks provided by someone else with the occasional opportunity to solo. In order to continue his development as a soloist, Armstrong would take what might seem to be a somewhat regressive step: Instead of taking a position as a lead trumpeter, he moved to New York to play third with a society dance band.

CHAPTER 12

FLETCHER HENDERSON
"That Big Fish Horn Voice of His"

FLETCHER HENDERSON SR. GRADUATED FROM ATLANTA UNIVERSITY and settled to teach at Douglas Academy, Cuthbert, Georgia, in 1880. He was known thereafter as "Professor" Henderson.[1] His son, Fletcher Hamilton Henderson Jr., was born in 1897.[2] Both parents taught the young Fletcher to play the piano, and he began formal piano lessons at the age of six. Although he did not enjoy his piano studies, he was proficient from an early age; his sister remembered as children playing the *Poet and Peasant Overture* and the *William Tell Overture* with her brother.[3] In 1911 Fletcher enrolled in Atlanta University's high school program, where the curriculum included "Latin, Bible, English, History, American Literature, Elocution, Cicero, Greek, Algebra, Geometry, Physiology, Botany, Physics, Manual Training, and Music."[4] He did well in all subjects, but his best grade—a 95% pass mark—was for music.[5] When he enrolled for his graduate studies in 1916, he no longer took lessons in music, but he did write about music for the student newspaper. His first known byline was an article about the college glee club and its rehearsals for a performance of Cadman's *Vision of Sir Launfal* to feature in the Annual Glee Club Concert of 1917.[6] This cantata published in 1910 was arranged for a "chorus of men's voices and tenor and baritone soli."[7] The quartet parts were scored for two tenors and two baritone voices, an arrangement similar to barbershop voicing. Glee clubs had their origin in English singing societies, and American educational establishments took up the tradition beginning with Harvard in 1858, and by 1875 Yale, Michigan, Kenyon, Hampton Institute, Boston College, Dartmouth, Wooster, New York University, Princeton, Ohio State, Hamilton, and the University of Rochester had all established glee clubs.[8] By the early twentieth century, glee clubs were a common feature of American academic establishments.

There are a number of similarities between glee club singing and barbershop practice. In its original usage, a glee is a specific type of unaccompanied song, but madrigals and drinking songs had become a part of the mix. According to one authority, "The glee is generally defined as an unaccompanied secular composition for solo voices. It is usually quite short and is written mostly for male voices, requiring a male alto for the top part. . . . This, in effect, adds a third to the top part of a male ensemble and gives more varied possibilities to the composer."[9] Given that the top voice in both the glee and barbershop tradition is a harmony voice that sings a third above the melody, there is scope for considerable overlapping of repertoire and practice between glee and barbershop singers. Further cross-fertilization of harmonic ideas and repertoire is evidenced in other African American academic establishments. "By 1872, the Fisk School had a glee club which gave a well-received concert at the Lyceum Hall. The pupils performed 'solos, duetts [sic] and choruses' which included the ballads 'Little Dolly's Vision,' 'I'll Love thee as long as I Live,' and 'Aria speak to me' as well as 'comic songs.'"[10] Also included in their repertoire was the barbershop favorite "Swanee River."[11] It seems doubtful that there was a clear delineation between the way that these singers harmonized spirituals, jubilee songs, glees, and popular songs.

Henderson graduated from Atlanta with a degree in chemistry in 1920.[12] He moved to New York City intending to continue his studies and roomed with a friend who worked playing piano on the riverboats.[13] When his friend became ill and needed someone to substitute for him, Henderson took his place. His friend did not recover quickly, and Henderson became the regular piano player for the orchestra.[14] In the fall of 1920, Henderson worked demonstrating at the piano for the Pace and Handy Music Company founded by the blues composer W. C. Handy and his business partner Harry H. Pace. It is possible that Pace and Henderson knew each other before they came to New York, as they had graduated from the same university.

Harry Pace had been a student of W. E. B. Du Bois at Atlanta University. Pace in association with Du Bois edited an African American newspaper called the *Moon Illustrated Weekly* that was based in Memphis and closed down in 1906.[15] Du Bois became one of the founders of the National Association for the Advancement of Colored People (NAACP) in 1909, and Pace founded a chapter of the NAACP in Atlanta, Georgia.[16] In 1918 Pace persuaded Handy to relocate the Pace and Handy Music Company to New

York.[17] After a split with Handy, in 1921 Pace established Black Swan Records. The label was the first recording company owned and managed by African Americans.[18] Although Black Swan was not officially sanctioned by the NAACP, Du Bois was on the board of directors, and the objectives of the company were closely associated with the concept of racial uplift. The company name, suggested by Du Bois, gave an indication of the company's aims and objectives. "Black Swan" was the stage name of Elizabeth Taylor Greenfield, who was considered the most prominent African American concert singer of the nineteenth century.[19] Born in Natchez, Mississippi, in 1809, she died in Philadelphia in 1876. In 1853 she appeared before an audience of four thousand in New York, before embarking on a tour of England to include a performance at Buckingham Palace. She was reputed to have had a "complete command of the standard concert repertoire of her day."[20] Du Bois was also on the board of directors of the Music School Settlement for Colored People that opened in Harlem in 1911. The founder, David Mannes, believed that "through music, which is a universal language, the Negro and white man can be brought to have a mutual understanding."[21]

Although Pace believed that "the problem of the races in this country is economic," Pace would also argue that, "unless we take hold vigorously of this matter of creating and shaping public opinion itself, all other efforts we may put forth in any line will be useless so far as our status among the races of the world is concerned."[22] It is clear that Black Swan was intended to shape public opinion, because De Bois published an editorial in the *Crisis*, the monthly journal of the NAACP, in February 1921 condemning "comic darky songs" and argued, "We must now develop a business organization to preserve and record our best voices."[23] He would further argue that the enterprise "will reveal the best music, not only of [our] own race but of all races and ages."[24] Black Swan was to provide "music of the better sort," to include arias by Verdi and Gounod, and the work of African American composer R. Nathaniel Dett.[25] What Du Bois considered the best music of the race is clear from his 1903 book; he reserved the last chapter of *The Souls of Black Folk* for "Sorrow Songs"; he considered these spirituals "the most beautiful expression of human experience born this side of the seas."[26]

New York was at the forefront of what would become known as the Harlem Renaissance and, to use Alain Locke's title from his 1925 anthology of African American writing, poetry, and art, the emergence of the New Negro.[27] Many middle-class African Americans had difficulty reconciling the aspiration for racial uplift with the commercial realities of the age. The *Chicago Defender*—a leading African American–owned newspaper—wrote editorials encouraging its readers to attend opera and classical concerts, and its columnists promoted the Café De Paris Orchestra, claiming "diners can sit and hear each other talk," as distinct from the noisy jazz it was critical of. A similar contradiction was evident in its advertising columns that regularly promoted the blues recordings that it distanced itself from editorially.[28] Opinions differed among black intellectuals about the merits or otherwise of jazz and the blues. Locke's understanding of the emergence of jazz was explored in *The Negro and His Music* (1936). He observed, in a chapter "Jazz and the Jazz Age: 1918–1926": "The Negro folk idiom in melody and syncopated rhythm gives us 'ragtime,' carried over to harmony and orchestration, it gives us jazz."[29] What distinguished jazz from ragtime was, according to Locke, its harmony and the way it was orchestrated. The two features were connected. Early jazz was polyphonic, in that there were many instruments (typically cornet, clarinet, and trombone) that had independent lines that despite being apparently improvised simultaneously nevertheless gave rise to consistent harmonic relationships between the instruments. Quite how this collective improvisation functioned, was, at the time, something of a mystery. He would go on to write:

> For the process of composing by group improvisation, the jazz musician must have a whole chain of musical expertness, a sure musical ear, an instinctive feeling for harmony, the courage and gift to improvise and interpolate, and a canny sense for the total effect. This free style that Negro musicians introduced into playing really has generations of experience back of it; it derives from the voice tricks and vocal habits characteristic of Negro choral singing.[30]

This understanding of how collective improvisation functioned and its relationship to black vocal tradition accords completely with Armstrong's explanation of how he used the methods of barbershop quartet singing to produce collectively improvised arrangements. However, some black intellectuals who contributed to the Harlem Renaissance were less understanding and supportive of the new music and thought of jazz as a primitive music that often conflicted with their desire for racial uplift. Historian Nathan Higgins has observed that, "except for Langston Hughes, none of then took jazz—the new music—seriously. . . . The promotors of the Harlem Renaissance were so fixed on a vision of *high* culture that they did not look very hard or well at jazz."[31] It was into this environment that Fletcher Henderson became the recording manager for Black Swan.[32]

Black Swan's initial focus on music of the "better sort" and its aspirations to promote uplift needed to be tempered with the needs of the business. Black Swan increasingly recorded vaudeville blues, jazz, and popular songs, alongside classical music and spirituals. Black Swan's first major hit was Ethel Waters's recording of "Down Home Blues" (1921). According to Henderson, it was he who discovered Ethel Waters and persuaded her to record: "I was walking along 135th Street in Harlem one night, and there, in a basement, singing with all her heart, was Ethel. I had her come down and cut four sides of which two—'Down Home Blues' and 'Oh Daddy'—became such hits that we [Black Swan] were made."[33] Harry Pace credits himself with bringing Waters to record. He said he visited a cabaret on the West Side of Atlantic City where she was singing "with a peculiar voice that I thought I might use." Although she initially declined his invitation, he subsequently sent her railroad tickets and "she came to New York and made two records."[34] In a third version of events, Ethel Waters remembered she had been approached by a freelance talent scout, who had arranged a recording for her at the Cardinal Company, and he also suggested an audition at Black Swan. She remembered meeting Henderson at the Black Swan offices as he sat behind a desk "looking very prissy and important," and there followed a discussion about whether she should record "cultural numbers."[35] Waters sang with the diction of a concert singer, but it was decided that she should instead sing popular songs. As such, the company could claim that in her recording of "Down Home Blues," she "changed the style of Blues singing overnight, and brought a finer interpretation of this work. She dignified the blues."[36] While this line of argument justified recording the blues as part of the racial uplift aspect of Black Swan's mission, it did so in the context of what had been—until Mamie Smith's recording of "Crazy Blues" in 1920—a monopoly on blues recordings by white singers.[37] Black Swan appear to have wanted black blues singers who could sing the blues closer to the manner of white performers, and famously rejected Bessie Smith when she auditioned to record. Her singing was considered "coarse and boisterous—'blacker,' according to the racial taxonomy of the period."[38]

To promote its star blues singer, the Black Swan Troubadours were formed to tour vaudeville headed by Waters and led musically by Fletcher Henderson.[39] Henderson was, if anything, too refined for Black Swan's star performer. She remembered Henderson as "a fine arranger and a brilliant band leader" who leaned "to the classical side." These were the qualities that Black Swan prized and that made Henderson suitable as their musical director. However, for Waters this caused arguments because he "wouldn't give me what I call 'the damn-it-to-hell bass,' that chump-chump stuff that real jazz needs."[40] Both Henderson and Waters were experiencing firsthand the inherent tensions and contradictions of the Harlem Renaissance. Unlike Henderson, Waters was not from a privileged middle-class background and classically trained. She may have been able to sing "cultural numbers," but her lack of formal training and perhaps her humble origins may have been a factor in why, instead, she was required by Black Swan to sing the blues.[41] They both had to compromise and adapt to their environment.

It was while Fletcher Henderson was on tour with Waters that he first met Louis Armstrong. As Henderson explained: "It was back in 1922, down in New Orleans, when I heard a young man playing the trumpet in a little dance hall. I was accompanist for Ethel Waters, who was the headline attraction at the Lyric Theatre, and I decided that the youthful trumpeter would be great in our act. I asked him his name and found he was Louis Armstrong."[42]

The Lyric Theater stood at the corner of Iberville and Burgundy streets in New Orleans, and from 1919 it was promoted as "America's Largest and Finest Colored Theatre."[43] Waters was booked to appear for one week in April 1922. Armstrong remembered being part of the audience during that week. He recalled, "Us boys went up into the peanut gallery to see Miss Waters. She was very young and was wonderful even then."[44] Although the Lyric principally catered to African American audiences, they also held "midnight frolics" for white patrons. The *New Orleans Item* of April 20, 1922, announced that "Ethel Waters, The Great Colored Singer of the Blues and Her Black Swan Troubadours" would appear at the midnight frolic at the Lyric, and the event was "For White Only."[45] Waters sang live on the WGV radio station in New Orleans that Friday evening along with "her famous Black Swan jazz masters." This would have given a substantial boost to the newspaper advertising.[46] This may also have been the first time that any black orchestra had performed on the airwaves. In his comprehensive exploration of Henderson's life and music, Walter C. Allen commented, "I know of no other such broadcast earlier than that of the Ethel Waters troupe from New Orleans in April, 1922."[47]

Henderson was impressed by Armstrong and tried to persuade him to join the tour, but Armstrong wanted drummer Zutty Singleton to go, too. Henderson recalled, "The next day Louis was backstage at the theater to tell me he'd have to be excused, much as he would love to go with us, because the drummer wouldn't leave New Orleans."[48] It is not clear what Henderson would have done if Singleton had been persuaded to leave. As Armstrong pointed out, "Fletcher did not have an opening for a drummer."[49] One possible reason for Singleton not wanting to leave New Orleans was that he may have had a regular job playing drums for the house orchestra at the Lyric. Singleton told the authors of *Jazzmen* (1939) that he played at the Lyric in 1922 with John Robichaux.[50] Robichaux formed his orchestra in New Orleans in the late 1890s, and led the Lyric Theater pit orchestra from as early as 1917 until the theater burned down in 1926.[51] This would have been a steady job and perhaps one that Singleton was reluctant to leave. On the other hand, he may not have been with Robichaux in early 1922, as an article in the *Chicago Defender* from November 11, 1922, said Robichaux "still has his orchestra intact, with the exception of the drummer, who is a late addition and whose name is Arthur [Zutty] Singleton."[52] The likelihood is that Singleton was playing with Armstrong in April—who left for Chicago in October—and Singleton only later took the job with Robichaux.

It would be another two years before Henderson would again offer Armstrong a job. Although Armstrong said that it was in "the latter part of 1923, I received a telegram to go to New York to join the great Fletcher Henderson's orchestra," it was actually around a year later.[53] Henderson had been retained for the fall season at the Roseland Ballroom in Harlem of 1924. The Roseland required continuous music for dancing and employed two bands. For the fall season, the Roseland employed Sam Lanin and his orchestra to appear opposite Henderson. Lanin had been with the Roseland since it had opened its first venue in Philadelphia in 1918.[54] Henderson was leading the only black orchestra playing in a midtown ballroom at that time. The Roseland authorized Henderson payment for two additional musicians: an extra clarinet, and a third trumpet.[55] The offer of a job with Henderson was timely for Armstrong. He had married Lil Hardin in February 1924, and she was ambitious for her husband. By this time Armstrong had left Oliver at Lil's insistence. She had explained to Armstrong, "We're married now . . . I don't want you playing second trumpet; you've got to play first . . . Well now it's one thing or the other . . . If you're going to stay with me, you'll have to play first . . . You can't be married to Joe and be married to me too."[56] Armstrong was very reluctant to leave Oliver, but in retrospect he came to realize that she was right: "If she did engineer my life, she had a perfect right to. We married and heard the preacher when he said to love, honor, and obey. And to me that's what was happening . . . I listened very carefully when Lil told me I should play first cornet. Play second to no one, she told me. They don't get great enough. She proved she was right, didn't she?"[57] Henderson thought that Armstrong was again likely to turn down his offer of work in New York and confided: "Truthfully, I didn't expect him to accept the offer, and I was very surprised when he came to New York and joined us."[58]

Although Henderson wrote arrangements for the orchestra, the talented multi-instrumentalist Don Redman (born Piedmont, West Virginia, 1900) shared, and increasingly took over, these duties. Redman played wind instruments from an early age and studied instrumental technique at the Boston Conservatory.[59] Given that Henderson and Redman were both classically trained, there has been some discussion regarding what role Henderson and Redman played in the development of jazz. Hugues Panassié, who founded the Hot Club of France and wrote some of the earliest books of jazz criticism, *Le Jazz Hot* (1934) and *The Real Jazz* (1942), dismissed Henderson as the "Paul Whiteman of the race."[60] Whiteman was classically trained and became popular for his recordings of orchestral arrangements of popular songs. By 1924 Whiteman introduced jazz to the concert stage, commissioning Gershwin's *Rhapsody in Blue* for a performance at the Aeolian Hall in New York. Described in the program notes as "an experiment in modern music," Gershwin's composition was orchestrated by Ferde Grofé to be performed by Whiteman's orchestra with Gershwin at the piano.[61] Billed as the "King of Jazz," Whiteman's efforts to make a "lady" out of jazz were diametrically opposed to Panassié's conception of "real jazz."[62] As Jeffrey Magee has commented, there is a "binary" that permeates much jazz criticism between black jazz as "improvisatory, authentic, and noncommercial and therefore 'true,' and white jazz [that] is written down, diluted, and commercial, and therefore 'false.'"[63] Henderson's band was a dance orchestra rather than a jazz band. The Roseland had specifically auditioned for "two high grade dance orchestras" and made it clear that "jazz bands will not be considered."[64] This would appear to place Henderson's orchestra on the *false* side of the jazz binary. The question is, what distinguished jazz of this period from dance music?

When audiences first heard jazz, they heard something that was different. Very few were able to express what they heard in musical terms. But there were exceptions. Carl Engel, the Chief of the Music Division of the Library of Congress, wrote a highly perceptive observation in "Jazz: A Musical Discussion" in August 1922:

> Between the earlier "rag" and the "blues," there was this distinction: the rag had been mainly a thing of rhythm, of syncopation; the blues were syncopation relished with spicier harmonies. In addition to these two elements of music, rhythm and harmony, the people—who in the beginning had known but one thing: melody, fastened upon a primitive and weak harmonic structure of "Barbershop" chords—the people, I say, who had stepwise advanced from melody and rhythms to harmony,

lastly discovered counterpoint. And the result of this last discovery is jazz. In other words, jazz is rag-time, plus "Blues," plus orchestral polyphony.[65]

This description of jazz is essentially a precursor of Locke's observation that ragtime when harmonized and orchestrated becomes jazz.[66] Given that the tonality of the blues is rooted in barbershop harmony, the two terms could be used interchangeably and Engel's description could be reformatted: jazz is a ragtime melody, plus barbershop harmony, plus orchestral polyphony. This, in turn, is strikingly similar to Louis Armstrong's explanation for how jazz counterpoint functioned. The feature that differentiated jazz from earlier ragtime was the presence of barbershop harmony, or, to put it another way, the tonality of the blues. This is not to say that barbershop harmony had no influence on ragtime composers—barbershop cadences can be found in ragtime—but rather that any suitable tune could be *jazzed* through the application of barbershop principles.[67] Armstrong, of course, through his early years singing in a quartet, and hearing this tonality all around him on the streets of New Orleans, could easily apply barbershop principles to his instrument, and from what he said consistently in interviews and biographies, he did this knowingly. One example of this is "Copenhagen" (1924). Gunther Schuller has argued that "Copenhagen" was a pivotal recording in the development of big band jazz: "Louis, who was in a transitional stage at this time, was still close enough to the New Orleans collective ensemble technique to permit a bridge between it and the newer solo-and-section style."[68] For Schuller, it is Armstrong's presence in Henderson's orchestra that makes the transition from arranged jazz (that we read as "false jazz") and the New Orleans collective ensemble style (that we read as "authentic jazz"). Analysis of how Redman and Henderson came to make their arrangement of "Copenhagen" suggests that the elements of New Orleans polyphony found in the Henderson orchestra arrangement had rather more complex origins than simply the presence of Armstrong.

"Copenhagen" was not named after the Danish capital, but rather after a brand of chewing tobacco. The composition has been traced back to white bandleader Charlie Davis and his Orchestra in Indianapolis, Indiana.[69] It is likely that the white Wolverine Orchestra learned "Copenhagen" from Davis and subsequently recorded the tune on May 6, 1924. Because of its popularity, the Melrose Brothers Music Company used the Wolverine Orchestra recording as the basis for a stock arrangement.[70] Redman seems to have used this commercial stock as the basis for his own orchestration. The Wolverines

Example 20: "Copenhagen," Melrose stock arrangement (1924)

recording of "Copenhagen" has a strain used by Redman as an introduction that also appears in the Melrose stock. The first four measures of Example 20 are an example of a barbershop cadence. The second cornet and the tenor saxophone follow the line taken by the baritone voice in a major third swipe ascending all the chromatic intervals between the fifth and the major seventh and then descending passing through its usual position on the fifth (see Ex. 20, m. 3). The note of G is sustained before continuing down chromatically through the major third and down to the minor third. This progression results in a barbershop chord on the flatted sixth of the scale. The following four measures are typical of New Orleans jazz counterpoint. Note the alternate major and minor thirds of the first cornet (see Ex. 20, mm. 5, 7) and the clarinet (see Ex. 20, m. 7). Note also the flatted seventh (B♭) in the tenor sax and trombone in (see Ex. 20, m. 7). Ironically, Rudi Blesh, who may or may not have been aware that this passage is a direct transcription of improvised polyphony, said, "Many of Armstrong's followers consider 'Copenhagen' a great record because of the magnificent Armstrong solo. Actually, except for Louis' few moments, it is inferior and boring"; he lectured, "No one has been able as yet to write the sort of free counterpoint which small bands improvise nor arrange for even the most gifted section to play it."[71] Had he known that this stock arrangement had been transcribed from a Wolverines recording, it is unlikely this would have softened his critique. He dismissed their lead cornetist, Bix Beiderbecke, as a "pervasive influence" on a "whole school of white playing, which pretends to be jazz."[72] Blesh also did not understand the significance of barbershop tonality in jazz, and complained that Al Gande on trombone "provides only the most obvious 'barber shop' harmony" in the Wolverines recording of "Jazz Me Blues" (1924).[73]

The Melrose stock arrangement of "Copenhagen" resulted from the transcription of a recording of a white jazz band who were playing a tune they probably learned directly from a white bandleader. What becomes apparent from this is that this tonality was ubiquitous. Although barbershop harmony had its origins in African American song, by the late nineteenth century, vocal quartets, both black and white, were a regular feature in touring shows and on early recordings.[74] It is likely that some white musicians were unaware of the association between barbershop singing and jazz and blues harmony; however, some prominent white musicians were.[75] Many perhaps only learned this harmony secondhand, either by listening to black bands who played jazz or from white bands who employed the same tonality. It is possible that the Wolverines learned this particular barbershop cadence in "Copenhagen" directly from hearing Charlie Davis and his Orchestra play it. On the other hand, as in "Jazz Me Blues," they may have been employing barbershop harmony independently.

"Copenhagen" also raises questions related to Armstrong's development as a soloist. Edward Brooks has argued that, in "Copenhagen," "we hear Armstrong in his brash, almost brutal solo embellishment of the twelve bar blues theme as a 'swing trumpeter' for the first time."[76] This may have as much to do with the rhythm section as with Armstrong himself. A comparison between

Example 21: Louis Armstrong's solo, "Copenhagen" (October 30, 1924)

the Wolverines recording of "Copenhagen" and Henderson's is informative. On the Wolverines recording the sousaphone bass plays predominantly on the first and third beat of each measure with the banjo strumming four even beats to the measure. This places the emphasis on the first and third beat of the measure, and this is consistent with contemporaneous practice. Arthur Lange, who published *Arranging for the Modern Dance Orchestra* (1926), claimed, "The most commonly used tempo played in American dance music is the Fox-Trot, which consists of four one-quarter beats to a measure."[77] He advised his readers, "It must be remembered that the basic principle of writing Fox-Trot tempo is to preserve the accented *first* and *third* beat of each measure, in *Alla-Breve* tempo."[78] Henderson's recording of "Copenhagen," by contrast, accents the second and fourth beat of the measure. These two different ways of placing emphasis has been described as Eastern and Western style. The Western style that Armstrong has been credited with bringing to Henderson's orchestra led to controversy. According to the trumpeter Louis Metcalf, this "came to a head when Louis Armstrong joined Fletcher Henderson."[79] In this solo (see Ex. 21) Armstrong rarely actually plays on the second beat of the measure and there is no particular emphasis on the fourth beat either.[80] It is the rhythm section that emphasizes these beats. As Magee argues, it was Redman's arrangement that was responsible for the "'western' style."[81] What Armstrong does, however, is begin and end his phrases between the down beats. The opening phrase begins half a beat before the 4 beat of the anacrusis (pick-up) measure and finishes half a beat before beat 2 of the opening measure. His note choices in terms of barbershop practice are derived from the tenor and baritone voices. The appoggiatura D♯ to E♮ that begins the phrase confirms the major third in the tenor voice. The A and G that follow confirm the baritone position on the fifth (G) and then a return to the tenor on E♮ (see Ex. 21, m. 1). The second phrase also accents half a beat after beat 2 (see Ex. 21, m. 2) as the tenor voice descends by a semitone to E♭. The E♮ is restored in the following measure (see Ex. 21, m. 3). This is followed by what could be interpreted as the lead voice descending chromatically through B♮ to B♭, rendering the underlying harmony C seventh instead of C major. Rhythmically the pick-up and phrase into measure 5 is identical to the opening phrase; only the note choice is different. The tenor voice now ascends a semitone to F♮. Measure 6 of Example 21 is arguably a continuation of the tenor voice as it ascends to the note usually taken by the baritone voice before returning to its usual position on the major third at the end of the measure. The following measure re-confirms a return of all voices to their usual positions: the lead voice on the tonic (C), the tenor on the major third (E), and the baritone on the fifth (G). The following phrase is particularly interesting as it is an example of a minor third swipe played against dominant harmony. As in Example 5 (Spaeth's "blues progression"), the baritone voice returns to the fifth via the major sixth. The effect of playing B♭ against a chord of G seventh is that harmonically it sounds the augmented ninth against the G seventh chord. This is a feature of Armstrong's playing that I will consider in more detail in relation to his Hot Five recordings.

Armstrong's playing in Henderson's orchestra contrasted with the trumpeter Joe Smith, who tended to play more on the beat. Joseph Emery Smith was born in Ripley, Ohio, in 1902, and joined Ethel Waters as a drummer in 1921. It was Waters who persuaded him to change to trumpet as his principal instrument.[82] Accounts from the time suggest that Armstrong's playing was initially not fully appreciated by the audience at the Roseland. Louis Metcalf remembered when Armstrong first played with the band: "The first number they played was 'Copenhagen.' And Louis solo was *so* good. But different [to Joe Smith], and the audience didn't know how much to applaud. The next number was even better and the people began to dig and they were sayin,' 'Here's another great trumpet player.' After the third piece, they really made up their minds. They were sayin,' 'Now here's another *King*!' And the house was his."[83] What made Armstrong different, according to Metcalf, was, "Louis represented the Western style of jazz, while Joe Smith was the Eastern."[84] Smith tended to phrase in a more predictable way than Armstrong and this may explain why audiences and some musicians initially found Armstrong's playing more challenging. Both Armstrong and Joe Smith recorded with Bessie Smith. Armstrong remembered, "I got to make some records with a lot of blues singers like Bessie Smith. She'd always have the words and tune in her head, and we'd just run it down once. Then she'd sing a few lines, and I'd play something to fill in, and some nice, beautiful notes behind her. Everything I did with her, I *like*."[85] However, Bessie Smith famously preferred

Joe Smith to Louis Armstrong. Perhaps this was because she preferred the predictability of Smith's Eastern style.

Whether Armstrong's solo on "Copenhagen" was improvised in the sense that contemporary musicians would use the term is open to question. There was a second take of "Copenhagen" recorded on the same day, and Magee argues that it was played "as if each note was etched in stone, or at least written in score. Although improvisatory in spirit, the lively, loose-limbed jazz classic 'Copenhagen' features virtually no improvisation."[86] This was also true of Armstrong's solo. On the two takes there are just two pitch changes and one rhythmic variation.[87] It seems that Armstrong's approach to soloing during this period was the same as he had applied with Oliver. He would work out his solo in advance and only make incremental changes in performance. Evidence of this can be found not only in "Copenhagen" but in other recordings that Armstrong made with Henderson. On two takes of "I'll See You in My Dreams," "Alabama Bound," "Money Blues," and three takes of "Why Couldn't It Be Poor Little Me?," William H. Youngren has argued, "Louis, made only the slightest changes from master to master: the basic solo was set beforehand, either in mind or perhaps on paper."[88] This was a method that Armstrong applied throughout his life: he told Richard Meryman in 1966, "Once you get a certain solo that fit in the tune, and that's it, you keep it. Only vary it two or three notes every time you play it—'specially if the record was a hit."[89] There is very little evidence to suggest that Armstrong's approach to soloing was informed by the methods employed by later jazz musicians who instead improvised in the moment.

Armstrong was initially uncomfortable in Henderson's orchestra: "I was a little lost with Henderson's arrangements, which I could read alright, but the restrictions of the scored music kept me from 'stretchin' out.'"[90] A week or so after Armstrong joined Henderson, Buster Bailey was employed at the Roseland.[91] As Armstrong recalled, "They had an opening for saxophone and clarinet, the man they hired didn't come and they asked me if I could find someone, and I knew Buster Bailey could play. So he comes in, and then I kind of had company in the band, and that made the difference."[92] Armstrong knew Bailey from the time he had toured with Joe Oliver. Johnny Dodds didn't want to tour, so, after the band completed their run at the Lincoln Garden, Bailey joined the band.[93] Bailey coming into Henderson's orchestra not only helped Armstrong settle in, it also increased the harmonic possibilities in the reed section. With three reed players, it was possible for Redman to write full triads for the section, and this became a distinctive feature in Redman's arranging.[94]

William C. "Buster" Bailey was born in Memphis, Tennessee, in 1902. He began playing clarinet at the age of thirteen. While still at school, he heard W. C. Handy and his band play "Memphis Blues" at a concert at Clay Street School.[95] He later began his musical career working with Handy and his band in 1917. Bailey recalled, "We were playing in Memphis at the same time they were playing in Storyville in New Orleans. The difference was the New Orleans bands did more improvising. Ours were more the note variety. We played from the sheets."[96] One way for the musicians of Memphis to keep abreast of the latest popular tunes, Bailey explained, "was through the magazine, *Etude*. Every month they'd publish two new numbers and we'd learn them—but with a beat."[97] Bailey's first experience of New Orleans jazz was hearing a recording of "Livery Stable Blues" (1917), and this initiated his earliest experiments with improvising.[98] In the winter of 1917 he was in New Orleans on tour for a week and heard Johnny Dodds playing at Tom Anderson's. He also heard Mutt Carey, the cornet player with Ory's band; Clarence Williams, and Armand J. Piron. Bailey's exposure to New Orleans music, he would later claim, "made it easier for me to adapt to the New Orleans musicians when I went to Chicago later on. After that trip, I came home and started jazzing it up in Memphis."[99] The principles that he employed to improvise were similar to those described by New Orleans musicians: he played embellishments around the melody.

> One of the jobs our band had, for example, was to accompany the draftees to the station in 1917 and '18. We played "Draftin' Blues," "Preparedness Blues," and I jazzed them up. Everybody would follow me. I was the center of attraction. They were playing straight lead, but I—as the principal of my school said—was embellishing around the melody. At that time, I wouldn't have known what they meant by improvising. But embellishment was a phrase I understood. And that was what they were doing in New Orleans—embellishment.[100]

Bailey came to Chicago in 1919. Bailey was also a good reader of music (who continued to study with Franz Schoeppe, first clarinet with the Chicago Symphony Orchestra). On his arrival Bailey found work with Erskine Tate's orchestra at the Vendome Theater. He later joining King Oliver.

Henderson's orchestra also helped Armstrong develop as a singer. Armstrong probably had a selective memory when it came to his opportunity to sing with Henderson. He said, "Fletcher never let me sing."[101] He would further claim, "All the singing that I did before I joined Fletcher Henderson's band went down the drain the whole time that I was with him."[102] But that was not quite how Henderson remembered it some years later. Henderson claimed, "About three weeks after he joined us, he asked me if he could sing a number. I know I wondered what he could possibly do with that big fish horn voice of his, but finally I told him to try it. He was great. The band loved it, and the crowd just ate it up. I believe that was the first time he sang anywhere. He didn't sing with Oliver, I'm sure."[103] It seems likely that Henderson may have assisted Armstrong's development as a singer, although his singing at this time was incidental rather than central to his musical activities in the Henderson orchestra.

Henderson may have summed up Armstrong's time with his orchestra accurately: "The band gained a lot from Louis, and he gained a lot from us. By that I mean he *really* learned to read in my band, and to read in just about every key. Although it's common today, it wasn't usual at that time to write in such keys as E natural, or D natural, so that Louis had to learn, and he did learn, much more about his own horn than he knew before he joined us."[104] Furthermore, "You might say we put the finishing touches on his playing. He was great when he came in the band, but he found out there were a lot of things that he didn't know, and he set about studying them—studied with himself, that is, not with a teacher."[105] "That's how we influenced him. But he influenced the band greatly, too, by making the men really swing-conscious with that New Orleans style of his."[106]

Whatever else Henderson's orchestra had done for Armstrong, he was still playing third. Lil Hardin had other ideas. It was time, she felt, for Armstrong to return to Chicago, where she would find work for him. The choice was not a difficult one. Armstrong was working for $55 a week with Henderson.[107] Lil wired him from Chicago for a job with her own band at the Dreamland Café at the unheard-of salary of $75 a week.[108] At first Armstrong thought she was kidding him.[109] He returned to his wife nevertheless.

CHAPTER 13

"THE PRIDE OF RACE"
When Louis Sang with Erskine Tate

ARMSTRONG CAME TO THE ATTENTION OF CHICAGO BANDLEADERS soon after his return from working with Fletcher Henderson in New York. Armstrong remembered, "early in 1926, Professor Erskine Tate started talking to me about joining his little symphony orchestra at the Vendome Theatre and before long I did and stayed with Erskine for a year."[1]

Erskine Tate was born December 19, 1895, in Memphis, Tennessee.[2] Tate was educated in music at Lane College, Jackson, Tennessee, and then at the American Conservatory in Chicago.[3] Tate led the pit orchestra at the Vendome on South State Street in Chicago. An advertisement in the *Chicago Defender* of May 10, 1919, boasted of its "1500 Comfortable Seats," its "Mammoth Pipe Organ," and the presence of "Erskine Tate's Symphony Orchestra." For the following decade, this was one of the foremost African American theaters in the city. The theater screened silent films and included some "race pictures" made by black directors using black actors, often depicting the contribution that African Americans made in World War I.

The work with Erskine Tate was challenging but rewarding for Armstrong. Tate had a pit orchestra that played to accompany silent films and they also played music between the films. Armstrong was concerned: "Well, I didn't know if I could do it. Never played any classical music—*Cavelleria* [sic] *Rusticana*, reading music, turning sheets and all that, but Lil said I could."[4] In fact, she may well have put it more forcibly than that. Reputedly, Lil told Louis that if he didn't take the job, "I'll skin you alive. Do you realize what this means? They didn't ask King Oliver—they came to *you*!"[5]

Although Armstrong's reading of notated music was by this time good enough for Tate, Armstrong was still playing second. This was, in part, the reason for Armstrong swapping from cornet to trumpet during this period. The lead player, James Tate, used a trumpet and according to Armstrong, Erskine Tate asked him to change to trumpet because "I looked funny there with a stubby little cornet."[6] Another change that working with Tate offered was the opportunity to develop as a singer. Armstrong remembered, "It was with Tate that my stage career began. It was great fun, once I got used to being up there alone. After the overture, I'd jump out of the pit onto the stage and do a feature number, 'Heebie Jeebies,' for instance, and the crowd would start swinging and swaying with me. That really got me started. Then I'd pick up a megaphone and sing a chorus or two."[7] Although he had sung occasionally with Oliver and Henderson, it was not until he was with Tate that singing became a regular part of his live performances.

The story of "Heebie Jeebies" was told many times by Armstrong. Throughout his life, Armstrong claimed that on the second chorus of the song he dropped the lyric sheet and not wanting to waste a master recording he continued to singing nonsense syllables and recorded a "scat" vocal. Armstrong claimed in an article for *Esquire* in 1951, "So when I dropped the paper, I immediately turned back into the horn and started to Scatting . . . Just as nothing had happened . . . When I finished the recording I just knew the recording people would throw it out . . . And to my surprise they all came running out of the control booth and said—'Leave That In.'"[8] Johnny St. Cyr who played banjo on the recording told interviewers in 1958 that the composer, Boyd Atkins, who played violin with Armstrong at the Sunset Café, had written the music but no lyrics. Armstrong (or maybe it was the recording engineers) wanted lyrics, so Armstrong wrote some out on a slip of paper. St. Cyr confirmed that Armstrong dropped the paper and then began scatting. This was a novelty number and it "went like wildfire," starting a craze for scat singing, he said.[9] There is an interesting piece of detail that St. Cyr added to this account in an interview with Bill Russell in 1969. He said that Louis had written the words for "Heebie Jeebies" before they got to the studio. Russell's notes quote St. Cyr as saying:

> We got to the studio to run over the numbers, you know, before getting to cut them—at that time he was making 3 test records—& a master— So we made the test records alright, on that number I think we made only 2 tests, said ah, we'll make a master now—so we went ahead to make the master, & got to singing the "Heebie Jeebies" & the paper slipped out of his hand.[10]

If this is an accurate account of the recording session, the band had twice rehearsed the number with complete lyrics. This seems to add credibility to Armstrong's version of events. However, Kid Ory, who was also on the session, had a more measured recollection. He confirmed that "Heebie Jeebies" was "what today would be called a hit record," and that when Louis started scatting "We had all we could do to keep from laughing. Of course, Louis said he forgot the words, but I don't know if he intended it that way or not. It made the record though."[11] Lil Hardin played piano on "Heebie Jeebies," and like others present that day she did not contradict Louis's version of events.[12] New Orleans piano player Richard M. Jones was working for OKeh Records and had played a role in getting Armstrong to record.[13] Jones was responsible for orchestrating "Heebie Jeebies" with Charles M. Cooke. They received copyright for the arrangements on July 16, 1926.[14] Jones added a rather doubtful piece of detail. He claimed that the lyric sheet was dropped because he was attempting to give Armstrong a microphone. Armstrong correctly remembered that he sang "Heebie Jeebies" into a horn. Electrical recording was not used in the OKeh studios in February 1926.[15] OKeh developed their own True Tone system of electrical recording, but this method was only used between April 19 and October 29, 1926.[16] Whether Armstrong did, or did not, drop the paper with the lyrics, Thomas Brothers claims that Armstrong was not the first to record a scat solo: "Preceding him on recordings were Ukulele Ike, Don Redman, and, all the way back to 1911, Gene Greene's 'King of the Bungaloos.'"[17] Gene Greene had published the sheet music to "King of the Bungaloos" in 1909 without a nonsense syllable chorus, but this was added in his later recordings.[18] There are elements of Greene's scat chorus (if that is what it is) that are similar to Armstrong's later scat recordings. Without further research, transcription, and analysis, it would be wise to not draw any firm conclusions, given that there is an earlier "Rag Chorus ad lib" with nonsense syllables in Ben Harney's "Cake Walk in the Sky" (1899).[19]

There has been a tendency among scholars to interpret scat singing as a subversive act. Daniel Stein has argued, "When we witness the subversive, disruptive, 'scatological' vocalizations in 'Heebie Jeebies,' in which Louis Armstrong plays the line between speech and song, we engage not merely the pure musicality of the grain [of the voice] but the compression of linguistic signification that is rich with racial meaning as well."[20] While Armstrong may have had a scatological concern with the use of laxatives, this did not relate to his singing. It is doubtful that Armstrong conceived of his scat vocal on "Heebie Jeebies" as somewhere "between speech and song." It is true that he argued that scat singing was "a lot of syllables [and] things," he was careful to

Example 22: Scat chorus, "Heebie Jeebies" (February 26, 1926)

say, "but you [are] still playing music. It is musical notes whatever I'm doing."[21] He would later explain, "To me, Scat Singing is just like playing an instrument . . . That is, when they sing with the right chords, and beautiful changes."[22] That Armstrong conceived of singing scat as the vocalization of an instrumental line is borne out by Gene Anderson's transcription of Armstrong's scat chorus in "Heebie Jeebies." Recorded in the key of A♭, Armstrong's scat chorus ranges from an E♭ below middle C to an F above middle C: a range of a little over an octave.[23] This scat vocal is, as Armstrong said, sung rather than spoken. The transcription also includes both minor thirds (B♮/C♭) and the major thirds (C♮). Both notes are associated with the voice leading of the tenor voice and, of course, these note choices are typical of Armstrong's cornet and trumpet solos.[24] Joshua Berrett observes that in his recording of "Heebie Jeebies" Armstrong "did not 'invent' scat at this session, he simply drew upon an old routine dating back to his days as a street singer in New Orleans."[25] This was confirmed by Armstrong in an interview with Bill Russell on May 5, 1970. Russell was researching to write a book on the New Orleans piano player Jelly Roll Morton. Russell referred Armstrong to a quote by Morton in the Library of Congress recording that Morton had made with Alan Lomax. In this recording, Morton had told Lomax that people had come to believe that "the first scat number was done by one of my hometown boys, Louis Armstrong. But I must take the credit away, since I know better. The first man that ever did a scat number in history of this country was a man from Vicksburg, Mississippi, by the name of Joe Sims, an old comedian."[26] Armstrong's reply to Russell was emphatic: "I never claimed that... The head man up at OKeh Records—when I dropped the paper—and I began to scat, and we used to do that in New Orleans in the quartet you know, when we singing—That's when Mr. Fearn said, 'Well Armstrong, that's when "scat" was born.' But I never did claim it."[27] Russell then asked for clarification: "So you used to do that down in New Orleans, before the recording date?" Armstrong replied, "Yeah, we used to do that in the quartet going down the street... scat-do-beep-de-do, etc. You know some old comedians used to do that."[28]

There is a clue to the origin of the song "Heebie Jeebies" because of the reference in the lyrics to "the Heebie Jeebies Dance." Around this period, Armstrong and Atkins were working with the married comedy and dance team Jodie and Susie Edwards, known as Butterbeans and Susie. As a married couple, they built their act around the conflict between man and wife. Nadine George-Graves explained in *The Royalty of Negro Vaudeville* (2000) how "Butterbeans tried to stand up to his domineering wife, but his small stature and less than imposing physicality only increased the hilarity of the situation."[29] Henry T. Sampson in *Blacks in Blackface* (1980) describes, "In their act they sang duets between which Susie sang the blues and cakewalked while Butterbeans performed eccentric dances."[30] Both writers comment on Butterbeans's trademark dance: "He was famous for his Heebie Jeebies, a dance routine known in the trade as 'the itch' in which he scratched in syncopated rhythm."[31] Butterbeans and Susie toured on the Columbia Burlesque Circuit in 1923 in a show "Heebie Jeebies" that took its title from Butterbeans's dance routine.[32] The Itch, described as "a spasmodic placing of the hands all over the body in an agony of perfect rhythm," had featured in African American vaudeville in a 1909 composition, "The Bull Frog Hop" by Perry Bradford.[33] Butterbeans claimed to have borrowed the Itch "from a great dancer named Stringbeans."[34] Butler "String Beans" May (born August 18, 1894) was a comedian, pianist, and pioneer blues performer, whose early death at the age of twenty-three, and the absence of recordings, as Doug Seroff and Lynn Abbott argue, led to him being overlooked in the historical narrative.[35] He was a great influence on Jelly Roll Morton, who imitated String Beans early in his stage career, inclusive of inserting a diamond stud in his teeth.[36] Butterbeans and Susie had worked with String Beans in October 1917 at the 81 Theater, Atlanta, Georgia, where they teamed together and went on to the Strand Theater, Jacksonville, Florida.[37] They reportedly "cleaned up" wherever they performed. The *Indianapolis Freemen* reported, "They don't need any more acts on the bill as these are standing them in the streets nightly. Edwards and Edwards [Butterbeans and Susie] opens and Beans closes with his Piano. Nuff Sed."[38] Within four months of recording "Heebie Jeebies," Armstrong accompanied Butterbeans and Susie on a recording of "He Likes It Slow" on June 18, 1926.[39]

In the audience at the Vendome Theater in 1926 was W. C. Handy, whose autobiography, *Father of the Blues*, describes how he composed many blues songs based upon the black folksongs he heard in his youth.[40] Handy had a similar musical education to that of Louis Armstrong. As a child, Handy learned music in the barbershops in his home town of Florence, Alabama. He recalled that travelling white bandleaders would set up headquarters in the barbershops of Florence and teach aspiring local musicians. Because Handy wanted to avoid paying, he would be "lurking at the entrance, in view of the board, clutching the antediluvian rotary-valve cornet which he had secretly obtained for $2.50."[41] Along with gaining a rudimentary musical education, Handy played in a quartet in the barbershop, and he also sang in a vocal quartet. They "gathered in the shop for the trying out of the new swipes; sang (for a consideration) at the whites' entertainments or even (for what might fall their way) on the street corner."[42] Handy, in a similar way to Armstrong, learned solfeggio singing at school. He remembered, "When I was a youngster in school, we studied music by the old tonic sol-fa system: Do, Re, Me, Fa, So, La Ti, Do." This grounding in music was based upon developing the recognition of relative pitches. Handy believed that this method ensured that "I could notice the peculiarities in music."[43] Having learned music in this way, Handy was able to accurately notate the music that he heard around him and capture the nuances of African American vocal music.

Handy began his musical career when he set out with his Lauzetta Quartet, and "twenty cents in the treasury," to sing at the 1892 World's Fair in Chicago.[44] When Handy discovered the World's Fair was postponed until the following year, he made his way to St. Louis. After St. Louis he went to Evansville, Indiana.[45] There he contacted Phil Jones, a local brass band leader. One of the songs that Phil Jones sang was "Got No Mo' Home Dan a Dog."[46] In 1938 Handy recorded an interview with Alan Lomax. Handy told Lomax he would sing for him a blues song, "Got No More Home than a Dog"—although the word "blues" was not in the title—that he "played around Evansville, Indiana in 1892 and 3."[47] There is some evidence that Handy may have known the song before he left for Chicago. Handy relayed, "The first strain with its words is at least thirty-five years old and written as it was sung around 1890" by his quartet in Florence.[48] Whether Handy did know this song from Florence or Evansville, it was associated with a vocal quartet,

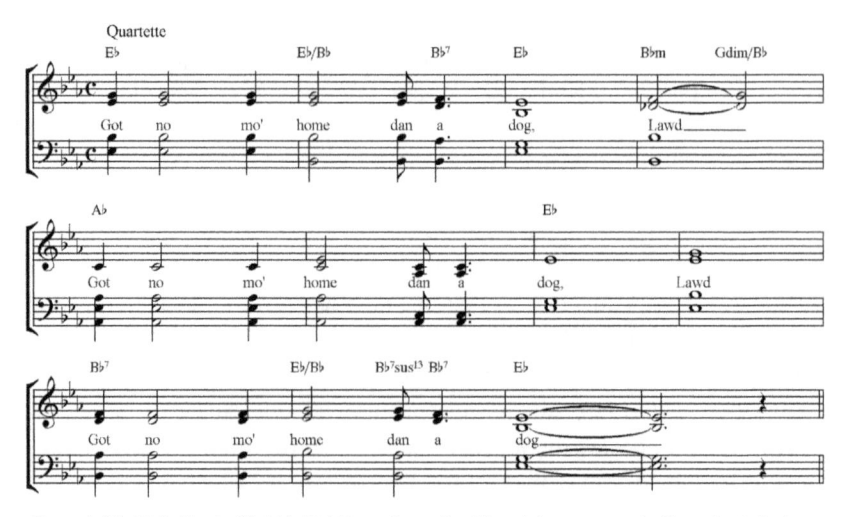

Example 23: W. C. Handy, "Got No Mo' Home Dan a Dog" (quartet arrangement, *Blues: An Anthology*, 1926) (Courtesy of Handy Bros Music Co. Inc.)

and it is presumably for this reason that Handy notated "Got No Mo' Home Dan a Dog" for a "quartette." Handy's arrangement of "Got No Mo' Home Dan a Dog" is significant because it is the earliest known transcription (albeit notated retrospectively) of a blues performance. Not only did Handy provide the lyrics: he also notated the melody and harmony. Handy claimed that this song "furnishes in short compass the transition between the folk-blues and their direct modern descendants."[49]

Handy was a prodigious blues composer. By 1926 his previous blues publications, combined with a few newer arrangements, were sufficient for him to publish *Blues: An Anthology*. This anthology contains four different arrangements of "Got No Mo' Home Dan a Dog." The first arrangement was as it was performed around 1892, whereas the next three versions were designed to show how this blues could be adapted and modified to become what was then a modern blues song.[50] With "Got No Mo' Home Dan a Dog," Handy was not presenting a finished composition; he was presenting the process that enabled him to convert folk material into a classic blues song of the 1920s. In so doing, he made explicit his role as "Father of the Blues." He also provided evidence of how vocal quartet music was transformed into a music performed on instruments. Handy as a composer was the counterpart to Armstrong the musician: they were both engaged in converting their knowledge of barbershop harmony into a form that could be performed on instruments. When Armstrong had the opportunity to record an album of W. C. Handy tunes in the 1950s, Armstrong said it was "no work making records like this! Them old time good ones, they play themselves, Mr. Handy. You get to blowing those beautiful changes right, and you have to play good. We was just having a ball, that's all."[51] Handy and Armstrong were rooted in the same musical tradition.

Handy had first heard Armstrong perform on the *S.S. Capitol*. Handy recognized Armstrong's ability: "I like naturalness . . . That's the thing I liked about Louis. If he likes a thing, he's just gonna put himself into it."[52] One of the songs that both Handy and Armstrong knew from childhood was "Careless Love." Handy claimed the song "narrated the death of the son of a governor of Kentucky. It had the mythical 'hundred stanzas' and is widely current in the South, especially in Kentucky, a number of years ago."[53] It is claimed that, before the dawn of the twentieth century, "In Henderson, Kentucky, the curbstone quartets improvised a song about a local scandal involving a prominent citizen. The roustabouts and musicians carried it to New Orleans. It became an American classic, 'Careless Love.'"[54] It is possible that the song was adapted from a ballad of Anglo-American origin. A version of "Careless Love" was collected in Mississippi in 1909 from "country whites."[55] It was nevertheless absorbed into the repertoire of early jazz bands in New Orleans and widely associated with Buddy Bolden.[56]

Handy produced an arrangement of "Careless Love" in *Blues: An Anthology* (1926); he also published a version called "Loveless Love" with new words.[57] Handy explained the inspiration for his new lyrics: "One day at noon, I heard a minister speaking to a crowd on Broadway, and he was charting them for adulterating goods, and merchandise, and food, and . . . They're adulterating everything, and I said, they are adulterating love even."[58] Handy said that after hearing the preacher he caught a train to Chicago where Armstrong was playing with Erskine Tate's Orchestra at the Vendome Theater. Handy continued, "And I sat down there and wrote 'Loveless Love,' and used the term that people were using then in the days of milk-less milk and silk-less silk. I orchestrated it, and carried it into Tate. Tate played it, and I sent it off and had it printed, and printed these words to 'Loveless Love' that Louis sang."[59] At the time, according to Handy, "Louis used to draw large crowds every night, singing just whatever number that he wanted to sing. They came that year to hear him play and sing . . . They realized that it was something different."[60] Although these audiences were attracted by both his playing and his singing, it was his singing that Handy drew particular attention to: "But they went to hear Louis sing. And I don't mind telling you, there was something in that voice that they appreciated: *the pride of race*."[61] Of particular interest is the end of the third line (see Ex. 24, m. 12). On the word "girl" the melody returns

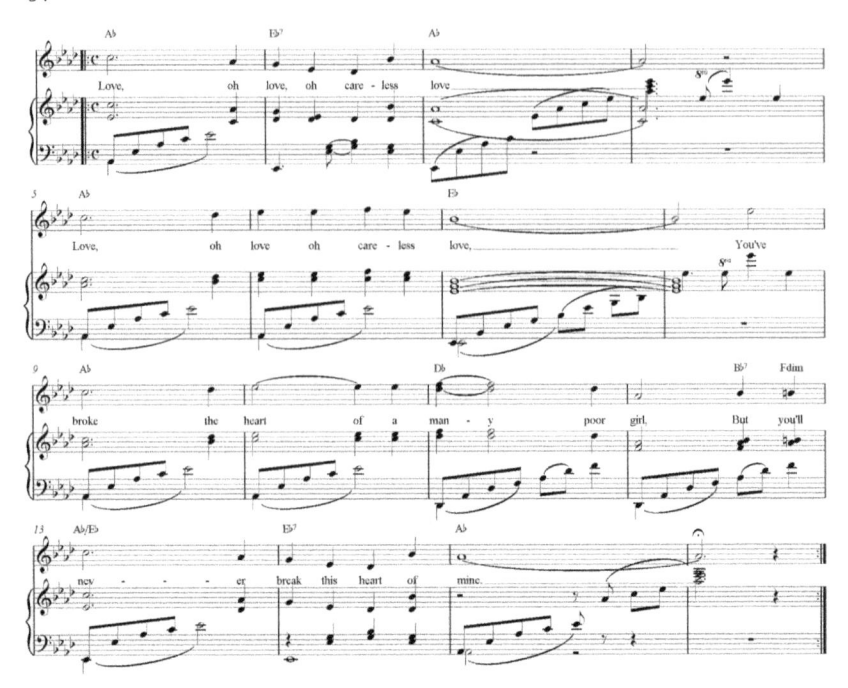

Example 24: W. C. Handy, "Careless Love" (*Blues: An Anthology*, 1926) (Courtesy of Handy Bros Music Co. Inc.)

to the tonic note of A♭. This note can be harmonized in a number of ways. In measure 15 of Example 24, for example, on the word "mine," Handy has chosen to harmonize this note with the tonic chord of A♭. Given that this is the final melody note of the chorus, a resolution to the tonic chord would be expected. In measure 12, although the melody note has returned to A♭, this is not a final resolution, and Handy has instead harmonized this note with a chord of D♭. D♭ is the subdominant chord of A♭, where the A♭ note forms the fifth of the chord. When Armstrong recorded "Loveless Love" many years later, this measure was harmonized with a subdominant chord as in the sheet music. Armstrong had recorded an earlier version of "Careless Love" with Bessie Smith and Fletcher Henderson in 1925.[62] In Bessie Smith's version of "Careless Love" (1925), Henderson played an inversion of the tonic diminished chord in this measure instead of the subdominant. A few years later in 1928 when the New Orleans guitarist Lonnie Johnson recorded "Careless Love," he too used an inversion of the tonic diminished in this measure. Another common variant in this measure of "Careless Love" is the barbershop chord on the flatted sixth. Examples include versions by New Orleans veterans Bunk Johnson and Wooden Joe Nicholas.[63] The songster Lead Belly, in his recordings for the Library of Congress, introduced a fourth variant in this measure by playing the tonic chord. What united all of these different chords is that the tonic note is one of the intervals of the chord. The tonic note can function as the root of the tonic chord; it is the major third of the flatted sixth chord; it is the flatted fifth of the tonic diminished chord, and it is the perfect fifth in Handy's original arrangement using the subdominant. Or to put it another way, the song was popular with barbershop quartets because these different chords are all possible variants of barbershop cadences as given in Example 12. Rather than chord substitution and reharmonization of a melody being advanced or modern devices in jazz composition and arranging, this suggests that these techniques were fundamental to the development of jazz and rooted in the practices of barbershop harmony. In barbershop, it is the harmony that is varied while the melody remains unchanged.

CHAPTER 14

LIL'S HOT SHOTS

THE AFRICANIST GERHARD KUBIK HAS ARGUED, "NO SERIOUS STUDENT of African-American music will subscribe today to all-encompassing formulations such as that 'harmony' in jazz and other African-American music is 'European' in origin, while 'Rhythm' is 'African.'"[1] Historically, in terms of harmony at least, many writers have. André Hodeir concluded his exploration of jazz harmony saying, "To sum up, jazz musicians have no special reason for taking pride in an harmonic language that, besides being easily acquired, does not really belong to them but rather to a 'light harmony' that North America borrowed from decadent Debussyism."[2] Gunther Schuller observed, "In a very real sense, European traditional harmony and melody are merely two sides of the same coin.... Melodies are very often horizontal projection of a harmonic substructure, and harmonies are just verticalizations of melodic segments."[3] By contrast, he argued, African music is "unilaterally melodic, that is, not harmonic in structure.... African music does not have the two-way cross-relationship between melody and harmony we have in European music."[4] While it may be that contemporary theorists take a less rigid view, there persists a view that harmony in jazz is predominantly of European derivation. An understanding of barbershop harmony does suggest that the influence of European harmonic practice has been overstated. However, there is clearly some influence.

The influence of European musical practice on Armstrong's playing has received some attention by music scholars in recent years.[5] Peter Ecklund has argued, in "'Louis Licks' and Nineteenth-Century Cornet Etudes: The Roots of Melodic Improvisation as Seen in the Jazz Style of Louis Armstrong" (2001), that it is "safe to say that it was the European tradition of mass-marketed popular music that provided most of the melodic material for early jazz, as well as its phrase structure and harmony."[6] Specifically, according to Ecklund,

Armstrong's licks, with the exception of the blues, "can be traced to the European tradition of melody, although it is difficult to identify their specific origins."[7] Part of the difficulty of identifying specific origin, as Ecklund acknowledges, is "we have no evidence from early in his career that Armstrong ever practiced from the St. Jacome, Arban, or any other nineteenth-century French instruction book."[8] We do know, however, that Joe Oliver did give Armstrong some lessons from an unidentified exercise book and they would "run down duets together."[9] We can be reasonably sure that this method book wasn't Arban because Armstrong dismissed Arban as "nothing but the rudiments of bop." Armstrong was openly critical of bebop when it came to prominence after World War II.[10] It is possible that Armstrong may have developed some of his improvisations from fragments of European melodies, as he had exposure to popular song that was heavily influenced by what has come to be known as "parlor" style.[11] Armstrong also had eclectic tastes. He told an audience of jazz fans, "You see, now we got to be not too partial to one kind of music. You've got to appreciate all kinds of music. That's what I'm trying to put in your head. Listen to all kinds of music. I got classics . . . Some of your best jazz musicians came from symphonies. And some of your best riffs."[12] Armstrong also said, during his time with Joe Oliver, "I picked up a lot of ideas from classical pieces I heard and got a kick out of putting a snatch of them in here and there when I played with the band."[13] Recorded examples include "Franz Drdla's light classical number, 'Souvenir', in his backing on Clara Smith's 'Court House Blues' in 1925, as well as his quoting of *Rigoletto* during a break on Johnny Dodds's 1927 recording of 'New Orleans Stomp.'"[14] If Armstrong's harmonic and melodic vocabulary was significantly affected by the European canon, it has become widely supposed that Lil Hardin was the person most responsible for this.

According to Armstrong's first autobiography, Hardin was not in Oliver's band when he arrived in Chicago in 1922. Armstrong said, one night after they finished a show, Oliver asked if he wanted to go over to the Dreamland and meet Lil. Oliver had previously sent Armstrong a photo of his band including Lil, and Armstrong had asked Oliver to "Tell Miss Lil I like her."[15] At the time he didn't think anything would come of it. Armstrong went on to say, "After that first night I didn't see much of Lil for two or three months, until she came back to join our band at the Lincoln Gardens."[16]

Lillian Beatrice Hardin was born in Memphis, Tennessee, telling interviewers that she was a "little younger" than Armstrong.[17] Census records show that she was actually a little older: she was born in February 1898.[18] She began piano lessons with Miss Violet White when she entered grade school.[19]

She claims to have then gone to Mrs. Hook's School of Music, "graduating in music" when she was eleven years old.[20] At school she studied the music of Edvard Grieg, Edward MacDowell, and other classical composers, along with some hymns and marches.[21] Away from school she was exposed to a little jazz by a guitar-playing cousin, and she remembered singing and playing "Buddy Bolden's Blues."[22] The extent of Hardin's education in classical music at the time she met Armstrong has probably been overstated. She claimed that she attended Fisk University as a "music special," but according to her biographer, James L. Dickerson, "Actually, Lil did not enroll in a [Fisk] university course of study and never received a degree. She was in a college preparatory program that offered high school courses chosen to prepare students for entry into the university."[23] She later enrolled at the Chicago College of Music to further her musical education and obtained her teaching certificate in 1928.[24] Armstrong was impressed by her studies:

> She was always going to music school to learn more about it, and she studies that way still. We used to practice together, "wood-shed" as we say . . . She would play on the piano and I, of course, on my trumpet. I had learned how to transpose from a piano part. We used to play classical music together sometimes. We bought classical trumpet music. Through this, later on, we played in church once in a while. All this was giving me more knowledge of my music.[25]

She continued with her musical education after her time with Armstrong. In 1939 the *Jazzmen* authors interviewed Hardin. They noted, "Lil is a graduate of Chicago College of Music, and a graduate of Fisk. Has two diplomas hanging up in her front room, over the piano. At the present time she is studying instrumentation and arranging."[26]

Lil assisted Louis with composing and gaining copyright for tunes. Armstrong remembered, "I used to sit on the back steps of Lil's house and write five or six songs a day—just lead sheets—and Lil would put the other parts to them, cornet, clarinet, trombone etc."[27] It is claimed, "Louis would play the melody and Lil would write it down as fast as Louis played it."[28] The first tunes that they got copyright for were "New Orleans Cut Out" and "Coal Cart Blues." Lawrence Gushee has observed, "Both 'Coal Cart Blues' and 'New Orleans Cut-Out' are copyrighted jointly by Armstrong and Lillian Hardin, leaving room for the argument that 'sophisticated touches' are attributable to Lil's formal education in music theory. I see no way to rule this out absolutely."[29] Moreover, Gushee drew attention to the "melodic outlining of the tonic diminished seventh" in "Coal Cart Blues." He would go on to say, "In fact, it is an important feature of all the early tunes, and may reveal Armstrong striving for a degree of harmonic sophistication."[30] While there is no way to completely rule out the possibility that Hardin inspired the use of tonic diminished harmony, the balance of probability is that this harmony was rooted in Armstrong's knowledge of barbershop cadences.[31] Tonic diminished harmony is featured in the opening break of "Dippermouth Blues" (see Ex. 13) and is, along with the flatted sixth, one of the most fundamental barbershop chords (see Ex. 12). The relationship between barbershop harmony and diminished harmony was evident to contemporary observers. Henry O. Osgood commented in 1926, "The celebrated 'barbershop chords' are, technically speaking, merely diminished sevenths." Unaware perhaps of the particular preference in barbershop for the tonic diminished (or one of its inversions), Osgood would go on to say that these chords were "the common property of composers for two centuries now."[32] While the chord itself was common property, basing the chord on the tonic note was not. In baroque and classical composition, the use of the diminished seventh is typically rooted on the leading note of the key rather than the tonic. As Arnold Schoenberg observed in *Theory of Harmony* (1911), "The most important and simplest function of the diminished seventh chord is . . . its resolution in the manner of a deceptive cadence: the root goes up a step (VII to I). It is most frequently found in this function."[33] It is rare to find examples of tonic diminished harmony used as part of a harmonic progression in the classical canon.[34]

The copyright for "Coal Cart Blues" was submitted two years before it was recorded with Clarence Williams in 1925, and it may have been played many years before that.[35] According to Armstrong, after working in the kitchen of Thompson's Restaurant in New Orleans, "I quit and went back to my old job in Andrews Coal Yard. That was when I wrote 'Coal Cart Blues.'"[36] This was, of course, many years before he met Lil Hardin. Whenever it was written, it contains many features that are typical of Armstrong's playing. Originally recorded in F major, in Example 25 it is transposed to C major.[37] In the first four measures Armstrong plays E♭ instead of the major third (E♮) against major harmony. The presence of minor thirds in a tune that is in a major key is a feature found in the barbershop cadence at the end of "Swanee River" (see Ex. 1); this feature was noted in "The Chimney Sweep's Song" (see Ex. 6); it is found in the "Charcoal Man's Cry" (see Ex. 7); and both major and minor thirds are found in the harmony parts in "Rock Mount Sinai" (see Ex. 8). This is a tonality that Armstrong knew well. A second feature of "Coal Cart Blues" is the use of A♭ against an F major chord in (see Ex. 25, m. 5). A♭ relative

Example 25: Louis Armstrong and Lil Hardin, "Coal Cart Blues" (October 8, 1925)

to F♮ is a minor third interval; however, the chord contains the major third (A♮). Gushee also commented on "the harmonic progression I-vi underlying the first strain of 'New Orleans Stomp' and the second strain of 'Coal Cart Blues.'"[38] The chord progression from the tonic major chord to the minor chord on the fourth degree of the scale is a fundamental barbershop cadence (see Ex. 12). The subdominant minor chord frequently appears in the sixth measure of a twelve-bar blues and it is often proceeded by a subdominant major chord. This is a characteristic of Armstrong's playing that has received attention from Brian Harker, who finds that Armstrong "developed the habit of playing a minor triad in the sixth bar, where the IV chord normally appeared."[39] The examples he cited were "See See Rider Blues," recorded with Ma Rainey, "Reckless Blues," and "You've Been a Good Ole Wagon," with Bessie Smith. Harker argues, "Such instances (and there are many) suggest that Armstrong was pursuing his own harmonic agenda with little regard, sometimes, for his surroundings."[40] Rather than harmonic disregard, a more convincing explanation is that the change of harmony from major to minor on a subdominant chord is a product of Armstrong's knowledge of the voice leading in a barbershop quartet in the baritone voice. Spaeth calls this a "twice over" ending as this produced a two-chord cadence.[41] This harmonic formulation was a feature that Sargeant recognized in blues tonality: "The sixth degree is also occasionally lowered by a flat and followed by a fifth. In this case the flatted tone usually serves as a passing tone between the major sixth and the fifth."[42] In some cases the subdominant minor chord can appear on its own. The blues guitarist Blind Lemon Jefferson on a number of recordings omitted the major chord IV and only played the minor chord. David Evans comments, "Jefferson features an unusual flatted sixth note in his playing, suggesting a minor IV chord in places where a major IV chord would normally be played."[43] What Armstrong has effectively done in composing "Coal Cart Blues" is to bring forward what would be in another context part

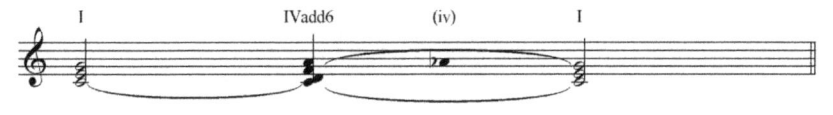

Example 26: Voice leading, "Skid-Dat-De-Dat" (November 16, 1926)

of a countermelody in the baritone voice to the main melody. He is playing countermelodies on his cornet that he sang and heard all around him as a child on the streets of New Orleans. Much as the street vendors had done before him, Armstrong is performing these countermelodies as a solo voice removed from the polyphonic texture of their origin. In so doing, he was composing and performing blues-inflected melodies and solos.

One Armstrong recording that has been explored in relation to Lil Hardin's classical education is "Skid-Dat-De-Dat" (1926). Described by Schuller as "a bit of scat-nonsense" written by the couple, Joshua Berrett finds "Skid-Dat-De-Dat" "strongly reminiscent of one of the staples of the European canon, Mozart's 'Jupiter' Symphony—specifically, the four whole notes with which its finale opens."[44] He goes on to say, "it comes as a revelation to realize that they [the four chords of "Skid-Dat-De-Dat"] are all anchored by a pedal point on the pitch of C, the key of Mozart's 'Jupiter' symphony. This kind of harmonic device, virtually unknown in New Orleans Dixieland jazz, provides strong evidence of Hardin's familiarity with European practice; it is a tradition harking back to early organ playing and its use of the pedal board, where a tone is sustained in the bass while harmonies above it change."[45]

Although Armstrong remembered spending evenings "running over some of the finest Classics" with his wife on their baby grand piano, it is unlikely that anything more than perhaps the four-note motif is derived from the *Jupiter Symphony*.[46] Example 26 is a voice leading reduction of the four chords of "Skid-Dat-De-Dat" as given by Gene H. Anderson in *The Original Hot Five Recordings of Louis Armstrong* (2007), and an example of the chord progression from subdominant major to subdominant minor.[47] As is evident from previous discussion, barbershop and blues tonality functions with reference to a tonal center, and the pedal tone that Berrett identified is fundamental to barbershop harmonic practice. The four-note motif may or may not be derived from Mozart, but the chords are not, because Mozart did not employ a pedal tone and instead used diatonic chords. Although a pedal tone may have been common in European church music, it was not employed by Mozart in this instance. He chose instead to use the leading note (B♮) in (see Ex. 27, m. 3) to produce this conventional interrupted cadence.[48] The ascending leading note and chromatic dissonance relative to the tonic is

Example 27: Mozart, *Jupiter Symphony* (Finale)

the hallmark of diatonic harmony and runs contrary to the basic principles of barbershop harmonization.

A further feature of "Skid-Dat-De-Dat" that strongly points toward the origin of this tune in barbershop practice is the opening break. As Schuller asks, "Does this look like a break for a piece in C major?"[49] He goes on to say that had the key of C already been established, the notes of B♭, E♭, and A♭ "would simply be heard as blue notes or lowered altered notes. But since the break starts the piece unaccompanied, our ears perceive this as some kind of E flat (or possibly C minor) melody, and it is therefore the tonic key of C *major* that sounds strange."[50] In the opening break to "Skid-Dat-De-Dat" (see Ex. 28), Armstrong and Hardin have opened the piece with the tenor and baritone voices unresolved. The anacrusis bar is a minor third swipe in the baritone voice—Spaeth's Blues Progression (see Ex. 5)—which is repeated in the first measure of the break. The tenor voice on the E♭ is unresolved, as is the following A♭ of the baritone voice. The only note that is resolved is the tonic (lead voice) note of C, the pedal tone that is present throughout.

"Skid-Dat-De-Dat" provides a further opportunity to explore the relationship between Armstrong's singing and playing, as he sings three scat vocal breaks on this recording. These breaks have been considered in some detail in an article by William Bauer, "Louis Armstrong's 'Skid Dat De Dat': Timbral Organization in an Early Scat Solo." Bauer observes, "Theorists have shown a remarkable lack of curiosity about jazz singers and about the peculiar techniques jazz singers use to give shape to their interpretations."[51] With the exception of Gunther Schuller, who did recognize what Bauer describes as "a conclusion that many reach intuitively: Armstrong is singing through his horn," Bauer can find little evidence of analysis of Armstrong's vocal work.[52] What is clear from his transcriptions of Armstrong's scat vocal breaks on

Example 28: Introductory break, "Skid-Dat-De-Dat" (November 16, 1926)

Example 29: Louis Armstrong's first scat break, "Skid-Dat-De-Dat" (November 16, 1926)

"Skid-Dat-De-Dat" is that they are typical of his instrumental note choices.[53] The first vocal break (see Ex. 29) is based upon two minor third swipes in the baritone voice interspersed with a brief transition to the tenor voice in the third measure. These are the note choices one would expect relative to barbershop practice and they are typical of the note choices Armstrong made on his cornet.

There are some examples of tunes where it is likely that Lil's background had a greater influence. One tune that is widely believed to have been a Hardin composition is "Struttin' with Some Barbecue," although Armstrong claimed that he wrote it:

> The tune was derived and thought of during the days that Zutty Singleton and I were playing at the Savoy Ballroom on the South Side of Chicago . . . And, after the dance was over every night, Zutty and I would drive out to 48th and State Street . . . There was an old man there who made the most delicious barbecue that anyone would love to smack their chops on (their lips) . . . One night, while Zutty and I were manipulating those "Chime Bones" (barbecue), a thought came into my head . . . I said to Zutty—"Say Zoot, as I sit here eating these fine-tasting ribs, it dawned on me that I should write a tune and call it, "Struttin with Some Barbecue" . . . Zutty said, "Dush, that's a real good idea" . . . So then and there, "Struttin with Some Barbecue" was born.[54]

Lil Hardin claimed instead that she had written the tune. She successfully gained inclusion on the copyright and a financial settlement many years after it was initially registered in only Armstrong's name.[55] The musical case to support the view that Hardin had written the tune is that the melody is based on the leading note on the major seventh interval of the scale. The use of this note in the melody converts the opening tonic chord into a major seventh chord. Frank Tirro argues that Lil Hardin's "compositions were far more adventurous, containing harmonies and melodic figures not common in the New Orleans repertoire. . . . The opening melody [of "Struttin' with Some Barbecue"], after the introduction, outlines a major seventh chord, an unusual and advanced harmonic idea not stemming from the New Orleans tradition."[56] This was a type of harmony that Joshua Berrett claims was "virtually unknown in 1920s jazz."[57] This is something of an overstatement. New Orleans jazz, as it was actually performed, did sometimes employ quite complex harmony. Although the major seventh chord was not common in the 1920s, increasingly major chords were often employed with an added sixth, and in the 1930s an added major seventh became common. The evolution of jazz harmony is a topic beyond the scope of this book, but an understanding of barbershop harmony is one method that may assist further enquiry.

Many writers have noted the absence of the major seventh in African American music making, but Winthrop Sargeant makes an interesting observation: he noticed that "even when the seventh degree of the major scale appears in the spirituals and in jazz, it seldom functions as the 'leading tone' of European melody."[58] Instead of ascending to the tonic, the tendency is for the melody of African American music to descend downward from the major seventh. An example of this can be found in the cry of the "Buttermilk Man" (see Ex. 4).

Lil's classical education, and her husband's open approach to all types of music, will of course have influenced Armstrong's development as a musician. A fundamental limitation to exploring how European and African American musical traditions influenced the development of jazz is that the only theoretical models and methods of analysis that have been available are the musical theories that developed to describe European music making. However, an understanding of barbershop harmony offers an alternative analytical approach to exploring jazz, blues, gospel, and other musics that have African American roots. There are limitations to this too: contemporary arrangers of barbershop harmony use theoretical concepts that may be far removed from the harmonic practices of the nineteenth and early twentieth century. There is much more that we need to know about the development of African American harmony, of which barbershop, as we know it today, is just one manifestation. However, if a more comprehensive understanding of barbershop, its history, its development, and its principles can be developed, then we may be able to explore in greater depth the role that African Americans had in the development of American music making.

CHAPTER 15

THE HOT FIVE AND SEVEN

ARMSTRONG CAME BACK TO CHICAGO AFTER PLAYING WITH HENDERSON for at least two reasons: in part because Lil could offer him work that paid better than Henderson and in part to record for OKeh Records. By the time Armstrong and his Hot Five recorded for OKeh in late 1925, OKeh had become the leading record company in the "race record" market.[1]

Lil Hardin seems to have played a pivotal role in negotiating with Ralph Peer, the director of production at OKeh, to enable Armstrong to record. Peer knew Lil and her husband from when Armstrong was performing at the Royal Gardens in Chicago before he joined Henderson in New York.[2] While Armstrong was in New York, Peer agreed, "Whenever we needed a New York trumpet player our first choice would be Louis Armstrong."[3] Armstrong's initial recordings for OKeh during this period were with Clarence Williams's Blue Five.[4] On November 9, 1925, Armstrong recorded four tracks all composed by New Orleans pianist Richard M. Jones with singers Bertha "Chippie" Hill and Blanche Calloway. It is possible that Jones played a role in persuading Armstrong to form the Hot Five, but it is clear that Lil Hardin and Ralph Peer were also involved.[5] Hardin spoke with Peer before Armstrong's return to Chicago to say that Louis "can't stand it in New York."[6] Hardin and Peer struck a deal. Peer told Hardin, "Well, if he goes back to Chicago, I will do this for you. We will create an Armstrong orchestra so that we can give you some work."[7] Armstrong subsequently received a call from Elmer A. Fearn, the president of OKeh Records, and Armstrong contacted the musicians' union and asked permission to hire Kid Ory, Johnny St. Cyr, and Johnny Dodds.[8] Ory was in California and received a letter from Armstrong who was still in New York to come to Chicago and record. Ory broke up his band and arrived in Chicago before Louis.[9]

Ory gave quite a detailed account of how the OKeh sessions were organized: "The OKeh people would call up Louis and say they wanted so many sides. They never told him what number they wanted or how they wanted them. Then Louis would give us the date, and sometimes he'd call and say, 'I'm short of a number for this next session. Do you think you can get one together?' I'd say, 'all right.'"[10] Ory explained:

> We would get to the studio at nine or ten in the morning. We didn't have to make records at night, with the lights out, or get drunk like some musicians think they have to do before they can play. In the beginning we made records acoustically, and there was a separate horn for each man. The recording engineer would motion to us if we played too loud or too soft, and then we'd know to move back or to move in closer. Then later, of course, we made records electrically.[11]

He expanded:

> When we'd get in the studio, if we were going to do a new number, we'd run it over a couple of times before we recorded it. We were a very fast recording band; in fact the records I made with the Hot Fives were the easiest I ever made. We spoiled very few records, only sometimes when one of us would forget a routine or the frame-up, and didn't come in when he was supposed to. Even then, we'd try to cover up. After we'd make a side, Louis would say: "was that all right?" And if one of us thought we could do it better, why Louis would tell them we wanted to do it again, and so we would do it over.[12]

Ory remembered that the Hot Five and Seven would usually record eight sides at a session and the "OKeh people were amazed."[13] This was because "Most of the other bands took all day to make a couple of sides. We would make eight in three hours."[14]

These tracks were arranged using the principles that Ory and the other New Orleans musicians had known since childhood. One musician would play the melody, and the other musicians would find their countermelodies and harmony parts by experimentation, as Ory described: "Often we didn't know the tunes when we got to the studio: one of us would suggest a melody; we'd run it through once and then record it. We never used any kind of arrangement. All we needed was a lead sheet and everybody would figure out his part."[15] Part of the reason that the Hot Five could arrange their material with little rehearsal was that a good number of the tunes that the Hot Five and Seven recorded were twelve-bar blues. This was a form and tonality that they knew well. Their ability to arrange these tunes derived from their shared knowledge of barbershop harmony, and this enabled them to work together without too much time-consuming preparation. While the chords usually found in the first eight measures of a twelve-bar blues can be derived from barbershop cadences, the dominant chord that usually appears in the closing measures is unlikely to be derived from barbershop practice. The reason for this is that the dominant chord contains the leading note a semitone below the tonic note. The dominant chord, rather than being derived from barbershop practice, is more likely a product of European harmony. Although the appearance of dominant harmony in the twelve-bar chord sequence of the blues would seem to undermine the theory that an understanding of barbershop harmony is fundamental to understanding blues tonality, in fact, closer inspection of how Armstrong approached the dominant chord confirms his claim to have applied barbershop principles to his playing. His treatment of dominant harmony in the accompanying chords indicates that Armstrong often approached the closing measures of a twelve-bar blues as a barbershop cadence rather than a conventional European cadence, and in so doing he introduced notes that were theoretically dissonant with the chord.

An example of Armstrong playing a dissonant note—in this instance, the tonic of the key—against dominant harmony was his solo on "Gut Bucket Blues" (1925), recorded at the first recording session of the Hot Five.[16] According to Johnny St. Cyr, Armstrong's Hot Five had only rehearsed three numbers for their recording session in Chicago, November 12, 1925, and the OKeh engineers wanted four sides to have both A and B sides for two discs.[17] When they were asked to record another tune, they decided to improvise a blues.[18] St. Cyr played an introduction.[19] The band then played two twelve-bar choruses with all instruments playing together in conventional New Orleans style before taking solos.[20] What seems surprising in comparison to European harmony is that in his solo on "Gut Bucket Blues" Armstrong chose to play three notes of C against a G seventh chord (see Ex. 30, m. 9). This should sound discordant as the C should clash with the B in the chord.[21] If this was an isolated example, it could be argued that this was a mistake, but there are many other examples including "S. O. L. Blues" (1927) and "Mahogany Hall Stomp" (1928). Rather than a mistake, a more convincing way to interpret this measure is that Armstrong superimposed a barbershop cadence on the underlying harmony. An explanation for the notes that Armstrong played (see Ex. 30, m. 9) is that this is an example of the D seventh omit third cadence

Example 30: Louis Armstrong's solo, "Gut Bucket Blues" (November 12, 1925)

(see Ex. 31): another of Spaeth's fundamental cadences where only two voices change notes.[22] In Example 30, if the D (m. 9) becomes E♭ (m. 10) before resolving to E♮ (m. 11), this is consistent with barbershop tenor voice leading. The A in measure 9 represents the baritone voice descending back to G in the final measure (see Ex. 31). Note also how the position of the baritone voice is reemphasized (see Ex. 30, m. 11). Example 32 is an embellishment of Spaeth's cadence, showing Armstrong's voice leading in Example 30, measures 9–12.

The process through which Armstrong applied barbershop cadences to dominant harmony could explain what has come to be known as II-V chord substitution. The principle is that a dominant V chord can be substituted with its minor II chord, such that a G seventh chord in the key of C can be substituted with a chord of D minor seventh. Example 33 is a transposed version of Armstrong's middle ensemble chorus on Sippie Wallace's "Have You

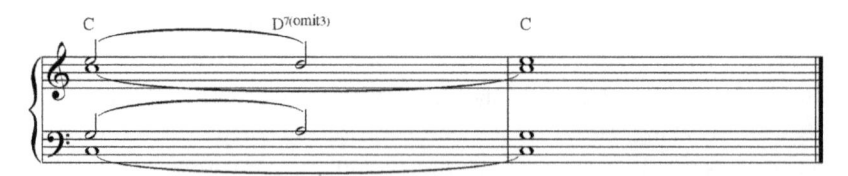

Example 31: Spaeth's barbershop ending number 6 (1940)

Example 32: Spaeth's barbershop cadence number 6 (1940), embellished

Example 33: Sippie Wallace, "Have You Ever Been Down?" (May 6, 1927)

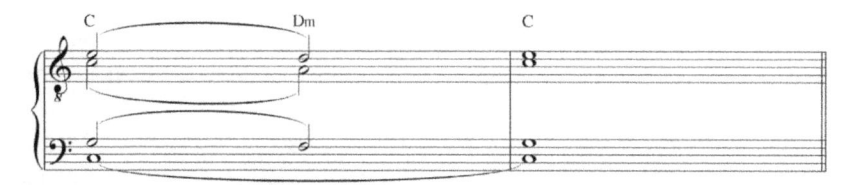

Example 34: Spaeth's barbershop cadence number 11 (1940)

Ever Been Down?" The notes that Armstrong played comprise a descending arpeggio of D minor seventh against G seventh harmony. As Brian Harker comments, "This substitution became standard practice on blues tunes of later jazz eras."[23] When viewed from the perspective of barbershop harmony, once again Armstrong can be observed to play the tonic note (C) against dominant harmony, and again he introduces the notes of D and A, consistent with Example 31. On this occasion, rather than omitting the third of the D chord, he played an F♮.[24] Similarly, Sigmund Spaeth provides examples of barbershop cadences where three pitches were changed to include the third of the II chord (see Ex. 34).[25] This would suggest that when Armstrong encountered a conventional European perfect cadence that included the leading note in the chord, he would on occasion superimpose a barbershop cadence, and in so doing would superimpose what observers would interpret as a II chord superimposed on a V chord: a practice that would later be described as II-V substitution.

The tonic note is not the only theoretically dissonant interval that Armstrong often played against dominant harmony. As discussed earlier in relation to "Copenhagen" (see Ex. 21, m. 9), Armstrong would sometimes play a minor third swipe in the baritone voice, sounding a flatted seventh relative to the tonic. When sounded against dominant harmony, this note extends the dominant chord with the augmented or sharpened ninth. An example is "Gully Low Blues" (1927). In this transposed example (see Ex. 35), Armstrong introduces two other harmonically dissonant notes against the dominant G seventh chord: B♭ (m. 9) and E♭ (m. 10–12).[26] These notes are the flatted or blues third and the flatted seventh in relation to the tonic key. The flatting of the third and seventh is often considered to be an essential characteristic of blues tonality and a significant element of "blues scales." Conventional

[Musical notation]

Example 35: Louis Armstrong's solo (meas. 9–12), "Gully Low Blues" (May 14, 1927)

analysis could therefore suggest that the E♭ and B♭ appear for this reason. Relative to the G seventh harmony, the E♭ and B♭ augment the fifth and the ninth of the chord respectively.

But there is a more convincing explanation for the presence of these harmonic alterations.[27] The appearance of B♭ is once again an example of a minor third swipe in the baritone voice played against a dominant chord. To demonstrate how a minor third swipe can be used in a twelve-bar blues, the second strain of Armstrong's solo on "Gully Low Blues" (see Ex. 36) provides further examples.[28] In measure 14 of this second twelve-bar solo strain (see Ex. 36), Armstrong plays a G followed by a B♭ against G seventh harmony. In so doing, he momentarily plays the augmented ninth of the chord before descending through the major ninth (A) and a return to G. In measures 20–21 he repeats the same swipe. The appearance a measure later of D♯ (see Ex. 36, m. 22) also momentarily augments the fifth of the chord. Note also the chromatic movement in measure 17 that can be interpreted as chromatic movement in the baritone voice. Applied as it is against subdominant harmony, the G♯ to A♮ produces a blues third appoggiatura against the prevailing harmony, but the resolution to the G♮ (the ninth of the chord) means that rather than playing notes that are part of the chord, Armstrong is instead resolving the baritone voice with a return to its usual position on the fifth of the scale.

Another example of what later theorists would describe as altered harmony is the use of the augmented fifth in "I'm Not Rough" (1927).[29] In Example 37, Armstrong could be understood to have added a sixth to the dominant

[Musical notation]

Example 36: Louis Armstrong's solo (meas. 13–24), "Gully Low Blues" (May 14, 1927)

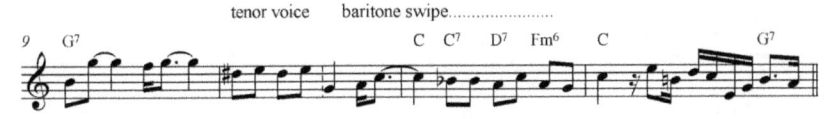

Example 37: Louis Armstrong's solo (meas. 9–12), "I'm Not Rough" (December 10, 1927)

chord to create a thirteenth chord (m. 10). Alternatively, the D♯ to E♮ could be considered as the minor and major thirds of a C blues scale. However, in the knowledge that the alternate thirds are the fundamental lines taken by the tenor voice in a barbershop quartet, a more convincing explanation is that Armstrong first plays the line taken by the tenor voice before switching to the baritone voice with a G (see Ex. 37, m. 10), and then plays a minor third swipe before resolving back to G (m. 11). Another interesting feature is the F minor chord (see Ex. 37, m. 11). This is not the product of Armstrong's line: he played an A♮. The harmony results from Kid Ory's line on trombone. As Gunther Schuller has noted of Armstrong's early recordings:

> The accidental intertwining and crossing of instrumental lines makes out of these innocuous tunes and chord progressions a piquant listening experience, one that is enhanced precisely by the accidents of voice-leading that might easily be considered wrong in another (especially "classical") context: such as the "wrong" notes, the chance parallelisms and convergence of lines, and their heterometric placement.[30]

Considering that both Armstrong and Ory had a background in barbershop harmony, and therefore both were familiar with the minor third swipe in the baritone voice that can be resolved in two different ways—either via the major sixth or passing through the minor sixth—it is almost inevitable that from time to time they would take different lines and give rise to this cross relation.

Alongside examples of Armstrong playing the augmented fifth and augmented ninth extensions against dominant chords, there are also examples that indicate the use of the flatted ninth. One example is Armstrong's second chorus on "Savoy Blues" (1927). The tune was written by Ory and "takes its title from Chicago's elegant new ballroom that opened on Thanksgiving Eve" that year.[31] Ory claimed this tune was composed two days before it was recorded.[32] Lawrence Gushee consulted the copyright deposit for the tune and it includes directions for "Brass intro break" and "Banjo or guitar solo" on the lead sheet. This, Gushee suggests, may be explained because "It could be that 'Savoy Blues' existed as a big band arrangement for the Carroll Dickerson band, but was recorded by the Hot Seven in a reduced version."[33]

Example 38: Louis Armstrong's solo (meas. 9–12), "Savoy Blues" (December 13, 1927)

What is interesting about Armstrong's use of the flatted ninth is that he played an ascending figure. Harmonically one might expect Armstrong to descend from the A♮, through A♭, to G (see Ex. 38, m. 9). That he does not do so suggests that he is conscious of the need to avoid resolving the baritone voice until the final measure. Note also the tonic note.[34]

Hugues Panassié observed, "Louis Armstrong was the first to use in his variations on a theme those altered notes that began to proliferate in the '30s."[35] These altered notes, he argued, "belonging to the black music tradition that were heard only in the many inflections of their singing. Louis Armstrong was the one who put them in the instrumental idiom."[36] Although Panassié thought that these altered notes were not related to flatted thirds and sevenths of the blues scale, some of them are. Relative to dominant harmony, the sharpened ninth and augmented fifth are related to the blues third and seventh. The flattened ninth is the product of baritone voice leading on the flatted sixth of the tonic key. Collectively, however, they all relate to voice leading in barbershop harmony. As Panassié correctly understood, all are rooted in African American vocal practice.

Superficially the harmony of jazz appears to be similar to European harmony. As Armstrong observed, "I never have liked a wrong harmony . . . Going right back to my earliest days singing in the quartet, as a kid it just came natural. I started to go through all that business of studying them big chords and harmonies way back, but then I found out I'd been playing them all the time."[37] The superficial similarity has led some observers to underestimate Armstrong's harmonic inventiveness. James Lincoln Collier has argued, "Although Armstrong frequently prepares a figure from a half-step below, he does not otherwise stray far from the chord changes." He argues "It is a mistake . . . to give Armstrong credit for much harmonic invention."[38] In relation to the first eight measures of a twelve-bar blues, this is often true. As these measures are compatible with barbershop cadences, it follows that Armstrong was able to stay close to the underlying harmony in these measures. However, because dominant harmony, often found in the concluding measures of a twelve-bar blues, contains the leading note in the chord—an interval that is dissonant to the tonic—Armstrong often played theoretically dissonant notes in these measures, and this gave rise to considerable harmonic variation.

CHAPTER 16

"I FIGURE SINGING AND PLAYING IS THE SAME"

THE TUNES DISCUSSED SO FAR, HAVE, FOR THE MOST PART, BEEN twelve-bar blues. During his early career, on twelve-bar blues tunes, Armstrong often played notes that were not part of the underlying harmony. He would typically play minor thirds against tonic major chords, or altered extensions to dominant harmony, and play the flatted sixth against subdominant major chords, converting the harmony to minor. Armstrong was not playing in a way that later jazz musicians approached improvising: playing arpeggios or scales that were appropriate to the chords of the tune. If chord scale analysis is applied to Armstrong's solos on non-blues chord progressions, it can be seen that this apparent disregard for the chords carried over into other recordings of the period. An example of this is "Muskrat Ramble" (see Ex. 39).[1]

Example 39: Armstrong's solo, "Muskrat Ramble" (February 26, 1926)

At the start of this solo, Armstrong seems to be oblivious to the D seventh chord in the opening measure. Instead of playing any of the notes from the chord (D, F♯, A, C) he plays a note of E that he introduced with two blues appoggiaturas in the anacrusis measure. This is a device he used frequently in blues solos to introduce the tenor voice on the tonic chord, but in this instance it is a II chord with a sharpened third, as discussed in relation to "Avalon" (see Ex. 11). This chord is commonly found in jazz tunes of the period and was often used in classical music as a way of modulating to the dominant key. In European music a modulation would be achieved because the sharpened third (usually referred to as the major third) of the chord (F♯) would form the leading note of the new key of G. The voice leading would therefore be in an upward direction. The presence of a II chord with sharpened third does not, in itself, determine whether this harmony is derived from European or African musical practice; however, the voice leading may be significant. Although the underlying harmony in the second measure is G seventh with chord tones of G, B, D, F, in the second measure, Armstrong plays an arpeggio of C major (C-E-G). Again, he seems completely oblivious to the underlying chord changes. The chord progression D seventh, G seventh, C or (II7, V7, I when related to any key) is a progression from the "dominant of the dominant" (D seventh) to the dominant (G seventh) to the tonic (C). Although this chord progression is common in early jazz, Armstrong seems—on the surface of things—not to know how to articulate this harmony. Then in measure 4 he seems to outline the notes of the G seventh chord (nevertheless still playing a note of C)—a measure too early—before a cadence back into C major in measure 7. The chords repeat and this time he appears to outline the notes of a B minor seventh (or maybe B minor eleventh) chord against a D seventh chord in measure 9, before once again playing the tonic note of C against dominant G-seventh harmony in measure 10. He then goes on to play what Schuller describes as "completely wrong harmonic changes" in the thirteenth measure of this solo.[2] It is not easy to analyze this solo in terms of chord scale analysis and come to any meaningful understanding of how Armstrong is relating the harmony of "Muskrat Ramble" to his note choices in this solo. It is as though, in the early measures at least, despite the chord changes not conforming to a twelve-bar blues, Armstrong is still attempting to approach this solo as though it *were* a twelve-bar blues. An alternative way to analyze this solo is to consider it from the perspective of barbershop cadences. Considered in this way, it is as though for the first three measures Armstrong is playing an arpeggio of a C major chord and then he plays a D minor cadence (see Ex. 34) for two measures before resolving back to C again. In effect, he is using the same II-V substitution that he used against dominant harmony in blues choruses to navigate these chord changes. The second eight measures are more complicated to explain, not least because of the appearance of the major seventh (B♮). But, despite Armstrong's solo not outlining the chords, this is a coherent solo. It strikes the ear as having its own melodic logic.

A tune that presents a similar analytical challenge is "Big Butter and Egg Man" (1926). However, if the comments of critics are correct, Armstrong's unusual approach to harmony transcends any concerns about Armstrong not playing over the chord changes. For André Hodeir, "It is not unreasonable to believe that this improvisation of a genius opened a new chapter in the evolution of jazz."[3] Frank Tirro found "Big Butter and Egg Man" to be "One of the most inventive cornet solos ever recorded."[4] Schuller enthused, "Not even a Mozart or a Schubert, composed anything more natural and inspired."[5] "Big Butter and Egg Man" has similar harmonic changes to "Muskrat Ramble," and Armstrong used much the same intervals and phrases that he did on "Muskrat Ramble" with apparent disregard for the harmony. Nevertheless, he triumphed.

"Big Butter and Egg Man" had its origins in a comedy number that Armstrong performed with Mae Alix at the Sunset Café.[6] Although Armstrong had had some experience taking center stage and singing with Erskine Tate, if piano player Earl Hines remembered correctly, Armstrong was at this time more comfortable in the orchestra than in the spotlight. According to Hines:

> Louis and I were both at home sitting up there on the bandstand, but we didn't realize what that floor meant. Louis had never had an opportunity to be out on that floor, and when he went out the first time to sing with Mae Alix he was frightened, and he wasn't sure of his lyrics. Also, although she didn't know it, he really liked Mae, and that probably made him a bit nervous. A number called "Big Butter and Egg Man" had been written for them. She'd sing part of it, he'd sing a part, and then blow his horn. Now Mae was a very good-looking girl, and she really had a lot on the ball. As a singer, she was one of those shouting-type girls. She knew Louis was timid and she took advantage of him. On opening night, when Louis went out there, he forgot his lyrics and everything else. He was just looking at Mae. Not having any experience on the floor, and being out there with a finished artist, it just took all of the run out of him. He didn't know whether to sit down, stand up, or what, but Mae got a kick out of it and had fun with him, and the whole house cracked up. He got accustomed to it finally.[7]

Example 40: Louis Armstrong's solo, "Big Butter and Egg Man" (November 16, 1926)

Unlike some of the other tunes recorded with the Hot Five and Seven, this was not a tune that had been hastily composed for a recording session, this was a tune that Armstrong knew well and performed often.[8] What is interesting when one compares the opening measures of Armstrong's solo on "Big Butter and Egg Man" with those in "Muskrat Ramble" (see Ex. 39) is that his approach to the harmony and his note choices and phrases are remarkably similar. The solo on "Big Butter and Egg Man" (see Ex. 40) opens on the tonic chord with an identical three notes of E in the first measure that Armstrong used to open his solo on "Muskrat Ramble." In "Big Butter and Egg Man" he plays these notes against a chord of C major and is therefore playing the major third of the chord. In the second measure where the harmony changes to D seventh, he does as he did in "Muskrat Ramble" (see Ex. 39, m. 1) and plays a note of E against the D seventh chord. Returning to "Big Butter and Egg Man," he then played a third rhythmic variant of the three notes of E motif (see Ex. 40, m. 5) against G seventh harmony. The opening measures of the "Muskrat Ramble" and "Big Butter and Egg Man" solos suggest that Armstrong had come to realize that by playing the major third of the key—the note usually taken by the tenor voice in a barbershop quartet—he could navigate through a II7, V7, I harmonic progression, and with the exception of the tonic chord, he would not be playing a chord tone, instead he would be playing an extension of the harmony of these chords.[9] In the second eight measures of "Big Butter and Egg Man" the harmony is similar to, although not exactly the same as, the first eight measures. This time (see Ex. 40, m. 11), instead of a chord of D seventh we find D minor seventh. In this measure, Armstrong appears to be far more harmonically secure. He plays a descending D minor seventh arpeggio, a figure he used often to navigate dominant harmony (see Ex. 33). In measures 13 and 14 Armstrong again plays repeated notes of E, and thereby confirms Brothers's observation that in this solo, "He is drawn to ninths and sixths [the extensions of the chords] because they occupy an uncertain middle ground that is neither fully consonant nor fully dissonant."[10]

Hodeir's assessment of the solo on "Big Butter and Egg Man" is that "Armstrong manages to transfigure completely a theme whose vulgarity might well have overwhelmed him; and yet his chorus is only a paraphrase. The theme is not forgotten for a moment; it can always be found there, just as it was originally conceived by its little known composer, Venable."[11] If we compare the opening eight measures of the melody of "Big Butter and Egg Man" with the first eight measures of Armstrong's solo, we can see that this observation is accurate. Again, we find a prominent E in the melody against the D seventh and G seventh chords, and this note technically extends the harmony of these chords. While Armstrong may be paraphrasing the melody as Hodeir suggests, this does not explain why Armstrong made the same note choices against the same chord changes in "Muskrat Ramble." Armstrong's own explanation for his solo on "Big Butter and Egg Man" does not really resolve the question: "In the first chorus I play the melody. The second chorus I play the melody round the melody, the third chorus I routines."[12] He only

Example 41: Percy Venable, "Big Butter and Egg Man" (melody)

played two choruses on the recording, although he may have played more in live performance. In his first chorus, there is a statement of the melody embellished with additional notes. His solo chorus is arguably a paraphrase, or to put it in Armstrong's terms a "melody round the melody." Given that he would have performed this often with Mae Alex, it seems reasonable to take Armstrong's reference to a "routine" at face value. The phrase to "routine" or to be a "routine player" was used by reading musicians in New Orleans as a kind of put-down for those musicians who could not read music fluently, but it seems unlikely that this is what Armstrong means in this instance. Just as in a barbershop quartet, once an improvised harmony part has been established it becomes a fixed routine.

For Gunther Schuller, "The bridge is certainly the imaginative climax to the solo."[13] An interesting feature of the bridge is the pick-up in measure 16. Harker has suggested that the explanation for the triplet eighth-note pattern may be that Armstrong played "Big Butter and Egg Man" with the husband and wife dance partnership of Brown and McGraw.[14] In "Louis Armstrong, Eccentric Dance, and the Evolution of Jazz on the Eve of Swing," Harker observes, "Few topics in the history of early jazz have been more neglected than dance."[15] While some writers have acknowledged the role that jazz played in influencing dance, Harker argues that *eccentric dance* may have played a role in influencing the development of the music.[16] Earl Hines described how Brown and McGraw "They used to go *bomp-bomp-bomp-bu-bomp, bomp-bomp-bomp-bu-bomp*, and Louis used to take his trumpet and do it right with them . . . Later all the acts used to have bands making the licks they were doing on the floor, especially the tap dancers . . . I must say Louis gained a lot of popularity from doing that thing with Brown and McGraw."[17] Rather than having the dancers follow the rhythms of the music, Armstrong is quoted as saying, "Every step they made, I put the notes to it."[18] It is therefore possible that the triplet eighth-note pattern, the triplet quarter-note pattern, and maybe some of the other rhythmic figures in this solo, may owe their rhythm—directly or indirectly—to Brown and McGraw's tap-dance steps.[19] In terms of Armstrong's note choice, the repeated note of G would suggest that Armstrong approached the bridge as though he was singing the baritone voice in a quartet, whereas in the first sixteen measures he had formed melodic patterns around tenor voice on the note of E. This would explain what is perhaps from a harmonic, melodic, and rhythmic point of view, the high point of the solo (see Ex. 40, mm. 20–22). What makes measure 21 of harmonic interest is that the chord of A seventh is a further extension of the cycle of fifths series of dominant chords. Where in the opening measures the chords were D seventh (the dominant of the dominant), G seventh (the dominant), and C major the tonic, now there is a cycle that extends back to A seventh (the dominant of the dominant of the dominant). In terms of jazz and ragtime harmony, this cycle of dominant chords often appears either as a chorus in its own right (as discussed in relation to "Down on the Amazon," see Ex. 9), as part of a bridge, or as a turnaround at the end of a chorus. In European music, this cycle is not nearly as common because each key has only one dominant chord. As there are three dominant chords in this harmonic cycle, it follows that technically there are three different modulations of key in just four measures (see Ex. 40, mm. 21–24). This would be challenging for even the most experienced European composers to navigate. So how does Armstrong successfully do this? Given that he has been playing the note of G (representing the baritone voice) in the first four measures of the bridge (see Ex. 40, mm. 17–20) he simply descends chromatically from G, through F♯, F♮, and E (the tenor voice), to resolve back onto the ninth of the D seventh chord (see Ex. 40, m. 23). From then on, Armstrong is back in the tenor voice right through to the end of the solo. A reference back to "Down on the Amazon" (see Ex. 9, mm. 8–16) is informative: its last eight measures are preceded by the same chromatic descent from the baritone voice to the tenor voice, and for the last eight measures there is an omnipresent E in the melody, and this extends the chords in the same way that Armstrong extended the harmony of "Big Butter and Egg Man." It seems that these harmonic and melodic devices were well known to Armstrong since childhood and had been internalized from his time singing with his quartet.

The dominant cycle of chords and the use of extended harmony—the result of a prominent melody note on the major third—was applied by Armstrong in his solo; by Percy Venable, the composer of "Big Butter and Egg Man," in the melody; by Billy Johnson, composer of "Down on the Amazon"; and also by Liszt in the opening of "Liebestraum," no. III. This chord sequence had become so common in popular music that it is sometimes referred to as the "ragtime progression."[20] To return to the earlier discussion regarding the origins of this harmonic cycle, Winthrop Sargeant believed that "from

Example 42: Sargeant's dominant chord cycle in barbershop harmony

'barbershop' harmony jazz adopted the formula of moving from dominant seventh to dominant seventh, or ninth, through cycles of related keys."[21] He explained:

> In "barbershop" harmony the voices tend to stick close together and to move in parallel formations. As often as possible the movement is by chromatic half-steps. Seventh- and ninth-chords are as common as, if not more common than triads—especially seventh- and ninth-chords of "dominant" formation. These later often succeed each other by parallel chromatic movement, and by such cyclical progression through related keys as the following:[22]

The top line of this descending cycle contains the same notes in chromatic descent that Armstrong used in "Big Butter and Egg Man" (see Ex. 40, mm. 21–22). It will be noticed that the opening note of G (see Ex. 42) is the seventh of the A seventh chord; the next note F♯ forms the third of the D seventh chord; then the F♮ is the seventh of the F seventh chord; and finally, the E is the third of the C chord. In terms of barbershop practice, the baritone voice has descended in semitones to the note usually taken by the tenor voice. Three whole tones (a tri-tone) below these notes are C♯, leading to C♮, and B♮. Up to this point the top notes and the notes a tri-tone below move in parallel descent, and when the top note is the seventh the lower is the third of the chord and vice versa. It is only when the lower note has reached B♮ that the parallel formation is disrupted, as the B♮ ascends to, C acting as the leading note associated with European harmony. The question this harmonic formulation raises is: how can this progression be reconciled with Spaeth's fundamental cadences where the note of C is omnipresent? In this cadence, only the D seventh chord and the final chord of C major contain the note of C. One way to approach this question is to explore how this descending four-note motif between the baritone voice (G) and its chromatic descent to (E) in the tenor voice is related to blues cadences.

One of the first published blues was "Dallas Blues" (1912) by Hart A. Wand.[23] The *Ada Evening News*, of 1905, advertised the services of WAND & SON, OKLAHOMA CITY, makers of rubber stamps, "notarial [sic] seals, chocks, stencils and badges."²⁴ Wand played the violin, and he often practiced in the back room of his father's store.

> There was a little tune he'd made up to play with his orchestra; he doesn't remember hearing it anywhere, and he used to play during the afternoons when he was practicing. There was a colored porter working for them, who had come into the territory from Dallas. He used to whistle the tune along with Hart's playing. One afternoon as he stood listening, leaning on his broom, he said, "That gives me the blues to go back to Dallas."²⁵

As a violinist, Wand was not able to arrange the tune. To produce a piano arrangement, he enlisted the help of a friend, Annabelle Robbins. He self-published the first edition of "Dallas Blues" in March 1912. The first printing was gone in a week. He didn't have time to copyright it until it was in its third edition, finally sending a copy to the copyright office on September 12, 1912.²⁶

The "Dallas Blues" has two strains. The first is introduced with the same four-note motif that Armstrong used in "Big Butter and Egg Man" (see Ex. 40, mm. 21–22) that appears in the top line of Sargeant's barbershop dominant chord progression (see Ex. 42). In both strains, Wand leads to the melody note of E by descending from G in semitones.²⁷ In his study of commercial blues before 1920, Peter Muir found that in both its ascending and descending forms "this motif is common in popular blues, occurring with various degrees of prominence in well over half of the total from the period between 1912 and 1920."²⁸ A working hypothesis is that there are at least two distinct types of fundamental barbershop cadences: those that center around a pedal tone of the tonic, as in Spaeth's barbershop cadences, and a second type of fundamental cadence that centers around the major third and are associated with the dominant cycle of chords.

Researchers have shown surprisingly little interest in Armstrong's early years singing with a quartet. Despite Armstrong saying time and again how important this was to his musical development, little effort has been made

Example 43: Heart A. Wand, "The Dallas Blues" (1912)

Example 44: "Sweet Adeline," Spaeth's barbershop arrangement (1925)

to explore in any detail what he sang, how he sang, or how his singing related to his cornet playing. What we do know is that when questioned on the relationship between his playing and singing, Armstrong offered "Sweet Adeline" as an example of how New Orleans jazz ensembles used the principles to develop their countermelodies. It is informative to take a look at "Sweet Adeline" and how it was performed by barbershop quartets early in the twentieth century. "Sweet Adeline" was published in 1903. It was a barbershop favorite and was almost certainly performed by Armstrong and his quartet. The second measure clearly demonstrates both the chromatic descent from the fifth to the third in the tenor voice and also the minor third swipe in the baritone voice. These swipes consistently appear in Armstrong's cornet playing. It will also be noticed that in measure 2 (see Ex. 44), when the tenor voice and baritone voice sing the chromatic descent simultaneously, this gives rise to what is the now familiar harmonies associated with barbershop, blues, and jazz tonality. We find the tonic dominant chord commonly found in the fourth measure of the twelve-bar blues; we find the tonic diminished chord, one of the most common chords in barbershop and a chord often found in the second and sixth measure of the twelve-bar blues; and then there is the subdominant minor chord that Armstrong (and others) employed in the sixth measure of the twelve-bar blues. In measure 4 of "Sweet Adeline" (see Ex. 44), we find the plagal tendency of blues and jazz harmony followed by a cycle of dominant chords: A seventh, D seventh, G seventh, and C. The dominant cycle of chord progression is found even more forcefully applied in measures 14–16, as the voices resolve toward the closing cadence. With this understanding of barbershop harmony and its attendant voice leading, we are able to consider, as Brian Harker observes, "Notwithstanding the major rhetorical advance represented by 'Big Butter and Egg Man,' . . . an important additional step to be taken along the path from the two-bar break of the ragtime age to the full-length solo of the swing age."[29] This step, according to Harker, was "Potato Head Blues." Harker goes on to say that the new concept that "Potato Head Blues" brought in "involved articulating the harmony or chord progression of a tune being played. Once the focus shifted to the harmony, solos became more abstract and large-scale routines more difficult to sustain."[30] He continued:

> In the place of routines, musicians created long extemporaneous solos, whose contours were harmonically fixed but melodically unpredictable. Free melody made possible the open-ended jam sessions of the 1930s and 1940s and the extended solo recordings of the 1950s. Possibly nothing was more important to the future of jazz as we know it than the developing of a robust harmonic approach to improvisation.[31]

But, as Harker questions, "The funny thing is, while Armstrong played a leading role in this development he also resisted taking full advantage of the new possibilities of the new approach."[32] Credited as an Armstrong composition, there is little in Armstrong's explanation of the origins of the tune that would explain why he applied a different or new concept to his solo on "Potato Head Blues." According to Armstrong:

> This particular recording really "gassed" me because of the perfect phrasing that was done by Johnny [Dodds] and Ory . . . I could look direct into the Pelican Dance Hall, at Gravier and Rampart Streets in New Orleans, during the days of the First World War . . . That was in the years of 1918–1919 . . ."Potato Head Blues" was a tune they really did swing out with . . . My man, Joe Oliver, bless his heart . . . Papa Joe (I used to call him) he really used to blow the kind of cornet I used to

just love to hear ... His playing still lingers in my mind ... There was never a creator of cornet any greater than Joe Oliver ... I've never heard anyone to come up to him as yet ... And he's been dead since 1938 ..."Potato Head Blues" ... Hmm ... Every note that I blew in this recording, I thought of Papa Joe ... Yass Lawd.[33]

This, like so much of his repertoire, referenced back to New Orleans and his mentor Joe Oliver, whose approach to soloing, as demonstrated in "Dippermouth Blues," was not based on playing chord tones from the underlying harmony. Throughout his famous solo on "Dippermouth Blues" (see Ex. 19), Oliver consistently played minor thirds against major chords and only played the major third in four measures of a three-chorus solo. If Armstrong was thinking of Joe Oliver with every note he played on "Potato Head Blues," why was he applying such a seemingly radically different approach to his solo?[34]

This is titled as a blues, but this tune is more complex harmonically and structurally than a twelve-bar blues. Despite the apparent complexity of the harmony, from an analytical perspective the chords can be categorized in two groups: those that can be formed around a pedal note of C, and those that are not formed in this way. The chords that can be formed around a C pedal tone are C major, C seventh, D minor, D minor seventh flat fifth, E♭ diminished, and F minor. All of these chords are found among Spaeth's fundamental barbershop cadences and progressions, and they conform to the barbershop principle of cracking up a chord around the tonic note. When we look at these chords and Armstrong's note choices in his solo, he does indeed seem to be able to conform closely to the chord tones. This is much as one would expect. He had known these chords and this harmony since childhood. However, there is another group of chords: A seventh, D seventh, and G seventh. These chords are not based on Spaeth's fundamental barbershop cadences. The chord of D seventh contains the note of C, but the chords before and after do not, and therefore C is not acting as a pedal tone. On these chords, Armstrong is far less likely to play a chord tone, and instead is more likely (see Ex. 45, mm. 11, 12, 13, 28, 29, 30, 45, 46) to play an E♮, thereby playing the fifth, sixth, or ninth of the underlying harmony. The fifth is a chord tone; the sixth and ninth are not. Having said that, the sixth and the ninth are not dissonant either. When chords are formed based upon a dominant cycle of fifths, Armstrong tends not to articulate the chord changes, instead privileging the major third of the scale. It is as though there are two cardinal notes, the tonic and the major third, that underpin Armstrong's approach to improvising on "Potato Head Blues."

Example 45: Louis Armstrong's solo (stop-time chorus), "Potato Head Blues" (May 10, 1927)

    Observers have believed that "Potato Head Blues" is an example of Armstrong playing over the chord changes, but this is not consistent with his own view. He never claimed that he analyzed chords or chord progressions in the way that later jazz musicians would. What he said was his understanding of harmony was rooted in barbershop: "I never have liked wrong harmony, going back to my earliest days singing in the quartet, as a kid it just came natural. I never was one for going on and on about the changes of a tune, if I've got my horn in my hand then I'll go, all I want to do is hear the chord."[35] It is likely that by the time he recorded "Potato Head Blues" Armstrong had some understanding of chord tones; however, as he made clear, he did not approach his solos in this way. It was not a theoretical but rather an aural approach that informed his note choices. If Armstrong had applied what knowledge he had of European harmony to this tune, it is very unlikely that there would have been a chord of F minor (see Ex. 45, m. 26) or D minor seventh flat fifth (m. 42). These chords form because of the appearance of A♭ in Armstrong's descending phrases.[36] The note of A♭, although it is one of the possible note choices of the baritone voice in a barbershop quartet, is not usually found in a tune in the key of C major, as A♭ is the minor sixth interval considered from the perspective of European melody and harmony, as discussed in relation to "Swanee River" (see Ex. 1). These chords can be described using European harmonic symbols, but they are not derived from European musical practice. Given that Armstrong was not soloing over the chords using a knowledge of chord tones to guide him, this explains why he never exploited this practice. He could solo over chord changes to tunes whose harmony was based on barbershop harmony by using his ears to guide him; he had done this all his life as both a singer and a cornet player. As the solo in "Potato Head Blues" shows, where chords are based around a tonic pedal Armstrong was able to solo over the changes. But there are also chord progressions in "Potato Head Blues" that are not based on a tonic pedal and on these chords, he did not play chord tones. An example of a tune that is entirely constructed from chords of this type, "Basin Street Blues" (1928), provides a further, particularly insightful example of Armstrong's approach to this type of harmony.

"Basin Street Blues" was composed by Spencer Williams, who was born on July 14, 1893, in Vidalia, Louisiana.[37] He later worked in New York for Oscar Hammerstein, and as a young man studied with the black comedian Bert Williams.[38] Armstrong recalled recording "Basin Street Blues," saying, "This was another recording date that was a real 'Gassuh' . . . 'Basin Street Blues' was also a tune written from the good old days of Storyville . . . In fact, there is a street named Basin Street in New Orleans . . . Lulu White, the Octoroon Chick, had a very famous house on that street in those days, called 'Mahogany Hall.'"[39]

The harmony of "Basin Street Blues" takes the cycle of dominant chords back one stage further: the melody is supported by the chord progression C, E seventh, A seventh, D seventh, G seventh, (C) (or I, III7, VI7, II7, V7,

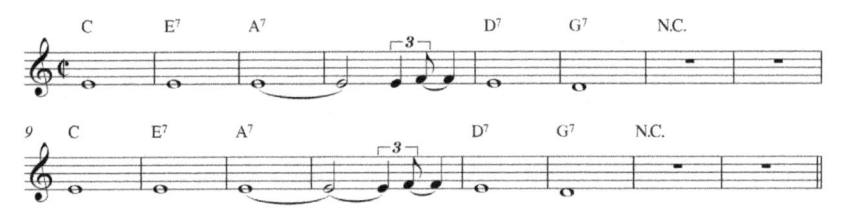

Example 46: Louis Armstrong's lead chorus, "Basin Street Blues" (December 4, 1928)

[I]). Where "Big Butter and Egg Man" has three changes of key in the bridge, "Basin Street Blues" has four in the chorus. As Brooks has pointed out. "Basin Street Blues" has lasted "as a jazz standard, its popularity a result of a stimulating 16-bar chorus chord sequence, admired enough to have been used in several other compositions before and since."[40] Other pieces that Brooks lists include: "That's a Plenty," "Please Don't Talk About Me When I'm Gone," "Music Maestro Please," "As Long As I live," "Mobile," "Carolina," and Bud Freeman's "The Buzzard."[41] Armstrong plays what Brooks has described as "an introspective lead in the first chorus, mostly on the same pitch."[42] The melody, as written, also gravitates around this pitch. In barbershop cadences discussed so far, the tonic note has been the note that has been sustained throughout the chord changes. In this example, Armstrong sustains the third of the scale—a note usually associated with the tenor voice in a barbershop quartet—and he does so against an extended dominant cycle of chords. The opportunity that this recording of "Basin Street Blues" affords, not generally available in other recordings, is the opportunity to hear how barbershop singers actually voiced these chord changes when unaccompanied. Notwithstanding Schuller's complaint that the recording is "spoiled by ... [a] badly balanced, slightly out-of-tune vocal ensemble," transcription of the voices in Armstrong's scat solo on this recording clearly demonstrates how barbershop singers navigate the dominant cycle of chords.[43] In Armstrong's scat vocal chorus, Earl Hines and Mancy Carr cease playing their instruments and instead sing harmony behind Armstrong's scat vocal.[44] This scat chorus once again confirms that Armstrong's approach to scat singing was the same as his approach to playing his cornet. When scatting over a dominant series of chords, he bases his solo around the major third, once again extending the harmony with sixths and ninths as he does in his playing. His other pitch choices are typical of his cornet solos played against these harmonic changes. As important, however, are the harmony vocals of Earl Hines and Mancy Carr, as this demonstrates how barbershop singers of this period actually voiced these chords.

168 "I FIGURE SINGING AND PLAYING IS THE SAME"

Example 47: Louis Armstrong scat chorus with vocal harmony, "Basin Street Blues" (December 4, 1928)

    Earl Hines was born in Duquesne, Pennsylvania, a section of Pittsburgh, on December 28, 1905.[45] He was brought up in a musical family. His mother had died when he was young. His stepmother played the organ.[46] His father ran a brass band that would play local events and picnics.[47] Around the age of ten or eleven, he played organ in a local Baptist church that the family belonged to.[48] He learned piano with a German teacher who used the Czerny method book and taught Hines to play compositions by Chopin.[49] Given his piano studies, he recalled, "I didn't find church music very hard."[50] During World War I people from the South began to migrate north to Pittsburgh for work in the steel mills. During the war, Hines learned to be a barber.[51] His first gigs were with the pianist Lois Deppe, who was also a barber in Monongahela City and who sang. It seems that initially Hines's principal role was to deputize in the barbershop while Deppe went out on gigs. Hines didn't seem to mind, saying, "I got nice money and transportation back."[52] Just after the war Hines's father bought his own barbershop.[53] Given Hines's background as a barber, it is likely that this was part of the reason that Hines was acquainted with barbershop singing, as his harmony chorus on "Basin Street Blues" testifies. Given Hines's musical education, it is also interesting that he confirms that in the 1920s head arrangements were often used in lieu of stock arrangements even by reading musicians. It would seem to follow from this that even reading musicians, like Hines, needed to have a well-developed ear for harmony:

> There weren't many arrangements made for bands in those days. It was a bit later that stocks became common. Mostly what we played were head arrangements, or something what would be call Dixieland now.... When King Oliver had his band, he played the lead trumpet and whoever was playing second trumpet, like Louis Armstrong did, had to sort of harmonize with him, and they would figure out what they call riffs today. They'd go over it again, and the second trumpet would try to put harmony to that, while the trombone worked out a part for himself. This was the beginning of a head arrangement. The reed section would do something similar. If one guy started on C, the second started on A and the third on F. They would begin the passage with one guy a third or fifth lower, and another a third or fifth higher, and that way you'd end up with harmony in it.[54]

Mancy Carr, along with Hines, was part of Carroll Dickerson's Orchestra at the Savoy Theater.[55] By the time of the "Basin Street Blues" recording, Armstrong was being recorded as Louis Armstrong and His Orchestra and was using his new bandmates from the Dickerson Orchestra rather than his New Orleans collaborators in the Hot Five. He did, however, still have his old friend Zutty Singleton on drums.[56]

There are just three voices in the scat chorus of "Basin Street Blues" (see Ex. 47). Armstrong sings the scat solo, and the harmony is provided by Hines and Carr. Armstrong sings a chorus that constantly references the major third, and this confirms that the role of lead voice in this instance is not taken by the second tenor as would usually be the case, but instead it is Armstrong's top line that is heard as the lead. In this voicing, the baritone sings the chromatic descent as Armstrong had played in the bridge of "Big Butter and Egg Man" (see Ex. 40, mm. 21–23) while the other harmony voice begins by descending a semitone to the leading note and then makes a minor third swipe up to the D to form the seventh of the chord E seventh (see Ex. 47, mm. 2, 10). From this point the voices descend chromatically in a tri-tone parallel formation. In this harmonization there are just two voices, and quite how this harmonic formula developed into a fully harmonized four-part harmony will require further research. What we can say with some certainty is that by the turn of the twentieth century, this harmonic formulation was common in barbershop song and ragtime tunes. By the time of the "barbershop revival" among white singers in the late 1930s, this formulation had become the defining feature of barbershop harmony as taught to the Society for the Preservation and Encouragement of Barber Shop Quartet Singing in America (SPEBSQSA), and it is still taught to aspiring barbershop singers up to the present day.[57]

There is much that we do not know about the relationship between European music, American popular song, and the harmonic formulations of barbershop, ragtime, and jazz. Developing a more complete understanding of how the dominant cycle of chords developed requires further research. While it seems beyond doubt that the origins of barbershop harmonization are to be found in African American vocal practice, there may be some aspects of this harmony, as it developed, that related to European musical practice. It is interesting that Liszt's "Liebestraum" no. III, a tune that uses the same harmonic sequence as "Basin Street Blues," also has a melody where the major third is prominent. There is no known causal link between the chords and melody of "Basin Street Blues" and Liszt's composition. But it is also unconvincing to argue that this is only a coincidence. Given that these harmonic and melodic devices were staples of barbershop song, as "Down on the Amazon" demonstrates, more research is needed. The availability of nineteenth-century sheet music may point a way forward for further investigation.

When Louis Armstrong was asked by an interviewer how his singing with a quartet influenced his playing, Armstrong was unequivocal: "I figure singing and playing is the same."[58] Time and again Armstrong tried to explain how he converted the lines that he sang with his quartet into the lines that he played on his cornet. Repeatedly he told interviewers about the importance of singing in his life. Armstrong was immersed from a young age in a culture where people sang: they sang in their work; they sang for leisure, and they sang in church. It is little wonder that Armstrong acknowledged singing as fundamental to his musicianship or that he would use these formative influences in his playing. In his time in the Waifs' Home, Armstrong learned how to convert the harmony lines that he sang to the cornet and the other instruments he played there. Once he was leading his own ensembles, the routines that he played as second parts with others formed the basis of his solos. He was not the first, or the only person, to do this. Buddy Bolden, Johnny Dodds, Kid Ory, and Sidney Bechet were all immersed in the vocal culture of New Orleans. More broadly, early jazz recordings of African American, white, and Creole musicians, suggest that this type of tonality was common to all races by the late nineteenth century.

Jazz, as a recorded music, has been with us now for a hundred years. In that time, observers have tried to understand how the blues tonality that underpinned the music functioned. One of the earliest and most successful was Winthrop Sargeant. He wrote, "The bread-and-butter basis of jazz harmonization exhibits the influence of two very important musical factors. The first of these is the type of close chromatic harmony known as 'barbershop.' The second is our old friend the blues scale."[59] What Sargeant could not have known, without further knowledge of barbershop harmony, was that the blues scales and tetrachords that he derived from recordings were the linearization of the voices in barbershop cadences. There were not two factors, as he believed, but only one: barbershop harmony was at the root of blues tonality, and this underpinned the harmony and melody of jazz. Just as in European music, African American music has a direct relationship between melody and harmony. Another early observer to understand the relationship between barbershop harmony and jazz was Carl Engel, who argued that early jazz musicians had fastened upon the "harmonic structure of 'Barbershop' chords'" and thereby converted ragtime into jazz.[60] Alain Locke, too, perhaps because of his African American heritage, understood that this tonality was rooted in "Negro choral singing."[61] Despite this, after World War II references to barbershop harmony and its influence on jazz are scant in the literature. This may have happened for a number of reasons. One reason could be that the nature of jazz changed. With a few notable exceptions, the war years brought to an end the era of the big bands. As bebop became the dominant form of jazz, the polyphony of arranged choruses of the big bands, and the earlier New Orleans–style counterpoint, were replaced by a rhythm section playing chords. These chord sequences increasingly became standardized. Given that the essence of barbershop practice is to re-harmonize a melody, in an era where the dominant paradigm was to improvise a melody over the chord changes, it is perhaps not surprising that barbershop's formative influence went unnoticed. But there could be other factors.

A further possible reason that barbershop's formative influence on jazz may have been overlooked after WWII is, separated by time and culture from early twentieth-century barbershop practice, theorists were informed about barbershop in the light of the white barbershop revival of the late 1930s. Although a strong quartet tradition continued among African Americans, communal singing in white society was in decline in the early years of jazz. In the industrial age, as one writer observed, amateur, recreational music and singing got caught "under the wheels of a Model A Ford on its way to the movies."[62] White barbershop received an unlikely revival with the chance meeting of two businessmen in Kansas City in 1938 after their flights had been cancelled. Having started singing barbershop in the hotel lobby with other guests, O. C. Cash and Rupert Hall went on to found the Society for the Preservation and Encouragement of Barbershop Quartet Singing in America (SPEBSQSA).[63] From its outset, the issue of whether African Americans should be allowed to become members of the organization and perform in its conventions and competitions was roundly rejected. The overriding impression left after many decades of excluding African Americans from the society was that barbershop singing was a white musical tradition. Now that the Barbershop Harmony Society has acknowledged and embraced the African American roots of barbershop harmony, we can begin to develop an integrated understanding of the development of barbershop and its relationship to jazz.

There is much that we do not know about the early years of barbershop singing. While its origins in African American vocal practice is beyond reasonable doubt, by the 1890s barbershop singing was enjoyed by all races.[64] One particularly interracial group singing in 1893, the Utopian Quartet of Bellevue, Nebraska, consisted of "one Indian, one Negro, and two Caucasians."[65] There are also reports of Chinese barbers in Hawaii singing barbershop in 1902.[66] This may, in part, explain why it has been so difficult for jazz researchers to state with any degree of certainty the racial origins of jazz. Given that the harmonic principles that underscore the music were the common property of all races in the United States by the time that jazz emerged, it has not been possible, in terms of musical criteria alone, to distinguish the music's racial origins. As a consequence, claims to being the "first man of jazz" (an African American, Buddy Bolden); the "first" to record jazz (the white Original Dixieland Jazz Band); or the "inventor" of jazz (Jelly Roll Morton, a Creole), have dominated the debate. An understanding of barbershop harmony and its practices could go some way toward informing this discussion.

More research into barbershop practice also has implications for jazz performance education. If we aspire to understand and perform early jazz in an authentic way, we need to rethink our approach to vocal culture in jazz. Much of jazz education today is based upon chord scale analysis and the application of these practices directly to an instrument. These principles are not appropriate to early jazz, and lacking a suitable alternative, the teaching of prewar jazz is largely bypassed and begins with the "classic" jazz of bebop. If we want to develop a firm musical foundation for jazz education, an understanding of barbershop harmony is one of the tools that can make this possible.

But, the musicology of jazz needs to be firmly grounded in historical research rather than abstract theory. We need to investigate oral histories, biographies, contemporaneous press reports, advertising, personal documents, and other materials. If we can bring together historically grounded research with appropriate musicology, we can begin to develop a history and theory of jazz that not only describes *what* Louis Armstrong and all the other musicians played and sang, but also *why* they played and sang as they did. It is also possible that in time we shall be able to begin to develop ways to teach jazz performance that is rooted in the way that the musicians themselves learned to play and perform the music and in a way that the jazz pioneers would have understood.

NOTES

ACKNOWLEDGMENTS

1. Extracts of the manuscript have been published. See Thomas Brothers, ed., *Louis Armstrong, In His Own Words: Selected Writings* (New York: Oxford University Press, 1999).
2. Trust Deed of the National Jazz Foundation Archive.

PREFACE

1. Lynn Abbott, "'Play That Barber Shop Chord': A Case for the African-American Origin of Barbershop Harmony," *American Music* 10, no. 3 (1992).
2. James Earl Henry, "The Origins of Barbershop Harmony: A Study of Barbershop's Musical Link to Other African American Musics as Evidenced through Recordings and Arrangements of Early Black and White Quartets" (PhD diss., Washington University, 2000). Frédéric Döhl, "From Harmonic Style to Genre: The Early History (1890s–1940s) of the Uniquely American Musical Term Barbershop," *American Music* 32, no. 2 (2014).
3. The use of chord symbols requires making judgments particularly in relation to inversions. Early fake books often will give a chord such as F minor sixth rather than D minor seventh flat fifth. Both interpretations have their merit. I trust that readers who have a preference for one form or the other will accept that such details have no bearing on the arguments made here.

CHAPTER 1: "SINGING WAS MORE INTO MY BLOOD, THAN THE TRUMPET"

1. The phrase "The First Great Soloist" comes from the chapter on Armstrong in Gunther Schuller, *Early Jazz: Its Roots and Musical Development* (New York: Oxford University Press, 1986), 89–133.
2. Gary Giddins, *Satchmo: The Genius of Louis Armstrong*, Kindle ed. (New York: Perseus, 2009), 22.
3. Dan Morgenstern, "Roses for Satchmo," *Down Beat* 37, no. 13 (1970): 16.
4. Morgenstern, "Roses for Satchmo," 16.
5. Morgenstern, "Roses for Satchmo," 15.
6. Morgenstern, "Roses for Satchmo," 16.
7. Morgenstern, "Roses for Satchmo," 15.
8. Morgenstern, "Roses for Satchmo," 15–16.
9. Morgenstern, "Roses for Satchmo," 18.

10. Morgenstern, "Roses for Satchmo," 17.

11. Morgenstern, "Roses for Satchmo," 16.

12. Terry Teachout, *Pops: A Life of Louis Armstrong* (New York: Houghton Mifflin Harcourt, 2009), 88.

13. Brian Rust, *Jazz Records 1897–1942* (Chigwell: Storyville, 1969; repr., New York: Arlington House, 1978).

14. Jeffrey Magee, *The Uncrowned King of Swing: Fletcher Henderson and Big Band Jazz* (New York: Oxford University Press, 2005), 95. The only time Armstrong sang on a recording with Henderson was a brief ending to the song "Everybody Loves My Baby" (1924). Fletcher Henderson and His Orchestra, ca. November 24, 1924, New York (Domino 3444). Rust, *Jazz Records 1897–1942*. Armstrong also told the *Jazzmen* editors that he "started singing with the Henderson band," and that he "used to scat around." He did however indicate in the interview that Henderson did not give him "much of a chance to sing in public." Louis Armstrong, "*Jazzmen* Interviews," in Papers of Frederic Ramsey Jr., MSS 559 (New Orleans: Williams Research Center, Historic New Orleans Collection).

15. Thomas Brothers, *Louis Armstrong, Master of Modernism* (New York: W. W. Norton, 2014), 190; "George Avakian's interview with W. C. Handy," *Louis Armstrong Plays W. C. Handy* (Columbia CD CK 64925).

16. For discussion of the impact of the Great Depression on the acceptance of jazz, see Neil Leonard, *Jazz and the White Americans: The Acceptance of a New Art Form* (Chicago: University of Chicago Press, 1962; repr., Jazz Book Club, 1964), 106–7.

17. Leonard, *Jazz and the White Americans*, 113.

18. Giddens, *Satchmo*, 9.

19. Louis Armstrong and his New Sebastian Cotton Club Orchestra, "Shine" (Los Angeles CA: OKeh 41486, March 9, 1931); Cecil Mack [R. C. McPherson] and Ford Dabney, "That's Why They Call Me Shine" (New York: Gotham-Attuck Music, 1910).

20. Teachout, *Pops*, 174.

21. Robert Moton, *What the Negro Thinks* (Garden City, NY: Doubleday, Doran, 1929), 187; *Chicago Defender*, January 7, 1933: 22; *Chicago Defender*, January 21, 1933: 14, as referenced in Brothers, *Louis Armstrong, Master of Modernism*, 439.

22. Lawrence Schenbeck, "Music, Gender, and 'Uplift' in the 'Chicago Defender,' 1927–1937," *Musical Quarterly* 81, no. 3 (1997).

23. Douglas Malcolm, "'Myriad Subtleties': Subverting Racism through Irony in the Music of Duke Ellington and Dizzy Gillespie," *Black Music Research Journal* 5, no. 2 (2015): 185.

24. Charles Hersch, *Subversive Sounds: Race and the Birth of Jazz in New Orleans* (Chicago: University of Chicago Press, 2007), 185.

25. Hersch, *Subversive Sounds*, 185.

26. Ricky Riccardi, "You've Got to Appreciate All Kinds of Music: Review of Thomas Brothers, Louis Armstrong: Master of Modernism," *Journal of Jazz Studies* 10, no. 1: 89.

27. First recorded by Louis Armstrong and His Orchestra, "When It's Sleepy Time Down South" (Chicago: OKeh 41504, April 20, 1931).

28. Barney Bigard, *With Louis and the Duke: The Autobiograhy of a Jazz Clarinetist*, ed. Barry Martyn (London: Macmillan, 1980; repr., 1985), 123; see also Ricky Riccardi, *What*

a Wonderful World: The Magic of Louis Armstrong's Later Years (New York: Pantheon, 2011), 59–61.

29. Riccardi, "You've Got to Appreciate All Kinds of Music," 89.

30. Louis Armstrong, *Swing That Music* (New York: Longmans, Green, 1936; repr., New York: Da Capo Press, 1995), xvi.

31. Armstrong, *Swing That Music*, xvi.

32. John Petters, "Louis Armstrong: The World's Greatest Jazz Vocalist," *Just Jazz* 40 (2001): 10.

33. Teachout, *Pops*, 88.

34. Leonard Feather, "The Real Louis Armstrong," *Down Beat* 29, no. 5 (1962): 21.

35. Max Jones, "The Hit No One Wanted," *Melody Maker*, May 23, 1964: 3.

36. See also Teachout, *Pops*, 342–51.

37. Gunther Schuller, *The Swing Era: The Development of Jazz, 1930–1945* (New York: Oxford University Press, 1989), 161.

38. Morgenstern, "Roses for Satchmo," 15.

39. A one-off magazine produced after Armstrong's death, *Satchmo: Collector's Copy*, Hollywood, CA: Matco Publishing, 1971 (William Ransom Hogan Jazz Archive, Tulane University: New Orleans, 1971), 16.

40. Schuller, *Early Jazz*, 100.

41. Lewis Porter, Michael Ullman, and Edward Hazell, *Jazz: From Its Origins to the Present* (New Jersey: Prentice Hall, 1993), 71.

42. Giddins, *Satchmo*, Introduction to New Edition.

43. Brian Harker, *Louis Armstrong's Hot Five and Hot Seven Recordings* (New York: Oxford University Press, 2011), 9.

44. "The Armstrong Story" manuscript, 1954, in Brothers, *Louis Armstrong, In His Own Words*, 64; Teachout, *Pops*, 88.

45. Brothers, *Louis Armstrong, In His Own Words*, 64.

46. Louis Armstrong, interview with Richard Hadlock (San Francisco, February 1962), in Joshua Berrett, ed., *Louis Armstrong Companion: Eight Decades of Commentary* (New York: Schirmer Books, 1999), 26.

47. Louis Armstrong, "Armstrong Heritage T.V. Program, Part 2, August 9, 1960," in *Audio Collection*, ed. Robert McCully and Adam Lynch (New Orleans: William Ransom Hogan Jazz Archive, Tulane University).

48. Armstrong, "Armstrong Heritage T.V. Program, Part 2, August 9, 1960."

49. Armstrong, "Armstrong Heritage T.V. Program, Part 2, August 9, 1960."

50. Armstrong, "Armstrong Heritage T.V. Program, Part 2, August 9, 1960."

51. Armstrong, "Armstrong Heritage T.V. Program, Part 2, August 9, 1960."

CHAPTER 2: "SINGING WAS MY LIFE"

1. Louis Armstrong, in Richard Meryman, *Louis Armstrong: A Self Portrait* (New York: Eakins Press, 1966), as quoted in Lynn Abbott, "Play That Barbershop Chord," 318.

2. Armstrong, *Swing That Music*, 4.

3. Armstrong, *Swing That Music*, 4.

4. Armstrong, *Swing That Music*, 4.

5. Armstrong, *Swing That Music*, 5.

6. Robert Goffin, *Horn of Plenty: The Story of Louis Armstrong*, trans. James F. Bezou (New York: Allen, Towne & Heath, 1947), 39, 43, 44. Some of the notebooks that Armstrong sent to Goffin are held at the Institute of Jazz Studies, Rutgers University, New Jersey.

7. Louis Armstrong, *Satchmo: My Life in New Orleans* (London: Peter Davies, 1955; repr., Sedgwick & Jackson, 1957), 35.

8. Harker, *Louis Armstrong's Hot Five and Hot Seven Recordings*, 101.

9. Armstrong, "*Jazzmen* Interviews."

10. Goffin, *Horn of Plenty*, 44.

11. Armstrong claimed that before he went to the Waifs' Home his ambition was to be a drummer. Armstrong, "*Jazzmen* Interviews."

12. Goffin, *Horn of Plenty*, 44. Although uptown of Canal Street, Maylie's had specialized in Creole cuisine since its opening in 1876.

13. Zutty Singleton, "Zutty First Saw Louis in Amateur Tent Show," *Down Beat*, July 14, 1950: 6.

14. Singleton, "Zutty First Saw Louis in Amateur Tent Show," 6.

15. Billy McBride and Mary McBride, "Interview November 23, 1970," in William Russell Jazz Collection, MSS 506 (New Orleans: Williams Research Center, Historic New Orleans Collection).

16. McBride and McBride, "Interview November 23, 1970."

17. McBride and McBride, "Interview November 23, 1970." Howard Avenue does not intersect with Louisiana Avenue. This could be two different lots.

18. Abbott, "'Play That Barber Shop Chord,'" 316.

19. Singleton, "Zutty First Saw Louis in Amateur Tent Show," 6.

20. Sigmund Spaeth, "Famous Tune Detective, Says Many Music Lovers Are Hypocrites," *Cornell Daily Sun*, January 7, 1935, 6.

21. Sigmund Spaeth, *Barber Shop Ballads and How to Sing Them* (New York: Prentice Hall, 1940), 3.

22. Sigmund Spaeth, *Barber Shop Ballads: A Book of Close Harmony* (New York: Simon and Schuster, 1925), 17.

23. Spaeth, *Barber Shop Ballads and How to Sing Them*, 4.

24. Spaeth, *Barber Shop Ballads and How to Sing Them*, 4.

25. Spaeth, *Barber Shop Ballads and How to Sing Them*, 4.

26. Armstrong, *Satchmo: My Life in New Orleans*, 35.

27. Lynn Abbott, interview with Dr. Laddie Melton, Beaumont, Texas, May 27, 1983, in Abbott, "'Play That Barber Shop Chord,'" 290.

28. Spaeth, *Barber Shop Ballads and How to Sing Them*, 5.

29. Spaeth, *Barber Shop Ballads and How to Sing Them*, 6.

30. Goffin, *Horn of Plenty*, 44.

31. E. P. Christy, "Old Folks at Home" (New York: Firth, Pond & Co., 1851).

32. S. C. Foster, "Old Folks at Home," ed. William G. Smith (Boston: Oliver Ditson & Co., 1887). It was republished with piano accompaniment by Charles E. Pratt and S. C. Foster, "Old Folks at Home (Way Down Upon the Swanee River)" (New York: H. Franklin Jones, 1894).

33. The original sheet music is in the key of A. The term "barbershop chord" became synonymous with the flatted sixth with the publication of Lewis F. Muir and William Tracey, "Play That Barbershop Chord" (1910). The first known use of the term "Barbershop Chord" appeared in 1894 in the *Leavenworth* [Kansas] *Herald*. "Although Emporia [a town about fifty miles southwest of Leavenworth] has a Haydn club it is not above singing 'I found a horseshoe,' with a 'barber-shop chord' on the second horseshoe." *Leavenworth Herald*, February 17, 1894; Lynn Abbott and Doug Seroff, *Out of Sight: The Rise of African American Popular Music 1889–1895* (Jackson: University Press of Mississippi, 2002), 358; Lynn Abbott and Doug Seroff, "'They Cert'ly Sound Good to Me': Sheet Music, Southern Vaudeville, and the Commercial Ascendancy of the Blues," *American Music* 14, no. 4 (1996): 404.

34. Spaeth, *Barber Shop Ballads and How to Sing Them*, 7.

35. W. C. Handy and George A. Norton, "The Memphis Blues" (New York: Joe Morris Music Co., 1913 [original edition 1912]). While other intervals have been claimed as "blue notes," the flatted fifth and sixth, for example, the flatted third and seventh are a consistent feature of blues note melodies. In his first blues composition "The Memphis Blues," Handy claimed he used "transitional flat thirds and sevenths in my melody, by which I was attempting to suggest the typical slurs of the Negro voice, were what have since been known as 'blues notes.'" W. C. Handy, *Father of the Blues* (New York: Macmillan, 1941; repr., London: Sedgwick & Jackson, 1961), 99.

36. John C. Cavendish, "Folk-Tunes as Material for Music," *American Mercury* (January 1925): 79. http://www.unz.org/Pub/AmMercury-1925jan-00079.

37. Eddy Gilmore, "Happy Ambassador for U.S. That's Our Satchmo Abroad," *Hartford Courant*, May 27, 1965, 16; Riccardi, *What a Wonderful World*, 124.

38. Cavendish, "Folk-Tunes as Material for Music," 81.

39. If a melody modulates to a different key, the harmony notes will be selected from the new key.

40. Deems Taylor, "Words and Music," unidentified publication, 1925; Karl Koenig, *The Scrap Book of R. Emmet Kennedy* (Running Springs, CA: Basin Street, 2007).

41. Cavendish, "Folk-Tunes as Material for Music," 81.

42. Unidentified newspaper article circa 1925; Koenig, *The Scrap Book of R. Emmet Kennedy*.

43. Sigmund Spaeth letter dated November 4, 1925, "America and Negro Spirituals," *New York Telegram*; Koenig, *The Scrap Book of R. Emmet Kennedy*.

CHAPTER 3: "ALWAYS HAD MUSIC ALL AROUND ME"

1. Meryman, *Louis Armstrong: A Self Portrait*, 11.

2. S. Frederick Starr, *Inventing New Orleans: Writings of Lafcadio Hearn* (Jackson: University Press of Mississippi, 2001), 99–107; Lyle Saxon, Edward Dreyer, and Robert Tallant, eds., *Gumbo Ya-Ya: Folk Tales of Louisiana* (Gretna, LA: Pelican, 1945; reprint, 1991), 27–49.

3. Saxon et al., *Gumbo Ya-Ya*, 36.

4. Saxon et al., *Gumbo Ya-Ya*, 36.

5. Saxon et al., *Gumbo Ya-Ya*, 11–12.

6. Thomas Brothers, *Louis Armstrong's New Orleans* (New York: W. W. Norton, 2006), 55–56.

7. Brothers, *Louis Armstrong's New Orleans*, 55.

8. Brothers, *Louis Armstrong's New Orleans*, 55.

9. Brothers, *Louis Armstrong's New Orleans*, 56.

10. Nat Shapiro and Nat Hentoff, eds., *Hear Me Talkin' to Ya: The Story of Jazz by the Men Who Made It* (New York: Rinehart, 1955; repr., Dover, 1966), 53.

11. Lawrence Bergreen, *Louis Armstrong: An Extravagant Life* (London: Harper Collins, 1997), 33.

12. Meryman, *Louis Armstrong: A Self Portrait*, 12.

13. R. Emmet Kennedy, *Mellows: A Chronicle of Unknown Singers* (New York: Albert & Charles Boni, 1925), 20.

14. Kennedy gave this melody in the key of F major.

15. Henry, "The Origins of Barbershop Harmony," 18.

16. Henry, "The Origins of Barbershop Harmony," 18.

17. Spaeth, *Barber Shop Ballads: A Book of Close Harmony*, 23.

18. Spaeth, *Barber Shop Ballads and How to Sing Them*, 17.

19. It is a convention in barbershop arranging to write the tenor and lead voice an octave above where they actually sound as Spaeth has done here.

20. Spaeth, *Barber Shop Ballads: A Book of Close Harmony*, 24.

21. Kennedy, *Mellows*, 22.

22. Goffin, *Horn of Plenty*, 43.

23. Goffin, *Horn of Plenty*, 43. The cry of "Stone-coal, Lady! Stone-coal" would be rarely heard on the streets of New Orleans in later years as steam and gas heating replaced the "old-fashioned grate fires." Saxon et al., *Gumbo Ya-Ya*, 38.

24. Bergreen, *Louis Armstrong: An Extravagant Life*, 42.

25. Kennedy, *Mellows*, 23.

26. There are two errors that I have not corrected. In measure 5 the first note should be dotted. In measure 7 the second note should be single dotted. The lyrics to the cry of the charcoal man were also remembered by "a Negro," called Leonard Parker. Saxon et al., *Gumbo Ya-Ya*, 38.

27. Johnny St. Cyr, "Interview August 27, 1958," in *Oral History Files*, ed. William Russell (New Orleans: William Ransom Hogan Jazz Archive, Tulane University).

28. Al Rose, *I Remember Jazz: Six Decades among the Great Jazzmen* (Baton Rouge: Louisiana State University Press, 1987), 174–76.

29. Ed "Montudi" Garland, "Interview April 16, 1957," in *Oral History Files*, ed. Nesuhi Ertegun and Robert Campbell (New Orleans: William Ransom Hogan Jazz Archive, Tulane University); John Wiggs, "Interview Digest August 26, 1962," in *Oral History Files*, ed. William Russell and Betty Hyman (New Orleans: William Ransom Hogan Jazz Archive, Tulane University).

30. Meryman, *Louis Armstrong: A Self Portrait*, 14.

31. Goffin, *Horn of Plenty*, 44.

32. Goffin, *Horn of Plenty*, 45.

33. Goffin, *Horn of Plenty*, 31.

34. Emile August Lacoume, born September 22, 1885, father Emile, mother Jennie, *New Orleans, Louisiana Birth Record Index, 1790–1899*, vol. 125, 1023; married Anna Lopresti, December 27, 1916, *Orleans Marriage Indices*, vol. 39, 360; 1917 *Draft Registration Card*, living 2723 Iberville Street, working as a musician at West End for Mr. H Martin and "totally blind." City of New Orleans, Division 3; 1920 Census at 2723 Iberville and working as a "Musician." New Orleans Ward 4, District 69 (Ancestry.com).

35. Henry O. Osgood, *So This Is Jazz* (Boston: Little, Brown & Co., 1926), 35–36.

36. Osgood, *So This Is Jazz*, 35–36.

37. Albert Glenny, "Interview Transcript, March 27, 1957," in *Oral History Files*, ed. Richard B. Allen and Nesuhi Ertegun (New Orleans: William Ransom Hogan Jazz Archive, Tulane University).

38. Garland, "Interview April 21, 1957."

39. Edmond "Doc" Souchon, "Interview February 17, 1962," in *Oral History Files*, ed. William Russell (New Orleans: William Ransom Hogan Jazz Archive, Tulane University).

40. "Kid" Thomas Valentine, "Interview Digest, March 22, 1957 (for *Life Magazine*)," in *Oral History Files*, ed. William Russell and Nesuhi Ertegun (New Orleans: William Ransom Hogan Jazz Archive, Tulane University); "Interview with Richard B. Allen, January 27, 1969," in *Oral History Files*, ed. Kay L. Wicker and Richard B. Allen (New Orleans: William Ransom Hogan Jazz Archive, Tulane University).

41. Clarence "Little Dad" Vincent, "Interview Digest, January 21, 1960," in *Oral History Files*, ed. Richard B. Allen and Ralph Collins (New Orleans: William Ransom Hogan Jazz Archive, Tulane University).

42. John Chilton, *Sidney Bechet: The Wizard of Jazz* (London: Macmillan, 1987), 3.

43. Ferdinand "Jelly Roll" Morton, "Transcript of the 1938 Library of Congress Recordings of Jelly Roll Morton," In John Szwed, ed., *Folklife Collection* (Washington, DC: Library of Congress, 2006); Nat Shapiro and Nat Hentoff, eds., *Hear Me Talkin' to Ya: The Story of Jazz by the Men Who Made It* (New York: Rinehart, 1955; repr., Dover, 1966), 53.

44. Brothers, *Louis Armstrong, Master of Modernism*, 110.

45. "Papa" Jack Laine, "Interview Transcript, March 26, 1957," in *Oral History Files*, ed. William Russell and Richard B. Allen (New Orleans: William Ransom Hogan Jazz Archive, Tulane University).

46. Meryman, *Louis Armstrong: A Self Portrait*, 7–8.

47. Louis Jones and Edmund Wise, "Interview Transcript, June 4, 1954," in Papers of Frederic Ramsey Jr., MSS 559 (New Orleans: Williams Research Center, Historic New Orleans Collection).

48. Louis Keppard, interview with Andy Ridley, quoted in Andy Ridley, "I'm Just a Plain Ordinary Guitar Player . . . But I'll Scare the Best of Them: The Autobiography of Louis Keppard," unpublished manuscript, 1985; Abbott, "'Play That Barber Shop Chord,'" 318; Jones and Wise, "Interview Transcript, June 4, 1954."

49. Vic Hobson, "Plantation Song: Delius, Barbershop, and the Blues," *American Music* 31, no. 3 (2013): 31.

50. Tim Brooks, *Lost Sounds: Blacks and the Birth of the Recording Industry, 1890–1919* (Urbana and Chicago: University of Illinois Press, 2004).

51. Armstrong, *Swing That Music*, 4.

CHAPTER 4: CHURCH IS WHERE "I ACQUIRED MY SINGING TACTICS"

1. Danny Barker, "Interview Digest June 30, 1959," in *Oral History Files*, ed. Richard B. Allen (New Orleans: William Ransom Hogan Jazz Archive, Tulane University); Ernest "Punch" Miller, "Interview, September 25, 1959," *Oral History Files*, ed. Richard B. Allen (William Ransom Hogan Jazz Archive, Tulane University).

2. Bill Russell and Paul Beaulieu, "Interview Summary, June 11, 1960," in *Oral History Files*, ed. William Russell and Ralph Collins (William Ransom Hogan Jazz Archive, Tulane University).

3. Berenice Phillips, "Interview September 3, 1960," in *Oral History Files*, ed. Richard B. Allen (William Ransom Hogan Jazz Archive, Tulane University).

4. Berenice Phillips, "Interview September 3, 1960."

5. Joseph René, "Interview Digest September 8, 1960," in *Oral History Files*, ed. Richard B. Allen and Majorie Zander (William Ransom Hogan Jazz Archive, Tulane University).

6. Johnny St. Cyr, "Interview Digest, August 27, 1958," in *Oral History Files*, ed. William Russell (William Ransom Hogan Jazz Archive, Tulane University).

7. Steve Angrum, "Interview Digest, August 8, 1961," in *Oral History Files*, ed. William Russell and Ralph Collins (William Ransom Hogan Jazz Archive, Tulane University).

8. Stella Oliver, "Interview Digest, April 22, 1959," in *Oral History Files*, ed. William Russell and Ralph Collins (William Ransom Hogan Jazz Archive, Tulane University).

9. Vic Hobson, *Creating Jazz Counterpoint: New Orleans, Barbershop Harmony, and the Blues* (Jackson: University Press of Mississippi, 2014), 104.

10. Stella Oliver, "Interview Digest, April 22, 1959."

11. Hersch, *Subversive Sounds*, 26.

12. Hersch, *Subversive Sounds*, 27.

13. Brothers, *Louis Armstrong, Master of Modernism*, 395.

14. Steve Brown, "Interview Transcript, April 22, 1958," in *Oral History Files*, ed. Richard Allen and William Russell (New Orleans: William Ransom Hogan Jazz Archive, Tulane University).

15. John McCusker, *Creole Trombone: Kid Ory and the Early Years of Jazz* (Jackson: University Press of Mississippi, 2012), 59; Steve Brown, "Interview Transcript, April 22, 1958."

16. "Papa Mutt Carey, Gene Williams and Marili Stuart," *Jazz* (1943): 5, as quoted in McCusker, *Creole Trombone*, 60.

17. Arthur "Bud" Scott, in Shapiro and Hentoff, *Hear Me Talkin' to Ya*, 37.

18. Edward "Kid" Ory, "Interview Transcript, April 20, 1957 (for *Life Magazine*)," in *Oral History Files*, ed. Nesuhi Ertegun and Robert Campbell (New Orleans: William Ransom Hogan Jazz Archive, Tulane University); McCusker, *Creole Trombone*, 60.

19. Armstrong, *Satchmo: My Life in New Orleans*, 31.

20. Armstrong, *Satchmo: My Life in New Orleans*, 32.

21. Abbott, "'Play That Barber Shop Chord,'" 324.

22. William Mark Cosey (born March 25, 1878). The 1915 New Orleans City Directory notes: "Cosey William Rev pastor Mt Zion Baptist Church 512 Howard" and he is resident at the same address. His WWI registration card (September 12, 1918) was recorded in Mississippi. His place of work is given as "minister" at Mount Zion Baptist Church at 512 Howard. His permanent address is given as 706 Bluff, Natchez, Adams County, Mississippi. He is "short" and "stout." He is Listed in the 1912, Natchez City Directory, at 704 Bluff. He appears in the 1920 Federal Census along with his wife (Marion) and son, living in rented accommodation at 215 Villere Street, New Orleans. His occupation is given as "minister," age 40, born Louisiana. 1920 United States Federal Census, Louisiana, New Orleans, Ward 3, District 0039; Armstrong, *Satchmo: My Life in New Orleans*, 32.

23. Goffin, *Horn of Plenty*, 81.

24. Louis Armstrong, Letter to L/Cpl. Villec, 1967, quoted in Daniel Stein, *Music Is My Life: Louis Armstrong, Autobiography, and American Jazz*, Kindle ed. (Ann Arbor: University of Michigan Press, 2012), 41–42. This extract is an example of Armstrong's unusual writing style.

25. Armstrong, *Satchmo: My Life in New Orleans*, 13.

26. http://www.jefferson.lib.la.us/news&events/kennedy.htm.

27. http://www.jefferson.lib.la.us/news&events/kennedy.htm.

28. Kennedy, *Mellows*, 38.

29. Koenig, *The Scrap Book of R. Emmet Kennedy*, 10.

30. Koenig, *The Scrap Book of R. Emmet Kennedy*, 10.

31. A copy of the article was later found in his papers in Czechoslovakia, and it had been annotated by his son who was with him in New York. Johann Tonsor, "Negro Music," *Music* (1892). Michael B. Beckerman, *Michael B. Beckerman, New Worlds of Dvořák: Searching in America for the Composer's Inner Life* (New York: W. W. Norton, 2003), 84.

32. Abbott and Seroff, *Out of Sight: The Rise of African American Popular Music 1889–1895*, 273. It is likely that that this is not a verbatim quote.

33. Koenig, *The Scrap Book of R. Emmet Kennedy*, 10–11.

34. R. Emmet Kennedy, *The Songs of Aengus* (New Orleans: Myers' Printing House, 1910).

35. Foreword, R. Emmet Kennedy, *Remnants of Noah's Ham (According to Genesis)* (New Orleans: Myers' Printing House, 1910).

36. Kennedy, *Mellows*, Music Index.

37. Kennedy, *Mellows*, 30.

38. Kennedy, *Mellows*, 45.

39. Frederika Bremer, *The Homes of the New World: Impressions of America* (New York: Harper Bros., 1853); Dena J. Polacheck Epstein, *Sinful Tunes and Spirituals: Black Folk Music to the Civil War* (Urbana: University of Illinois Press, 1977), 297.

40. Alexander Dromgoole Sims, A *View of Slavery, Moral and Political* (Charleston: Miller, 1834); Epstein, *Sinful Tunes and Spirituals*, 221.

41. William Faux, *Memorable Days in America* (London: W. Simpkins and R. Marshall, 1832), 77–78; Epstein, *Sinful Tunes and Spirituals*, 167, 290.

42. William Francis Allen, Charles Pickard Ware, and Lucy McKim Garrison, *Slave Songs of the United States* (New York: A. Simpson & Co., 1867; repr., Dover, 1995), iv–v, xxi.

43. Henry Edward Krehbiel, *Afro-American Folksong: A Study in Racial and National Music* (New York: G. Schirmer, 1914), 43.

44. Krehbiel, *Afro-American Folksong*, 43. The melodies described as "Major with flatted seventh" could also have been harmonized using conventional European harmony based on the Mixolydian mode.

45. H. L. Mencken, "Negros' Contribution to Music Condensed in a Book of Spirituals," newspaper article in unidentified publication, 1925 in Koenig, *The Scrap Book of R. Emmet Kennedy*.

46. Andre Hodeir, *Jazz: Its Evolution and Essence* (Grove Press, 1956), 42.

47. Leroy Ostransky, *Understanding Jazz* (Englewood Cliffs, NJ: Prentice-Hall, 1977), 92–93.

48. Alain Locke, *The Negro and His Music* (Washington, DC: Associates in Negro Folk Education, 1936; repr., New York: Arno Press, 1969), 22.

49. Bergreen, *Louis Armstrong: An Extravagant Life*, 17.

CHAPTER 5: "WHEN I WAS AT SCHOL, I PLAYED ALL CLASSICAL MUSIC"

1. There appear to have been three schools named after Abijah Fisk in New Orleans: the school Armstrong attended at Franklin and Perdido; a rented building on South Dorgenois between Gravier and Perdido that was used from around 1909–10 onward for the lower grades and known as Fisk Branch; and Abijah Fisk Elementary School, which was operational in 1957. Public school records held in New Orleans University's Special Collections contains an "initial copy of our handbook" written by Mrs. Mildred L. Reese "Principle [sic]—Fisk School—Community Committee," dated October 18, 1957, setting out the history of the Abijah Fisk School. "School History," *Abijah Fisk Elementary School Handbook*, 1957 (Public School Records, New Orleans University Special Collections).

2. Charles Piper and Judy Piper, "A Passport to History," *The Jazz Archivist: A Newsletter of the William Ransom Hogan Jazz Archive* 23 (2010): 36.

3. Piper and Piper, "A Passport to History," 35–36.

4. Thirteenth Census of the United States: 1910, New Orleans City, Ward 3, sheet 10 A. (Ancestry.com).

5. Louis Armstrong, "Typescript for Satchmo: Life Story of Louis Armstrong" (New Jersey: Institute of Jazz Studies, Rutgers University), 9.

6. Brothers, *Louis Armstrong, in His Own Words*, vii.

7. Brothers, *Louis Armstrong, in His Own Words*, vii.

8. Brothers, *Louis Armstrong, in His Own Words*, 10.

9. Al Kennedy, *Chord Changes on the Chalkboard: How Public School Teachers Shaped Jazz and the Music of New Orleans* (Langham, MD: Scarecrow Press, 2002), xxi.

10. Armstrong, *Satchmo: My Life in New Orleans*, 30.

11. Thirteenth Census of the United States: 1910, New Orleans, Ward 3, District 0031 (Ancestry.com). In 1911 she is described as the "portress Fisk School, 507 S. Franklin," and her residential address is give as the "same." *Soards' City Directory*, New Orleans, Louisiana, 1911, 814 (Ancestry.com).

12. Armstrong, *Satchmo: My Life in New Orleans*, 30.

13. Armstrong, *Satchmo: My Life in New Orleans*, 31.

14. John McCusker gives "Coochie" Martin's real name as "Albert." McCusker, *Creole Trombone*, 109.There is no Albert in the family living in Franklin Street in1910. Rose and Souchon give "Coochie's" date of birth as ca. 1887. Al Rose and Edmond Souchon, *New Orleans Jazz: A Family Album*, third ed. (Baton Rouge: Louisiana State University Press, 1984), 84. Carmelite sons in the census are: James, thirty years old; Odonell, twenty-nine; Casimere, twenty-eight; Walter, twenty-five; and Henry, seventeen. Given that she bore thirteen children and eight were still living in 1910, and all eight are listed in the census, one of these older sons must be "Coochie."

15. Twelfth Census of the United States: 1900, New Orleans, Ward 3, District 0028 (Ancestry.com).

16. New Orleans *Times-Picayune*, June 24, 1905, 4.

17. Armstrong, *Satchmo: My Life in New Orleans*, 31.

18. Goffin, *Horn of Plenty*, 27. Orleania's age is given as ten years old in the 1910 census. School hours were typically from 9 a.m. to 2:30 p.m. "Wisdom in the School Board," New Orleans *Times Picayune*, December 14, 1895, 3.

19. Armstrong, *Satchmo: My Life in New Orleans*, 31. Wilhelmina's age is given as thirteen years old in the 1910 census.

20. Armstrong, *Satchmo: My Life in New Orleans*, 31.

21. "Armstrong Heritage Program, Part 4, August 23, 1960," in *Audio Collection*, ed. Robert McCully and Adam Lynch (New Orleans: William Ransom Hogan Jazz Archive, Tulane University).

22. *Manual of Music Work: New Orleans Public School* (New Orleans: Maubrret's Printing House, 1902).

23. *Manual of Music Work: New Orleans Public School*, 6.

24. *Manual of Music Work: New Orleans Public School*, 6.

25. *Manual of Music Work: New Orleans Public School*, 6.

26. *Manual of Music Work: New Orleans Public School*, 6.

27. *Manual of Music Work: New Orleans Public School*, 7.

28. *Manual of Music Work: New Orleans Public School*, 8.

29. *Manual of Music Work: New Orleans Public School*, 8.

30. *Manual of Music Work: New Orleans Public School*, 10.

31. *Manual of Music Work: New Orleans Public School*, 11.

32. *Manual of Music Work: New Orleans Public School*, 11.

33. Brothers, *Louis Armstrong, Master of Modernism*, 41.

34. *Manual of Music Work: New Orleans Public School*, 22.

35. *Manual of Music Work: New Orleans Public School*, 22.

36. *Manual of Music Work: New Orleans Public School*, 23.

37. Eleanor Smith, *The Eleanor Smith Music Course: Book 1* (New York: American Book Company, 1908; repr., Kessinger Legacy Reprints).

38. Smith, *The Eleanor Smith Music Course: Book 1*, iii.

39. Smith, *The Eleanor Smith Music Course: Book 1*, iii.

40. In February 1919. The minutes of the Education Board record: "It has come to the attention of the committee that there are songs of German origin that are being taught from the text books in music now in use. Such action is in direct violation of the orders of the Board. This Board is unalterably opposed to using such material and has ordered the elimination of all books of German flavor or propaganda. We, therefore, recommend that the use of the *Eleanor Smith Music Series* be discontinued and that the substitutes for these books be recommended by the Superintendent's Department for adoption." Minutes of the Orleans Parish School Board February 21, 1919, Volume 1916–1919 (New Orleans: Special Collections, New Orleans University), 475–76.

The minutes of July that year recommended that the revised *Eleanor Smith Music Series* by American Books Company be adopted for use in all grades. Minutes of the Orleans Parish School Board July 11, 1919, Volume 1916–1919 (New Orleans: Special Collections, New Orleans University), 562.

41. William Buckingham, "Musical Training and Early Jazz in New Orleans' Black Institutions of Education" (Masters, Tulane, 2011), 30.

42. Thomas "Papa Mutt" Carey, in Shapiro and Hentoff, *Hear Me Talkin' to Ya*, 47.

CHAPTER 6: "MY BRAZILIAN BEAUTY"

1. "Second City Criminal Court," *New Orleans Daily Item*, July 19, 1906.

2. "Juvenile Round-up," *New Orleans Daily Picayune*, October 22, 1910, as reproduced in, James Karst, "Secrets of Satchmo," New Orleans *Times-Picayune*, December 21, 2014.

3. Reproduction of a report in the *New Orleans Daily Picayune*, October 22, 1910, in James Karst, "Secrets of Satchmo."

4. Reproduction of a report in the *New Orleans Daily Picayune*, October 22, 1910.

5. Reproduction of a report in the *New Orleans Daily Picayune*, October 22, 1910.

6. Armstrong, *Satchmo: My Life in New Orleans*, 36.

7. Herbert Asbury, *The French Quarter: An Informal History of the New Orleans Underworld* (London: Alfred A. Knopf, 1936; repr., London: Basic Books, 2008), 437.

8. Robert Goffin, *La Nouvelle-Orléans Capital Du Jazz* (New York: Éditions De La Maison Française, 1946), 37.

9. This is possibly a mistranslation by Robert Goffin and should read "White Folks' Yard." The phrase appears in African American song. An example is "Get You a Kitchen Mechanic (Out the White Folks' Yard)," in Lynn Abbott and Doug Seroff, *The Original Blues* (Jackson: University Press of Mississippi, 2017), 75.

10. Goffin, *La Nouvelle-Orléans Capital Du Jazz*, 39–40. In later years Gregson had the task of going from cabaret to cabaret, from sporting-house to sporting-house, to announce that the City Council had voted the day before to enforce the July ordinance to close Storyville. Goffin, *Horn of Plenty*, 112.

11. "Few Juveniles Arrested," *New Orleans Times Democrat*, January 2, 1913.
12. Armstrong, "Armstrong Heritage T.V. Program, Part 1, August 9, 1960."
13. Armstrong, "Armstrong Heritage T.V. Program, Part 1, August 9, 1960."
14. Armstrong, "Armstrong Heritage T.V. Program, Part 1, August 9, 1960."
15. Armstrong, "Armstrong Heritage T.V. Program, Part 1, August 9, 1960."
16. Armstrong, "Armstrong Heritage T.V. Program, Part 1, August 9, 1960."
17. Meryman, *Louis Armstong: A Self-Portrait*, 14; Abbott, "'Play That Barber Shop Chord,'" 316; Billy Johnson, "Down on the Amazon" (New York: Dowling Sutton Music Company, 1903). My thanks to Lynn Abbott for passing this on to me.
18. The *New York Clipper*, December 19, 1903. My thanks to Lynn Abbott for passing this on to me.
19. Meryman, *Louis Armstrong: A Self Portrait*, 14–15.
20. Meryman, *Louis Armstrong: A Self Portrait*, 14.
21. Meryman, *Louis Armstrong: A Self Portrait*, 14.
22. Billy Johnson, "Down on the Amazon." The right-hand part in the first measure is as given (transposed) in the sheet music. This is almost certainly in error. There should be a C$^\sharp$ in the first measure as there is in measure 9.
23. Gage Averill, *Four Parts, No Waiting: A Social History of Barbershop Harmony* (New York: Oxford University Press, 2003), 163.
24. Art Merrille, "You Can Call Off the Search—for We've Found the Lost Chord," *Harmonizer* 10, no. 3 (1951): 27.
25. Deac Martin, *Martin's Book of Musical America* (Englewood Cliffs, NJ: Prentice-Hall, 1970), 180.
26. Merrille, "You Can Call Off the Search—for We've Found the Lost Chord," 27; Averill, *Four Parts, No Waiting*, 164.
27. Maurice Reagan, "The Mechanics of Barbershop Harmony," *Harmonizer* 3, no. 3 (1943): 10.
28. Donald Johns, "Funnel Tonality in American Popular Music, Ca. 1900–70," *American Music* 11, no. 4 (1993): 460.
29. Martin, *Martin's Book of Musical America*, 180.
30. Winthrop Sargeant, *Jazz: Hot and Hybrid* (New York: Arrows Editions, 1938; repr., New York: Da Capo,1976), 147; Martin, *Martin's Book of Musical America*, 180.
31. Ostransky, *Understanding Jazz*, 88.
32. Peter Van Der Merwe, *Origins of the Popular Style* (Oxford: Clarendon Press, 1989), 250. The second piece he cites is Chopin, Waltz in D$^\flat$, Op. 70, no. 3.
33. Van Der Merwe, *Origins of the Popular Style*, 251.
34. Van Der Merwe, *Origins of the Popular Style*, 251.
35. Scott Joplin, "Please Say You Will" (New York: M. A. Manfell, 1895).

CHAPTER 7: "ME AND MUSIC GOT MARRIED IN THE HOME"

1. Armstrong, *Swing That Music*, 5.
2. Teachout, *Pops*, 36.

3. Louis Armstrong, "The First Complete Pictorial Life Story of Louis Armstrong as Told to Inez Caveanaugh," *Band Leaders* (January 1945): 16.

4. Will Buckingham, "Louis Armstrong and the Waifs' Home," *Jazz Archivist: A Newsletter of the William Ransom Hogan Jazz Archive* XXIV (2011): 2.

5. Goffin, *La Nouvelle-Orléans Capital Du Jazz*, 159.

6. Goffin, *La Nouvelle-Orléans Capital Du Jazz*, 160.

7. John Fogarty became presiding judge of the First Recorders Court in 1904. *Behrman Administration Biography* (1912) (New Orleans: William Ransom Hogan Jazz Archive, Tulane University).

8. Goffin, *La Nouvelle-Orléans Capital Du Jazz*, 160.

9. Goffin, *La Nouvelle-Orléans Capital Du Jazz*, 161; Buckingham, "Louis Armstrong and the Waifs' Home," 7.

10. Goffin, *La Nouvelle-Orléans Capital Du Jazz*, 161.

11. Joe Rene, "Interview April 7, 1960," in *Oral History* (Tulane University, New Orleans: William Ransom Hogan Jazz Archive).

12. Goffin, *La Nouvelle-Orléans Capital Du Jazz*, 161.

13. Goffin, *La Nouvelle-Orléans Capital Du Jazz*, 161–62.

14. Goffin, *La Nouvelle-Orléans Capital Du Jazz*, 161.

15. Armstrong, "Typescript for Satchmo: Life Story of Louis Armstrong," 16.

16. Armstrong, *Swing That Music*, 6.

17. Armstrong, *Swing That Music*, 7.

18. Janet Rink, "Satchmo Comes Home," *Dixie*, October 31, 1965, 8.

19. Goffin, *La Nouvelle-Orléans Capital Du Jazz*, 162–63.

20. Meryman, *Louis Armstrong: A Self Portrait*, 15.

21. James Lincoln Collier, *Louis Armstrong: An American Genius* (New York: Oxford University Press, 1983), 37.

22. Armstrong, "Typescript for Satchmo: Life Story of Louis Armstrong," 17. My italics.

23. Goffin, *La Nouvelle-Orléans Capital Du Jazz*, 164. Louis Armstrong recorded "Swanee River" later in his career, on one occasion with the Mills Brothers. Louis Armstrong with the Mills Brothers, "Old Folks at Home" (New York: Decca 1360, June 29, 1937).

24. Rink, "Satchmo Comes Home," 8.

25. Meryman, *Louis Armstrong: A Self Portrait*, 15–16.

26. Goffin, *La Nouvelle-Orléans Capital Du Jazz*, 164.

27. Rink, "Satchmo Comes Home," 8.

28. Singleton, "Zutty First Saw Louis in Amateur Tent Show," 6.

29. "Juvenile Band," *New Orleans Daily Picayune*, May 31, 1913, as reproduced in James Karst, "Armstrong Already the Leader of Waifs' Home Band at 11," New Orleans *Times-Picayune*, December 21, 2014, A-14.

30. A similar view is expressed in Bruce Boyd Raeburn, "Early New Orleans Jazz in Theaters," *Louisiana History: The Journal of the Louisiana Historical Association* 43, no. 1 (2002): 41–52.

31. Goffin, *Horn of Plenty*, 65.

32. McCusker, *Creole Trombone*, 102.

33. "Lively Music Provided," *New Orleans Times-Democrat*, December 27, 1913 (New Orleans: Williams Research Center, Historic New Orleans Collection).

34. "Lively Music Provided."

35. Armstrong, *Swing That Music*, 5.

36. Buckingham, "Louis Armstrong and the Waifs' Home," 7.

37. Buckingham, "Louis Armstrong and the Waifs' Home," 8.

38. Buckingham, "Louis Armstrong and the Waifs' Home," 8.

39. Rose and Souchon, *New Orleans Jazz: A Family Album*, 81.

40. Rose and Souchon, *New Orleans Jazz: A Family Album*, 81.

41. Manuel Manetta, "Interview Digest, March 28, 1957," in *Oral History Files*, ed. William Russell et al. (New Orleans: William Ransom Hogan Jazz Archive, Tulane University).

42. Kid Shots Madison, "Interview with Bill Russell, August 8, 1944 (New Orleans: Williams Research Center, Historic New Orleans Collection), in Abbott, "'Play That Barber Shop Chord,'" 318.

43. Rose and Souchon, *New Orleans Jazz: A Family Album*, 106.

44. Rose and Souchon, *New Orleans Jazz: A Family Album*, 106.

45. Buckingham, "Louis Armstrong and the Waifs' Home," 6.

46. U.S. World War I Draft Registration Cards, 1917–1918, Louisiana, New Orleans City, 02, Draft Card B, serial no. 876, order no. 4876 (Ancestry.com).

47. Brothers, *Louis Armstrong, Master of Modernism*, 212.

48. Goffin, *La Nouvelle-Orléans Capital Du Jazz*, 166.

49. Karst, "Secrets of Satchmo."

50. Preston Jackson, in Shapiro and Hentoff, *Hear Me Talkin' to Ya*, 97.

51. Preston Jackson, "Interview June 2, 1958," in *Oral History Files* (New Orleans: William Ransom Hogan Jazz Archive, Tulane University).

52. Sally Asher, *Stories from the St. Louis Cemeteries of New Orleans* (Charleston, SC: History Press, 2015), 203–4.

53. Preston Jackson, "Autobiography," in William Russell Jazz Collection MSS 519 (New Orleans: Williams Research Center, Historic New Orleans Collection).

54. Asher, *Stories from the St. Louis Cemeteries of New Orleans*, 204.

55. "Playground Dedicated: First in the South for the Use of Negro Children," New Orleans *Times-Picayune*, August 29, 1915, 15.

56. "To Dedicate First Negro Playgrounds: Thorny [sic] Lafon Recreation Center to Be Formally Opened Saturday," *New Orleans Item*, August 28, 1915, 2.

57. Singleton, "Zutty First Saw Louis in Amateur Tent Show," 6; "Lively Music Provided."

58. *Louis Armstrong and His Dixieland Seven, Maryland My Maryland, New Orleans* (film) (Los Angeles: United Artists, 1946). Recorded September 5–October 8, 1946.

59. W. S. Mygrant, "My Maryland," ed. Maurice F. Smith (New York: Leo Feist, 1906), in John Robichaux Sheet Music Collection (New Orleans: William Ransom Hogan Jazz Archive, Tulane University).

60. "The New Orleans All Stars," an unidentified handwritten article located in Folder 2 of the William Russell Collection, "Jazz Files M (Miscel.)" (New Orleans: Williams Research Center, Historic New Orleans Collection); Buckingham, "Louis Armstrong and the Waifs' Home," 64.

61. John Casimir, "Interview, January 17, 1959," in *Oral History Files*, ed. Richard B. Allen (New Orleans: William Ransom Hogan Jazz Archive, Tulane University); Buckingham, "Louis Armstrong and the Waifs' Home," 65.

62. *Remick Orchestra Folio 14*, "Sailing Down the Chesapeake" (1913), Sheet Music Collection (New Orleans: William Ransom Hogan Jazz Archive, Tulane University).

CHAPTER 8: "I WAS SINGING SELLING COAL"

1. Brothers, *Louis Armstrong, in His Own Words*, 5.
2. Brothers, *Louis Armstrong, in His Own Words*.
3. Brothers, *Louis Armstrong, in His Own Words*, 11–12.
4. Brothers, *Louis Armstrong, in His Own Words*, 12.
5. Brothers, *Louis Armstrong, in His Own Words*, 13.
6. Brothers, *Louis Armstrong, in His Own Words*, 18.
7. Brothers, *Louis Armstrong, in His Own Words*, 11.
8. Brothers, *Louis Armstrong, in His Own Words*, 15.
9. The Louis Armstrong House Museum in Queens, shows an introductory video that begins with the Karnofsky family and what is believed to be Louis's first cornet.
10. Brothers, *Louis Armstrong, in His Own Words*, 12.
11. Goffin, *Horn of Plenty*, 42–43.
12. Goffin, *Horn of Plenty*, 53. He is also referred to as "Morris" Konowski, 59.
13. Brothers, *Louis Armstrong, in His Own Words*, 13.
14. Armstrong, "The First Complete Pictorial Life Story of Louis Armstrong as Told to Inez Caveanaugh," 16.
15. Armstrong, *Swing That Music*, 24.
16. Goffin, *Horn of Plenty*, 73.
17. Goffin, *Horn of Plenty*, 74.
18. Armstrong, *Satchmo: My Life in New Orleans*, 59.
19. Armstrong, *Satchmo: My Life in New Orleans*, 59.
20. Charter Number 01000490D,12/10/1899, Louisiana Business Files, Louisiana Department of State; *Soards' New Orleans City Directory*, 1901–1910 (New Orleans: Williams Research Center, Historic New Orleans Collection). It gained switch rights to link its coal yard at Arabella Street and Lenke Avenue with the Illinois Central Railroad Company tracks in 1905. *New Orleans Daily Item*, September 13, 1905, 7.
21. 1911 *Soards' New Orleans City Directory* (New Orleans: Williams Research Center, Historic New Orleans Collection).
22. Armstrong, *Satchmo: My Life in New Orleans*, 73.
23. *New York Times*, September 30, 1915, 1.
24. Armstrong, *Satchmo: My Life in New Orleans*, 83.
25. Armstrong, *Satchmo: My Life in New Orleans*, 58.
26. Armstrong, *Satchmo: My Life in New Orleans*, 83.
27. Armstrong, *Satchmo: My Life in New Orleans*, 83.
28. "Typescript for Satchmo: Life Story of Louis Armstrong," 39.

29. Brothers, *Louis Armstrong, in His Own Words*, 12.

30. US WWI Draft Registration Card (Ancestry.com). He was registered on June 5, 1917. His occupation is given as "Merchant 26 [?]" and he was working "for himself."

31. There is a reference to Louis Kornofsky at a "second store" at "205 S Rampart" in the 1900 *Soards' New Orleans City Directory*.

32. Thirteenth Census of the United States 1910, Third Ward of New Orleans, District 30, sheet 13 A. There is an Abraham Kornofsky, "Junk Dealer" at 722 S. Basin in 1902 *Soards' New Orleans City Directory*; Abraham Karanofsky, "Junk Dealer" at 722 Saratoga in 1903 *Soards' New Orleans City Directory*. There is no reference to Louis Karnofsky in *Soards' New Orleans City Directory* up to 1904.

33. Brothers, *Louis Armstrong, in His Own Words*, 7.

34. Fourteenth Census of the United States 1920, Third Ward of New Orleans, District 34, sheet 3A (Ancestry.com).

35. US WWII Draft Cards Young Men, 1940–1947, New Orleans (Ancestry.com).

36. Brothers, *Louis Armstrong, in His Own Words*, 30.

37. Thirteenth Census of the United States 1910, Third Ward of New Orleans, District 30, sheet 13A (Ancestry.com).

38. 1914 *Soards' New Orleans City Directory*.

39. Brothers, *Louis Armstrong, in His Own Words*, 23.

40. Fourteenth Census of the United States 1920, Third Ward of New Orleans, District 34, sheet 3A (Ancestry.com).

41. Fourteenth Census of the United States 1920, Third Ward of New Orleans, District 34, sheet 3A (Ancestry.com).

42. Bergreen, *Louis Armstrong: An Extravagant Life*, 107.

43. Louis Keppard, "Interview Transcript, December 25, 1969," in William Russell Jazz Collection MSS 519 (New Orleans: Williams Research Center, Historic New Orleans Collection).

44. Pops Foster quoted in a review of his autobiography, *Oakland Tribune*, October 31, 1971, Vertical File (New Orleans: William Ransom Hogan Jazz Archive).

45. "Lincoln Park Notes," Indianapolis *Freeman*, June 8, 1907; Lynn Abbott, "Remembering Mr. E. Belfield Spriggins: First Man of Jazzology," *78 Quarterly* 1, no. 10, 1999: 41.

46. "Lincoln Park Auditorium—New Orleans, L. A.," Indianapolis *Freeman*, September 7, 1907; Lynn Abbott, "Remembering Mr. E. Belfield Spriggins: First Man of Jazzology," *78 Quarterly* 1, no. 10 (1999): 41.

47. Chicago *Defender*, June 5, 1915; Abbott, "Remembering Mr. E. Belfield Spriggins: First Man of Jazzology," 45.

48. Hayward, Joseph, bartender, r. 1318 Gravier, 1910 *Soards' City Directory of New Orleans*. Haywood, Joseph, Saloon 1301 Gravier, *1913 Soards' City Directory of New Orleans*.

49. Keppard, "Interview Transcript, December 25, 1969."

50. Meryman, *Louis Armstrong: A Self Portrait*, 16; Manetta, "Interview Digest, March 28, 1957." Keppard mentions that "Manuel, 'course we used to call him horse'" was playing with Oliver at Bottlers. "Hoss" or "Fess" are both nicknames associated with Manetta. Keppard, "Interview Transcript, December 25, 1969."

51. Goffin, *Horn of Plenty*, 77.

52. Jeff Nussbaum, Niles Eldridge, and Robb Stewart, "Louis Armstrong's First Cornet?" *Historic Brass Society Journal* 15 (2003): 355–57.

53. Meryman, *Louis Armstrong: A Self Portrait*, 16.

54. James Lincoln Collier has argued (62) that Tonk Bros. are "a company nobody has heard of since." In the 1930s Tonk Bros. claimed to be the "World's Largest Exclusive Wholesalers of Musical Merchandise," *Tonk Bros. Inc. Catalogue*, No. 47, 1930. Foreword. http://www.acousticmusic.org/userfiles/file/pdfs/historical-data/Musical%20Distributors/Tonk%20Bros%201930%20Catalog%2047.pdf.

55. Meryman, *Louis Armstrong: A Self Portrait*, 16–17.

56. Larry Gara, *The Baby Dodds Story: As Told to Larry Gara* (Baton Rouge: Louisiana State University, 1959; repr., 1992), 8.

57. Armstrong, *Satchmo: My Life in New Orleans*, 99.

58. Edward "Kid" Ory, in Shapiro and Hentoff, *Hear Me Talkin' to Ya*, 48.

59. Edward "Kid" Ory, "The Hot Five Sessions," *Record Changer* 9, no. 6–7 (1950): 17 (Loughton UK: National Jazz Archive).

60. Ory, "The Hot Five Sessions."

61. Ory, "The Hot Five Sessions."

62. Edward "Kid" Ory, in Shapiro and Hentoff, *Hear Me Talkin' to Ya*, 48.

63. Bergreen, *Louis Armstrong: An Extravagant Life*, 90.

64. Tom Stoddard, *Pops Foster: The Autobiography of a New Orleans Jazzman* (Berkeley: University of California Press, 1971; repr., San Francisco: Backbeat Books, 2005), 51.

65. Ory, in Shapiro and Hentoff, *Hear Me Talkin' to Ya*, 48.

66. Ory, in Shapiro and Hentoff, *Hear Me Talkin' to Ya*, 49.

67. Pops Foster, quoted in Richard Hadlock, "Pops Foster," *San Francisco Examiner*, Vertical File (New Orleans: William Ransom Hogan Jazz Archive).

68. Bigard, *With Louis and the Duke*, 10–11.

69. Bigard, *With Louis and the Duke*, 10–11.

70. Ory, "Interview Transcript, April 20, 1957 (for *Life Magazine*)."

71. Ory, "Interview Transcript, April 20, 1957 (for *Life Magazine*)."

72. Ory, "Interview Transcript, April 20, 1957 (for *Life Magazine*)."

73. Ory, in Shapiro and Hentoff, *Hear Me Talkin' to Ya*, 28.

74. Ory, "Interview Transcript, April 20, 1957 (for *Life Magazine*)."

75. G. E. Lambert, *King of Jazz Johnny Dodds* (New York: Barnes, 1961), 3.

76. Gara, *The Baby Dodds Story*, 1.

77. Gara, *The Baby Dodds Story*, 2.

78. Gara, *The Baby Dodds Story*, 2.

79. Gara, *The Baby Dodds Story*, 2.

80. Gara, *The Baby Dodds Story*, 4.

81. Lambert, 3.

82. Gara, *The Baby Dodds Story*, 4. It is likely that Johnny was playing clarinet rather than the tin flute by the time Baby was playing his homemade drums.

83. Ory settled in New Orleans in the spring of 1910. McCusker, *Creole Trombone*, 84.

84. Stoddard, *Pops Foster: The Autobiography of a New Orleans Jazzman*, 51.
85. Manetta, "Interview Digest, March 28, 1957."
86. Manetta, "Interview Digest, March 28, 1957"; 1914 *Soards' City Directory, New Orleans*.
87. Manetta, "Interview Digest, March 28, 1957."
88. Meryman, *Louis Armstrong: A Self Portrait*, 17.
89. Bergreen, *Louis Armstrong: An Extravagant Life*, 106.
90. Armstrong, *Satchmo: My Life in New Orleans*, 89.
91. Armstrong, *Satchmo: My Life in New Orleans*, 90.
92. Goffin, *Horn of Plenty*, 86.
93. Goffin, *Horn of Plenty*, 86.
94. Goffin, *Horn of Plenty*, 87.
95. Goffin, *Horn of Plenty*, 91.
96. Goffin, *Horn of Plenty*, 94.
97. Goffin, *Horn of Plenty*, 102–3.
98. Goffin, *Horn of Plenty*, 104.
99. Goffin, *Horn of Plenty*, 124.
100. Goffin, *Horn of Plenty*, 116–25.
101. Meryman, *Louis Armstrong: A Self Portrait*, 25.
102. Ory, in Shapiro and Hentoff, *Hear Me Talkin' to Ya*, 49; McCusker, *Creole Trombone*, 126.
103. Stella Oliver, "Interview Digest, April 22, 1959."
104. Stella Oliver, "Interview Digest, April 22, 1959."
105. Edward "Kid" Ory and Manuel "Fess" Manetta, "August 26, 1958," *Oral History Files*, ed. William Russell, Richard B. Allen, and Ralph Adamo (New Orleans: William Ransom Hogan Jazz Archive, Tulane University). Prohibition was implemented throughout the United States in 1920.
106. Ory, in Shapiro and Hentoff, *Hear Me Talkin' to Ya*, 49; McCusker, *Creole Trombone*, 126.
107. McCusker, *Creole Trombone*, 127.
108. Armstrong, *Satchmo: My Life in New Orleans*, 122–23; McCusker, *Creole Trombone*, 127.
109. McCusker, *Creole Trombone*, 126–27.
110. Armstrong, *Satchmo: My Life in New Orleans*, 124; McCusker, *Creole Trombone*, 128.
111. Ory, in Shapiro and Hentoff, *Hear Me Talkin' to Ya*, 49; McCusker, *Creole Trombone*, 128.
112. Armstrong, *Satchmo: My Life in New Orleans*, 130; McCusker, *Creole Trombone*, 128.
113. William "Baba" Ridgley, "Interview Summary June 2, 1959," in *Oral History Files*, ed. Betty B. Rankin et al. (New Orleans: William Ransom Hogan Jazz Archive, Tulane University).
114. "Interview Summary, April 11, 1961," in *Oral History Files*, ed. John Handy, Richard B. Allen, and Marjorie T. Zander (New Orleans: William Ransom Hogan Jazz Archive, Tulane University).

115. "Interview Summary, April 11, 1961."
116. "Interview Summary, April 11, 1961."
117. "Interview Summary, April 11, 1961."
118. "Interview Summary, April 11, 1961."
119. "Interview Summary, April 11, 1961."
120. William "Baba" Ridgley, "Interview, April 7, 1961," in *Oral History Files*, ed. Richard B. Allen and Dave Dutcher (New Orleans: William Ransom Hogan Jazz Archive, Tulane University). Ridgley had some knowledge of harmony and could play piano chords.
121. Ridgley, "Interview, April 7, 1961."
122. Ridgley, "Interview, April 7, 1961."
123. Morris French and Ernest "Punch" Miller, "Interview Digest, June 24, 1960," *Oral History Files*, ed. Richard B. Allen and Marjorie T. Zander (New Orleans: William Ransom Hogan Jazz Archive, Tulane University).
124. William "Baba" Ridgley, "Interview, April 7, 1961" *Oral History Files*, ed. Richard B. Allen and Dave Dutcher (New Orleans: William Ransom Hogan Jazz Archive, Tulane University).
125. Ridgley, "Interview, April 7, 1961."
126. Ridgley, "Interview, April 7, 1961."
127. "Interview Summary, April 11, 1961."
128. Ridgley, "Interview, April 7, 1961."
129. "Interview Summary, April 11, 1961."
130. Sally Newhart, *The Original Tuxedo Jazz Band: More Than a Century of a New Orleans Icon*, Kindle ed. (Charleston SC: History Press, 2013), loc. 479–80. This would not have been a steam railway service. This service was ended in 1903. In the spring of 1911, an electric street car began to serve the recently redeveloped resort of Spanish Fort. Louis C. Hennick and E. Harper Charlton, *The Streetcars of New Orleans* (Gretna, LA: Jackson Square Press, 1975), 32.
131. Ridgley, "Interview Summary, April 11, 1961."
132. Ridgley, "Interview Summary, April 11, 1961."
133. Ridgley, "Interview Summary, April 11, 1961."
134. Ridgley, "Interview Summary, April 11, 1961."
135. Newhart, *The Original Tuxedo Jazz Band*, 484.
136. Mike Hazeldine and Barry Martyn, *Bunk Johnson: Song of the Wanderer* (New Orleans: Jazzology Press, 2000), 48–49.

CHAPTER 9: DID BUNK TEACH LOUIS?

1. Brothers, *Louis Armstrong, in His Own Words*, 40.
2. Hobson, *Creating Jazz Counterpoint*, 32–47.
3. Brothers, *Louis Armstrong, in His Own Words*, 40.
4. Park Breck, "This Isn't Bunk; Bunk Taught Louis," *Down Beat* 6, no. 6 (1939): 4.
5. Breck, "This Isn't Bunk; Bunk Taught Louis," 4.
6. Breck, "This Isn't Bunk; Bunk Taught Louis," 4.

7. Louis Armstrong, in Shapiro and Hentoff, *Hear Me Talkin' to Ya*, 39.

8. Armstrong gave Johnson a signed photo of himself dedicated to Johnson, who was, Armstrong claimed, "my musical insparation [sic] all my life—'yea man.'" Hazeldine and Martyn, *Bunk Johnson: Song of the Wanderer*, 48–49.

9. Meryman, *Louis Armstrong: A Self Portrait*, 50.

10. Lillian Hardin-Armstrong, "Jazzmen Interviews," in Papers of Frederic Ramsey Jr., MSS 559 (New Orleans: Williams Research Center, Historic New Orleans Collection).

11. Breck, "This Isn't Bunk; Bunk Taught Louis," 4.

12. Danny Barker, in Shapiro and Hentoff, *Hear Me Talkin' to Ya*, 52.

13. Bigard, *With Louis and the Duke*, 71.

14. Chilton, *Sidney Bechet: The Wizard of Jazz*, 1.

15. Chilton, *Sidney Bechet: The Wizard of Jazz*, 2–3.

16. Goffin, *La Nouvelle-Orléans Capital Du Jazz*, 151.

17. Goffin, *La Nouvelle-Orléans Capital Du Jazz*, 151.

18. Goffin, *La Nouvelle-Orléans Capital Du Jazz*, 151.

19. Goffin, *La Nouvelle-Orléans Capital Du Jazz*, 152.

20. Lizzie Miles, letter to David Griffiths (May 18, 1959), in Chilton, *Sidney Bechet: The Wizard of Jazz*, 3.

21. Goffin, *La Nouvelle-Orléans Capital Du Jazz*, 156.

22. Sidney Bechet, *Treat It Gentle: An Autobiography*, Kindle ed. (London: Cassell, 1960; repr., New York: Da Capo,1978), 83.

23. Bechet, *Treat It Gentle: An Autobiography*, Loc. 1253.

24. Bechet, *Treat It Gentle: An Autobiography*, Loc. 1269.

25. Bechet, *Treat It Gentle: An Autobiography*, Loc. 1294.

26. Bechet, *Treat It Gentle: An Autobiography*, Loc. 1294.

27. Bechet, *Treat It Gentle: An Autobiography*, Loc. 1294.

28. Bechet, *Treat It Gentle: An Autobiography*, Loc. 1278.

29. Bechet, *Treat It Gentle: An Autobiography*, Loc. 1286.

30. Bechet, *Treat It Gentle: An Autobiography*, Loc. 1304.

31. William "Bunk" Johnson, in Shapiro and Hentoff, *Hear Me Talkin' to Ya*, 47.

32. Lawrence Gushee, "The Improvisation of Louis Armstrong," in Bruno Nettl and Malinda Russell, eds., *In the Course of Performance: Studies in the World of Musical Improvisation* (Chicago: University of Chicago Press, 1989), 293.

33. William "Bunk" Johnson, in Shapiro and Hentoff, *Hear Me Talkin' to Ya*, 47–48.

34. William "Bunk" Johnson, in Shapiro and Hentoff, *Hear Me Talkin' to Ya*, 47.

35. Armstrong, "The First Complete Pictorial Life Story of Louis Armstrong as Told to Inez Caveanaugh," 16.

36. Bergreen, *Louis Armstrong: An Extravagant Life*, 64.

37. Louis went on to talk about the Waifs' Home after discussing being with Bunk in Dago Tony's. Armstrong, "The First Complete Pictorial Life Story of Louis Armstrong as Told to Inez Caveanaugh," 16.

38. Bechet, *Treat It Gentle: An Autobiography*, Loc. 1294.

39. Bechet, *Treat It Gentle: An Autobiography*, Loc. 93.

40. Bechet, *Treat It Gentle: An Autobiography*, Loc. 1304.

41. Armstrong, *Satchmo: My Life in New Orleans*, 120.

42. Bechet, *Treat It Gentle: An Autobiography*, Loc. 1294.

43. Louis Armstrong, "60-Year-Old 'Bunk' Johnson, Louis' Tutor, Sits in the Band," *Down Beat* (August 15, 1941): 11.

44. Meryman, *Louis Armstrong: A Self Portrait*, 50.

45. Louis Armstrong, "Bunk Didn't Teach Me," *Record Changer* 9, no. 6–7 (1950): 30 (Loughton, UK: National Jazz Archive).

46. Armstrong, "Bunk Didn't Teach Me," 30.

47. Armstrong, "Bunk Didn't Teach Me," 30.

48. For discussion of "Buddy Bolden's Blues," see Vic Hobson, "Buddy Bolden's Blues," *Jazz Archivist: A Newsletter of the William Ransom Hogan Jazz Archive* XXI (2008): 1–18.

49. Will Handy, "Oh! Didn't He Ramble," New York: Jos. Stern & Co., 1902 (Performing Arts Reading Room, Library of Congress, Washington, DC).

50. Edith Maida Lessing and Jimmie V. Monaco, "Oh, You Circus Day" (Chicago: Will Rossiter, 1912). It is less likely to be Albert Gumble and Jack Yellen, "Circus Day in Dixie" (New York: Jerome H. Remick, 1915).

51. Chris Smith and Jim Burris, "Ballin' the Jack" (New York: Jos. W. Stern, 1913).

52. Bunk Johnson, "Letter from Bunk Johnson to William Russell," undated, in William Russell Collection, MSS 501 (New Orleans: Williams Research Center, Historic New Orleans Collection).

53. Brothers, *Louis Armstrong, in His Own Words*, 197–98. Quoting Stoddard, *Pops Foster: The Autobiography of a New Orleans Jazzman*, 56–57.Pops Foster interview, August 24, 1958, is in the William Russell Jazz Collection MSS 519 (New Orleans: Williams Research Center, Historic New Orleans Collection).

54. Stoddard, *Pops Foster: The Autobiography of a New Orleans Jazzman*, 57.

55. Hazeldine and Martyn, *Bunk Johnson: Song of the Wanderer*, 4.

56. Hazeldine and Martyn, *Bunk Johnson: Song of the Wanderer*, 231.

57. Hazeldine and Martyn, *Bunk Johnson: Song of the Wanderer*, 231.

58. Hazeldine and Martyn, *Bunk Johnson: Song of the Wanderer*, 231.

59. Hazeldine and Martyn, *Bunk Johnson: Song of the Wanderer*, 231.

60. Hazeldine and Martyn, *Bunk Johnson: Song of the Wanderer*, 231.

61. Hazeldine and Martyn, *Bunk Johnson: Song of the Wanderer*, 231–32.

62. Bechet, *Treat It Gentle: An Autobiography*, Loc. 2334.

63. Breck, "This Isn't Bunk; Bunk Taught Louis," 4.

64. Gushee, "The Improvisation of Louis Armstrong," 293.

65. Meryman, *Louis Armstrong: A Self Portrait*, 50.

66. Frederick J. Spencer, *Jazz and Death: Medical Profiles of Jazz Greats* (Jackson: University Press of Mississippi, 2002), 28.

67. Armstrong, *Swing That Music*, 26.

68. Les Tompkins, "Playing with King Oliver Was Still the Real High Spot," *Crescendo* 3, no. 12 (1965): 23 (Loughton, UK: National Jazz Archive).

69. Louis Armstrong, "Scanning the History of Jazz," *Jazz Review* 3, no. 6 (1960): 8. (Loughton, UK: National Jazz Archive).

70. "Joe Oliver Is Still King," *Record Changer* 9, no. 6–7 (1950): 10 (Loughton, UK: National Jazz Archive).

71. Louis Armstrong, in Shapiro and Hentoff, *Hear Me Talkin' to Ya*, 43.

CHAPTER 10: "GOING TO THE CONSERVATORY"

1. Willie E. Humphrey (the elder) and Willie J. Humphrey (the younger), "Interview Digest, March 15, 1959," in *Oral History Files*, ed. William Russell and Ralph Collins (New Orleans: William Ransom Hogan Jazz Archive, Tulane University).

2. David Chevan, "Riverboat Music from St. Louis and the Streckfus Steamboat Line," *Black Music Research Journal* 9, no. 2 (1989): 153.

3. Chevan, "Riverboat Music from St. Louis and the Streckfus Steamboat Line," 153–54.

4. Chevan, "Riverboat Music from St. Louis and the Streckfus Steamboat Line," 154.

5. Chevan, "Riverboat Music from St. Louis and the Streckfus Steamboat Line," 160.

6. Chevan, "Riverboat Music from St. Louis and the Streckfus Steamboat Line," 154, 60; Verne Streckfus, "Digest September 22, 1960," ed. Paul R. Crawford Richard B. Allen (New Orleans: William Ransom Hogan Jazz Archive, Tulane University).

7. Beulah Schacht, "Riverboat Jazz and the Story of a Legendary St. Louisian Who Made It Click," *St. Louis Globe-Democrat*, July 22, 1945, 5. http://www.doctorjazz.co.uk/marabletjr.html.

8. Fate Marable, *Autobiography*, unpublished and undated manuscript, in the private collection of Wilma Dobie; Chevan, "Riverboat Music from St. Louis and the Streckfus Steamboat Line," 161, 77.

9. Marable, *Autobiography*; Chevan, "Riverboat Music from St. Louis and the Streckfus Steamboat Line," 161, 77.

10. Chevan, "Riverboat Music from St. Louis and the Streckfus Steamboat Line," 160–61.

11. Streckfus, "Digest September 22, 1960."

12. Schacht, "Riverboat Jazz and the Story of a Legendary St. Louisian Who Made It Click," 5. http://www.doctorjazz.co.uk/marabletjr.html.

13. Schacht, "Riverboat Jazz and the Story of a Legendary St. Louisian Who Made It Click," 5; Chevan, "Riverboat Music from St. Louis and the Streckfus Steamboat Line," 161.

14. Chevan, "Riverboat Music from St. Louis and the Streckfus Steamboat Line," 154.

15. Chevan, "Riverboat Music from St. Louis and the Streckfus Steamboat Line," 159.

16. Streckfus, "Digest September 22, 1960."

17. Arthur "Zutty" Singleton, in Shapiro and Hentoff, *Hear Me Talkin' to Ya*, 76.

18. William Howland Kenney, *Jazz on the River* (Chicago: University of Chicago Press, 2005), 45.

19. Kenney, *Jazz on the River*, 45.

20. Kenny's footnote: Marable as quoted by Wilma Dobie. Interview with Dobie, September 19, 2001. Kenney, *Jazz on the River*, 58.

21. Streckfus, "Digest September 22, 1960."

22. Streckfus, "Digest September 22, 1960"; Schacht, "Riverboat Jazz and the Story of a Legendary St. Louisian Who Made It Click," 5. http://www.doctorjazz.co.uk/marabletjr.html.

23. http://www.doctorjazz.co.uk/marabletjr.html.

24. http://www.doctorjazz.co.uk/marabletjr.html.

25. Streckfus, "Digest September 22, 1960."

26. Stoddard, *Pops Foster: The Autobiography of a New Orleans Jazzman*, 108.

27. Gara, *The Baby Dodds Story*, 21.

28. Peter Bocage, "Interview Transcript, January 29, 1959," in *Oral History Files*, ed. Richard B. Allen and William Russell (New Orleans: William Ransom Hogan Jazz Archive, Tulane University).

29. Stoddard, *Pops Foster: The Autobiography of a New Orleans Jazzman*, 106.

30. Bocage, "Interview Transcript, January 29, 1959." Bocage said that Manuel Perez was also playing in the Marable band at this time.

31. Bocage, "Interview Transcript, January 29, 1959."

32. Bocage, "Interview Transcript, January 29, 1959."

33. Stoddard, *Pops Foster: The Autobiography of a New Orleans Jazzman*, 115.

34. Streckfus, "Digest September 22, 1960."

35. Streckfus, "Digest September 22, 1960."

36. Armstrong, *Swing That Music*, 36.

37. Streckfus, "Digest September 22, 1960."

38. Armstrong's recollection of buying himself a new horn for his first trip on the riverboats is not supported by other accounts. Armstrong, *Swing That Music*, 41–42.

39. Gara, *The Baby Dodds Story*, 24. In another account, Armstrong and Beiderbecke did not meet until Armstrong was with Oliver at the Lincoln Gardens; see Goffin, *Horn of Plenty*, 180–81.

40. Meryman, *Louis Armstrong: A Self Portrait*, 26.

41. Meryman, *Louis Armstrong: A Self Portrait*, 26.

42. Ridgley, "Interview Summary June 2, 1959." He also recalled that John Porter played "bass violin . . . the first year they went to St. Louis." Given that "Pops" Foster was in the orchestra when Armstrong joined, it is likely that Porter had left by this time.

43. Gara, *The Baby Dodds Story*, 24.

44. Gara, *The Baby Dodds Story*, 26.

45. Stoddard, *Pops Foster: The Autobiography of a New Orleans Jazzman*, 115.

46. Bocage, "Interview Transcript, January 29, 1959."

47. Bocage, "Interview Transcript, January 29, 1959."

48. Ed Crowder and A. F. Niemoeller, "Norman Mason: Riverboat Jazzman," *Record Changer*, no. 2 (1952): 8.

49. Crowder and Niemoeller, "Norman Mason: Riverboat Jazzman."

50. "Freddie Pratt Writes from 'A Rabbit Foot. Co.' Helena, Ark.," *Indianapolis Freeman*, November 21, 1914; Lynn Abbott and Doug Seroff, *Ragged but Right: Black Travelling Shows, "Coon Songs," and the Dark Pathway to Blues and Jazz* (Jackson: University Press of Mississippi, 2007), 276.

51. Crowder and Niemoeller, "Norman Mason: Riverboat Jazzman," 8.
52. Crowder and Niemoeller, "Norman Mason: Riverboat Jazzman."
53. Crowder and Niemoeller, "Norman Mason: Riverboat Jazzman."
54. Crowder and Niemoeller, "Norman Mason: Riverboat Jazzman."
55. Crowder and Niemoeller, "Norman Mason: Riverboat Jazzman."
56. In Abbott and Seroff's notes: "'David James,' the mellophonist mentioned here, may be David Jones of New Orleans, who had recently toured in the band with Tolliver's Smart Set." Abbott and Seroff, *Ragged but Right*, 415.
57. Meryman, *Louis Armstrong: A Self Portrait*, 25.
58. Armstrong, *Swing That Music*, 47.
59. Rose and Souchon, *New Orleans Jazz: A Family Album*, 64; Abbott and Seroff, *Ragged but Right*, 138.
60. Meryman, *Louis Armstrong: A Self Portrait*, 26.
61. Gara, *The Baby Dodds Story*, 24.
62. Stoddard, *Pops Foster: The Autobiography of a New Orleans Jazzman*, 115.
63. Meryman, *Louis Armstrong: A Self Portrait*, 26.
64. Armstrong, *Swing That Music*, 48.
65. Armstrong, *Swing That Music*, 64–65.
66. Armstrong, *Swing That Music*, 48.
67. Gara, *The Baby Dodds Story*, 22.
68. Gara, *The Baby Dodds Story*, 22.
69. Streckfus, "Digest September 22, 1960."
70. Gara, *The Baby Dodds Story*, 79.
71. Gara, *The Baby Dodds Story*, 25.
72. Gara, *The Baby Dodds Story*, 25.
73. Gara, *The Baby Dodds Story*, fn. 32.
74. Gara, *The Baby Dodds Story*, 25.
75. Gara, *The Baby Dodds Story*, 29.
76. Gara, *The Baby Dodds Story*.
77. "Frankie and Johnny," Fate Marable's Society Syncopators (New Orleans: OKeh 40113, March 16, 1924).
78. Schacht, "Riverboat Jazz and the Story of a Legendary St. Louisian Who Made It Click," 5. http://www.doctorjazz.co.uk/marabletjr.html.
79. Schacht, "Riverboat Jazz and the Story of a Legendary St. Louisian Who Made It Click," 5. http://www.doctorjazz.co.uk/marabletjr.html.
80. Gara, *The Baby Dodds Story*, 31.
81. Gara, *The Baby Dodds Story*, 32.
82. Joseph Streckfus, "Manuscript, March 18, 1958," in Vertical Files (New Orleans: William Ransom Hogan Jazz Archive, Tulane University).
83. Streckfus, "Manuscript, March 18, 1958."
84. Streckfus, "Manuscript, March 18, 1958."
85. Streckfus, "Manuscript, March 18, 1958."
86. "Manuscript, February 20, 1958," in Vertical Files (New Orleans: William Ransom Hogan Jazz Archive, Tulane University); Kenney, *Jazz on the River*, 47.

87. Streckfus, "Manuscript, March 18, 1958."

88. "Japanese Sandman" was the first recording made by Paul Whiteman. Both Hickman and Whiteman recorded medleys of "Avalon" and "The Japanese Sandman." The sheet music for "The Japanese Sandman" had the first page of "Avalon" printed at the back. This was a common advertising strategy at the time to encourage further sales. Perhaps this is why the idea of a medley took hold. "The Japanese Sandman," by Richard A. Whiting and Raymond B. Egan (New York: Jerome H. Remick, 1920); Al Jolson and Vincent Rose, "Avalon" (New York: Jerome H Remick, 1920).

89. Streckfus, "Manuscript, March 18, 1958."

90. "Love Nest," Columbia A2955, New York (June 11, 1920); "A Young Man's Fancy," Columbia A2970, New York (July 10, 1920); "Avalon," Columbia A3322, New York (October 1, 1920). http://www.redhotjazz.com/hickman.htm.

91. Mr. and Mrs. Vernon Castle, *Modern Dancing* (New York: Harper & Row, 1914; repr., New York: Da Capo, 1980), Foreword.

92. Castle, *Modern Dancing*, 43.

93. Castle, *Modern Dancing*, 20.

94. Armstrong commented on the "famous Castle Walk" and considered the Castles "The greatest ballroom dance team ever known up to the time of Mr. Fred Astaire and his sister, Adele, and later, of course, Mr. Astaire and Ginger Rogers." Armstrong, *Swing That Music*, 11.

95. Al Jolson and Vincent Rose, "Avalon: Fox Trot Song" (New York: Jerome H. Remick, 1920).

96. The "Toodle" was a dance popular after 1917. It was a form of Fox Trot.

97. Small numbers were provided as suffixes to indicate which octave the notes were sung in. These are not shown.

98. Streckfus, "Manuscript, March 18, 1958."

99. Streckfus, "Manuscript, March 18, 1958."

100. John W. Work III, *American Negro Songs and Spirituals: 230 Folk Songs and Spirituals, Religious and Secular* (New York: Bonanza, 1940; repr., New York: Dover, 1998), 46.

101. The seventh of the G seventh chord is sounded on the second beat of measure 2.

102. Kenney, *Jazz on the River*, 48.

103. Streckfus, "Manuscript, March 18, 1958."

104. Chevan, "Riverboat Music from St. Louis and the Streckfus Steamboat Line," 164.

105. Chevan, "Riverboat Music from St. Louis and the Streckfus Steamboat Line," 165; Schuller, *The Swing Era: The Development of Jazz, 1930–1945*, 786–87.

106. DeDroit was among the best paid of the New Orleans bandleaders. He earned $68 a week leading the pit orchestra at the Orpheum Theatre. Johnny DeDroit, "Interview, December 4, 1969," in *Oral History Files*, ed. Betty B. Rankin, Richard B. Allen, and Keith V. Abramson (New Orleans: William Ransom Hogan Jazz Archive, Tulane University).

107. DeDroit recalled that he played the Grunewald Hotel for four years. DeDroit earned $25 a week for playing two hours a night. His sidemen earned $20 a week, which was $2 a week above union scale. DeDroit, "Interview, December 4, 1969."

108. Streckfus, "Manuscript, February 20, 1958."

109. Streckfus, "Manuscript, February 20, 1958."
110. Streckfus, "Manuscript, February 20, 1958."
111. Chevan, "Riverboat Music from St. Louis and the Streckfus Steamboat Line," 159.
112. Leon King, *Leon King Memoir: Jazz in the St. Louis Area: An Oral History Project* (Evansville: Southern Illinois University, 1982); Chevan, "Riverboat Music from St. Louis and the Streckfus Steamboat Line."
113. Streckfus, "Manuscript, March 18, 1958."
114. Streckfus, "Manuscript, March 18, 1958."
115. Streckfus, "Manuscript, March 18, 1958."
116. Streckfus, "Manuscript, February 20, 1958."
117. Brothers, *Louis Armstrong, in His Own Words*, 70.
118. Armstrong, *Swing That Music*, 68.
119. "The First Complete Pictorial Life Story of Louis Armstrong as Told to Inez Caveanaugh," 18.
120. Jackson, "Interview June 2, 1958."
121. George "Pops" Foster, "Interview Digest, April 21, 1957 (for *Life Magazine*)," in *Oral History Files*, ed. Nesuhi Ertegun and Robert Campbell (New Orleans: William Ransom Hogan Jazz Archive, Tulane University).
122. Stoddard, *Pops Foster: The Autobiography of a New Orleans Jazzman*, xviii.
123. Stoddard, *Pops Foster: The Autobiography of a New Orleans Jazzman*, Loc. 145.
124. This is explored further in an as yet unpublished essay for *Jazz Perspectives*. Vic Hobson, "Making the Changes: Countermelodies in the Basslines of George "Pops" Foster and Ed "Montudi" Garland."
125. Meryman, *Louis Armstrong: A Self Portrait*, 27.
126. "Storyville," *Satchmo: Collector's Copy*, 13.
127. Louis Armstrong, in Shapiro and Hentoff, *Hear Me Talkin' to Ya*, 104.

CHAPTER 11: "DIPPERMOUTH BLUES"

1. Stella Oliver, "Interview Digest, April 22, 1959."
2. Stella Oliver, "Interview Digest, April 22, 1959."
3. Volume 33, page 460, New Orleans, Louisiana, Marriage Records Index, 1831–1925. (Ancestry.com). Stella told her interviewers that she was married in 1912. Stella Oliver, "Interview Digest, April 22, 1959."
4. Edmond Souchon, "King Oliver: A Very Personal Memory," *Jazz Review* 3, no. 4 (1960): 8.
5. Preston Jackson, in Shapiro and Hentoff, *Hear Me Talkin' to Ya*, 41.
6. Richard M. Jones, in Shapiro and Hentoff, *Hear Me Talkin' to Ya*, 96.
7. Meryman, *Louis Armstrong: A Self Portrait*, 56.
8. Brothers, *Louis Armstrong, Master of Modernism*, 65.
9. Gushee, "The Improvisation of Louis Armstrong," 292.
10. Brothers, *Louis Armstrong, Master of Modernism*, 65.

11. John W. Work II, *Folk Song of the American Negro* (Nashville, TN: F. A. McKenzie, 1915), 92; Abbott, "'Play That Barber Shop Chord,'" 306.

12. Armstrong, "The First Complete Pictorial Life Story of Louis Armstrong as Told to Inez Caveanaugh," 18.

13. Armstrong, "Scanning the History of Jazz," 8 (Loughton, UK: National Jazz Archive).

14. Gushee, "The Improvisation of Louis Armstrong," 294.

15. Preston Jackson, in Shapiro and Hentoff, *Hear Me Talkin' to Ya*, 103.

16. Armstrong, "Scanning the History of Jazz"; *Esquire's World of Jazz*, ed. Lewis W. Gillenson (New York: Thomas Y. Crowell, 1975), 153.

17. Louis Armstrong, in Shapiro and Hentoff, *Hear Me Talkin' to Ya*, 104.

18. Gara, *The Baby Dodds Story*, 38.

19. Gara, *The Baby Dodds Story*.

20. Buster Bailey, in Shapiro and Hentoff, *Hear Me Talkin' to Ya*, 103.

21. Hardin-Armstrong, "Jazzmen Interviews."

22. Louis Armstrong, "Interview with Donald MacIsaac," Boston University radio station WBUR-FM, September 1951, Armstrong Vertical File (William Ransom Hogan Jazz Archive, Tulane University, New Orleans).

23. Shapiro and Hentoff, *Hear Me Talkin' to Ya*, 103.

24. Gara, *The Baby Dodds Story*, 36.

25. Gara, *The Baby Dodds Story*.

26. Gara., *The Baby Dodds Story*.

27. King Oliver and the Creole Jazz Band, "Dippermouth Blues" (Richmond, IN: Gennett 5132, April 6, 1923); "Dippermouth Blues" (Chicago: OKeh 8402-A, June 23, 1923).

28. Spaeth, *Barber Shop Ballads: A Book of Close Harmony*, 18.

29. It is convention in writing barbershop harmony that for clarity the lead and tenor voices are written an octave above where they sound.

30. Lewis F. Muir and William Tracy, "Play That Barber Shop Chord" (New York: J. Fred Helf, 1910).

31. King Oliver and the Creole Jazz Band, "Dippermouth Blues."

32. As transcribed by Brian Harker, "Louis Armstrong and Clarinet," *American Music* 21, no. 2 (2003): 145.

33. Meryman, *Louis Armstrong: A Self Portrait*, 38.

34. Elmer Schoebel and Herman Openneer Jr., "The Elmer Schoebel Story," *Doctor Jazz* 32 (1968): 6.

35. Louis Armstrong, *Louis Armstrong's 50 Hot Choruses for Cornet* (Chicago: Melrose Brothers, 1927; repr., *Louis Armstrong's 44 Trumpet Solos and 125 Jazz Breaks*, New York: Charles Hansen Music and Books, 1951). The breaks were given with a concert pitch piano chord and transposing breaks for B♭ cornet. The cornet breaks are transposed to concert pitch.

36. King Oliver and the Creole Jazz Band, "Dippermouth Blues." This melody is as given in David Littlefield, *Dixieland Fake Book*, vol. 1, 55. Also reproduced is Oliver's copyright deposit for the melody. Although some of the note timings are slightly different between the two versions, the pitch choices are much the same.

37. There is also the occasional appearance of G♯/A♭. This note is included in other blues scales constructed by other theorists. See, for example, Lou Harrison's blues scale in Rudi Blesh, *Shining Trumpets: A History of Jazz* (London: Cassell, 1949; repr., 4th edition, enlarged, 1958), 415. Musical Examples ex. 14 C.

38. Sargeant, *Jazz: Hot and Hybrid*, 160.
39. Musical Examples 14 C; Blesh, *Shining Trumpets*, 106–7.
40. Sargeant, *Jazz: Hot and Hybrid*, 167.
41. Sargeant, *Jazz: Hot and Hybrid*, 167–68.
42. King Oliver and the Creole Jazz Band, "Dippermouth Blues."
43. Porter, Ullman, and Hazell, *Jazz: From Its Origins to the Present*, 43.
44. Porter, Ullman, and Hazell, *Jazz: From Its Origins to the Present*.
45. King Oliver and the Creole Jazz Band, "Dippermouth Blues."
46. Sargeant, *Jazz: Hot and Hybrid*, 156.
47. Sargeant, *Jazz: Hot and Hybrid*, 198.
48. Sargeant, *Jazz: Hot and Hybrid*, 169.
49. Schuller, *Early Jazz: Its Roots and Musical Development*, 51.
50. Schuller, *Early Jazz: Its Roots and Musical Development*, 85.
51. Armstrong, "Joe Oliver Is Still King," 10.
52. Armstrong, "Scanning the History of Jazz," 8.
53. Transcription by Porter, Ullman, and Hazell, *Jazz: From Its Origins to the Present*, 43.
54. Bocage, "Interview Transcript, January 29, 1959."
55. Mutt Carey, in Shapiro and Hentoff, *Hear Me Talkin' to Ya*, 42.
56. Preston Jackson, in Shapiro and Hentoff, *Hear Me Talkin' to Ya*.
57. Tommy Brookins, in Shapiro and Hentoff, *Hear Me Talkin' to Ya*, 98.
58. Tommy Brookins, in Shapiro and Hentoff, *Hear Me Talkin' to Ya*.
59. Eddie Condon, *We Called It Music: A Generation of Jazz* (New York: H. Holt, 1947; repr., New York: Da Capo, 1992), 112; Kathy J. Ogren, *The Jazz Revolution: Twenties America and the Meaning of Jazz* (New York: Oxford University Press, 1989), 78.
60. Brothers, *Louis Armstrong, in His Own Words*, 50.

CHAPTER 12: FLETCHER HENDERSON: "THAT BIG FISH HORN VOICE OF HIS"

1. Walter C. Allen, *Hendersonia: The Music of Fletcher Henderson and His Musicians* (Highland Park, NJ: Walter C. Allen, 1973), 3.
2. Allen, *Hendersonia*, 2.
3. Allen, *Hendersonia*, 3.
4. Allen, *Hendersonia*, 4.
5. Allen, *Hendersonia*.
6. Fletcher Henderson, *The Scroll* 21, no. 4 (January 1917): 4; Allen, *Hendersonia*, 9.
7. Charles Wakefield Cadman, *The Vision of Sir Launfal* (New York: G. Schirmer, 1910).
8. Frank Albinder and Jeremy D. Jones, "Male Choirs: A Brief Historical Overview of the European Tradition of Male Singing Societies and Their Influence of the Development of Collegiate Glee Clubs in America (Part 2)," *Choral Journal* 49, no. 4 (2008): 87.

9. J. Merrill Knapp, "Samuel Webbe and the Glee," *Music and Letters* 33, no. 4 (1952): 347.

10. "Concert," *Weekly Louisianian*, June 29, 1872, 2; Buckingham, "Louis Armstrong and the Waifs' Home," 36.

11. Lynn Abbott and Doug Seroff, *To Do This, You Must Know How*, Kindle ed. (Jackson: University Press of Mississippi, 2013), 22.

12. Porter, Ullman, and Hazell, *Jazz: From Its Origins to the Present*, 121.

13. Allen, *Hendersonia*, 6–7.

14. Allen, *Hendersonia*, 7.

15. David Robertson, *W. C. Handy: The Life and Times of the Man Who Made the Blues* (New York: Alfred A. Knopf, 2009), 12.

16. David Suisman, "Co-Workers in the Kingdom of Culture: Black Swan Records and the Political Economy of African American Music," *Journal of American History* 90, no. 4 (2004): 1311.

17. Suisman, "Co-Workers in the Kingdom of Culture," 1301.

18. Suisman, "Co-Workers in the Kingdom of Culture," 1297.

19. Suisman, "Co-Workers in the Kingdom of Culture," 1302.

20. Locke, *The Negro and His Music*, 39.

21. David Mannes, Founder of MSSCP, quoted in R. Reid Badger, *A Life in Ragtime: A Biography of James Reese Europe* (New York: Oxford University Press, 1995), 61; Suisman, "Co-Workers in the Kingdom of Culture," 1303.

22. Suisman, "Co-Workers in the Kingdom of Culture," 1304.

23. W. E. B. Du Bois, "Phonograph Records," *Crisis*, February 1921, 152; Suisman, "Co-Workers in the Kingdom of Culture," 1304.

24. Du Bois, "Phonograph Records," 152; Suisman, "Co-Workers in the Kingdom of Culture," 1304.

25. Suisman, "Co-Workers in the Kingdom of Culture," 1306–7.

26. W. E. B. Du Bois, *The Souls of Black Folk* (Chicago: A. C. McClurg & Co., 1903; repr., New York: Vintage, 1990), 181.

27. Alain Locke and Winold Reiss, *The New Negro: An Interpretation* (New York: Albert & Charles Boni, 1925).

28. Schenbeck, "Music, Gender, and 'Uplift' in the 'Chicago Defender,' 1927–1937," 349.

29. Locke, *The Negro and His Music*, 70.

30. Locke, *The Negro and His Music*, 79.

31. Nathan Huggins, *Harlem Renaissance* (New York: Oxford University Press, 1971), 9–11; Ogren, *The Jazz Revolution*, 117.

32. Suisman, "Co-Workers in the Kingdom of Culture," 1305.

33. "Fletcher Henderson, as told to Felix Manskleid," *Jazz Monthly*, December 1957; Allen, *Hendersonia*, 13.

34. Harry H. Pace, letter November 17, 1939, in Roi Ottley and William J. Weatherby, *The Negro in New York: An Informal Social History* (New York: Oceana Publications, 1967), 233; Allen, *Hendersonia*, 13.

35. Ethel Waters, *His Eye Is on the Sparrow: An Autobiography by Ethel Waters and Charles Samuels* (New York: Doubleday, 1951; repr., Westport, CT: Greenwood Press, 1978), 134.

36. Suisman, "Co-Workers in the Kingdom of Culture," 1308.

37. Adam Gussow, "'Shoot Myself a Cop': Mamie Smith's 'Crazy Blues' as Social Text," *Callaloo* 25, no. 1 (2002): 9.

38. Suisman, "Co-Workers in the Kingdom of Culture," 1310.

39. Suisman, "Co-Workers in the Kingdom of Culture," 1309.

40. Waters, *His Eye Is on the Sparrow*, 146–47; Suisman, "Co-Workers in the Kingdom of Culture," 1310.

41. Suisman, "Co-Workers in the Kingdom of Culture," 1307.

42. Fletcher Henderson, Shapiro and Hentoff, *Hear Me Talkin' to Ya*, 203.

43. Lynn Abbott, "'For Ofays Only': An Annotated Calendar of Midnight Frolics at the Lyric Theater (Part 1)," *Jazz Archivist: A Newsletter of the William Ransom Hogan Jazz Archive* XVII (2003): 2.

44. Armstrong, *Swing That Music*, 27.

45. Abbott, "'For Ofays Only': An Annotated Calendar of Midnight Frolics at the Lyric Theater (Part 1)," 5.

46. Abbott, "'For Ofays Only': An Annotated Calendar of Midnight Frolics at the Lyric Theater (Part 1)."

47. Allen, *Hendersonia*, 7. It must have been on this visit to New Orleans that Henderson first met Armstrong, as Waters next appeared at the Lyric in February 1923; by that time Armstrong was in Chicago. Abbott, "'For Ofays Only': An Annotated Calendar of Midnight Frolics at the Lyric Theater (Part 1)," 6–7.

48. Fletcher Henderson, in Shapiro and Hentoff, *Hear Me Talkin' to Ya*, 203.

49. Armstrong, *Swing That Music*, 35.

50. Abbott, "'For Ofays Only': An Annotated Calendar of Midnight Frolics at the Lyric Theater (Part 1)," 3; Zutty Singleton, "Jazzmen Interview Notes," in Papers of Frederic Ramsey Jr., MSS 559 (New Orleans: Williams Research Center, Historic New Orleans Collection).

51. Abbott, "'For Ofays Only': An Annotated Calendar of Midnight Frolics at the Lyric Theater (Part 1)," 3; Karl Koenig, *Trinity of Early Jazz Leaders: John Robichaux, "Toots" Johnson, Claiborne Williams* (Running Springs, CA: Basin Street, undated), 10.

52. Abbott, "'For Ofays Only': An Annotated Calendar of Midnight Frolics at the Lyric Theater (Part 1)," 3.

53. Louis Armstrong, in Shapiro and Hentoff, *Hear Me Talkin' to Ya*, 203.

54. Allen, *Hendersonia*, 112.

55. Allen, *Hendersonia*, 118.

56. Lil Hardin, *Satchmo and Me* (Riverside, R LP 12–120).

57. Max Jones and John Chilton, *Louis: The Louis Armstrong Story 1900–1971* (Boston: Little, Brown, 1971), 80; Joshua Berrett, *Louis Armstrong and Paul Whiteman: Two Kings of Jazz* (New Haven: Yale University Press, 2004), 46.

58. Fletcher Henderson, in Shapiro and Hentoff, *Hear Me Talkin' to Ya*, 203.

59. Porter, Ullman, and Hazell, *Jazz: From Its Origins to the Present*, 121.

60. Hugues Panassié, *The Real Jazz* (New York: Smith & Durrell, 1942; repr., New York: A. S. Barnes, 1960), 198; Jeffrey Magee, "Before Louis: When Fletcher Henderson Was the 'Paul Whiteman of the Race,'" *American Music* 18, no. 4 (2000): 391.

61. Edward N. Waters, "Gershwin's 'Rhapsody in Blue,'" *Quarterly Journal of Current Acquisitions* 4, no. 3 (1947): 65–66.

62. Bruce Boyd Raeburn, "Early New Orleans Jazz in Theaters," *Louisiana History: The Journal of the Louisiana Historical Association* 43, no. 1 (2002): 50.

63. Magee, "Before Louis: When Fletcher Henderson Was the 'Paul Whiteman of the Race,'" 392.

64. *New York Clipper*, February 22, 1924. Magee, "Before Louis: When Fletcher Henderson Was the 'Paul Whiteman of the Race,'" 391.

65. Carl Engel, "Jazz: A Musical Discussion," *Atlantic Monthly* 130, no. 2 (1922); in Karl Koenig, ed., *Jazz in Print (1859–1929): An Anthology of Selected Early Readings in Jazz History* (Hillsdale, NY: Pendragon Press, 2002), 200.

66. Locke, *The Negro and His Music*, 79.

67. See the introduction to Scott Joplin, "Please Say You Will" (New York: M. L. Mantell, 1895). Brun Campbell, "From Rags to Ragtime Riches," *Jazz Journal*, July, 1949, wrote: "Joplin wrote his first two songs that year [1894] titled "A Picture of Her Face" and "Please Say You Will." [Otis] Saunders and Joplin formed the Medley Quartette that sang in and around Sedalia at parties, plugging Joplin's songs." As Peter Gammond has noted, "the song is obviously written with barber-shop type singing in mind." Peter Gammond, *Scott Joplin and the Ragtime Era* (Aylesbury, UK: Abacus, 1975), 121.

68. Schuller, *Early Jazz: Its Roots and Musical Development*, 260.

69. Jeffrey Magee, "Revisiting Fletcher Henderson's 'Copenhagen,'" *Journal of the American Musicological Society* 48, no. 1 (1995): 50.

70. Magee, "Revisiting Fletcher Henderson's 'Copenhagen,'" 50–52.

71. Blesh, *Shining Trumpets*, 278; Rudi Blesh, "This is Jazz Lectures" (San Francisco: Museum of Art, 1943) in *Shining Trumpets*.

72. Blesh, *Shining Trumpets*, 229.

73. Blesh, *Shining Trumpets*, 228.

74. Abbott, "'Play That Barber Shop Chord'"; Tim Brooks, *Lost Sounds*; Henry, "The Origins of Barbershop Harmony."

75. Trombonist George Brunies, for example, in Hobson, *Creating Jazz Counterpoint*, 104–5.

76. Edward Brooks, *The Young Louis Armstrong on Record: A Critical Survey of the Early Recordings, 1923–1928* (Lanham, MD: Scarecrow Press, 2002), 119.

77. Arthur Lange, *Arranging for the Modern Dance Orchestra* (New York: Robbins Music, 1926), 10.

78. Lange, *Arranging for the Modern Dance Orchestra*, 12.

79. Magee, *The Uncrowned King of Swing*, 76.

80. Fletcher Henderson and His Orchestra, "Copenhagen" (New York: Vocalion 14926, master 13929, October 30, 1924). Transposed from $B^\flat$ in Magee, *The Uncrowned King of Swing*, 83.

81. Magee, *The Uncrowned King of Swing: Fletcher Henderson and Big Band Jazz*, 76.

82. "Joe Smith Obituary," *Ripley Bee*, December 10, 1937. http://www.ohiomemory.org/cdm/singleitem/collection/p267401c01136/id/11719/rec/1.

83. Louis Metcalf, in Shapiro and Hentoff, *Hear Me Talkin' to Ya*, 206.
84. Magee, *The Uncrowned King of Swing*, 84.
85. Meryman, *Louis Armstrong: A Self Portrait*, 32.
86. Magee, *The Uncrowned King of Swing*, Loc. 1183.
87. Magee, "Revisiting Fletcher Henderson's 'Copenhagen,'" 64. Magee provides a transcription of matrix 13928 and the variations found on matrix 13929 of Fletcher Henderson and His Orchestra, "Copenhagen" (New York: Vocalion 14926, master 13928, October 30, 1924); "Copenhagen."
88. William H. Youngren, "Louis," *Hudson Review* 29, no. 2 (1976): 243.
89. Meryman, *Louis Armstrong: A Self Portrait*, 43.
90. Armstrong, "The First Complete Pictorial Life Story of Louis Armstrong as Told to Inez Caveanaugh," 18.
91. Magee, "Revisiting Fletcher Henderson's 'Copenhagen,'" 49.
92. Louis Armstrong, quoted in Fletcher Henderson, "He Made the Band Swing," *Record Changer* 9, no. 6–7 (1950): 16 (Loughton, UK: National Jazz Archive).
93. Brothers, *Louis Armstrong: In His Own Words*, 63.
94. Magee, "Revisiting Fletcher Henderson's 'Copenhagen,'" 49.
95. William C. "Buster" Bailey, in Shapiro and Hentoff, *Hear Me Talkin' to Ya*, 77.
96. William C. "Buster" Bailey, in Shapiro and Hentoff, *Hear Me Talkin' to Ya*.
97. William C. "Buster" Bailey, in Shapiro and Hentoff, *Hear Me Talkin' to Ya*.
98. William C. "Buster" Bailey, in Shapiro and Hentoff, *Hear Me Talkin' to Ya*.
99. William C. "Buster" Bailey, in Shapiro and Hentoff, *Hear Me Talkin' to Ya*, 78.
100. William C. "Buster" Bailey, in Shapiro and Hentoff, *Hear Me Talkin' to Ya*.
101. Meryman, *Louis Armstrong: A Self Portrait*, 32.
102. *Brothers, Louis Armstrong, Master of Modernism* 496.
103. Henderson, "He Made the Band Swing," 15.
104. Henderson, "He Made the Band Swing."
105. Henderson, "He Made the Band Swing."
106. Henderson, "He Made the Band Swing."
107. Hardin-Armstrong, "Jazzmen Interviews." In Papers of Frederic Ramsey Jr. (New Orleans: Williams Research Center, Historic New Orleans Collection).
108. Armstrong, "The First Complete Pictorial Life Story of Louis Armstrong as Told to Inez Caveanaugh," 18.
109. Hardin-Armstrong, "Jazzmen Interviews."

CHAPTER 13: "THE PRIDE OF RACE": WHEN LOUIS SANG WITH ERSKINE TATE

1. Armstrong, *Swing That Music*, 84.
2. Erskine Tate's Vendome Symphony Orchestra Including a Review of his Chicago Recording Sessions 1923 & 1926. http://littlebeatrecords.dk/LittleBeatDK/Projekter_files/Erskine%20Tate's%20Vendome%20Symphony%20Orchestra.pdf.
3. Erskine Tate's Vendome Symphony Orchestra Including a Review of his Chicago Recording Sessions 1923 & 1926. http://littlebeatrecords.dk/LittleBeatDK/Projekter_files/Erskine%20Tate's%20Vendome%20Symphony%20Orchestra.pdf.

4. Meryman, *Louis Armstrong: A Self Portrait*, 33.

5. Goffin, *Horn of Plenty*, 215.

6. Meryman, *Louis Armstrong: A Self Portrait*, 33. It is possible that Armstrong had played trumpet on an earlier recording with Perry Bradford in November 2, 1925. See Gushee, "The Improvisation of Louis Armstrong," 329.

7. Armstrong, "The First Complete Pictorial Life Story of Louis Armstrong as Told to Inez Caveanaugh," 19.

8. Brothers, *Louis Armstrong, in His Own Words*, 32.

9. St. Cyr, "Interview August 27, 1958."

10. Johnny St. Cyr, "Interview January 31, 1969," in William Russell Jazz Collection MSS 519, ed. William Russell (New Orleans: Williams Research Center, Historic New Orleans Collection).

11. Edward "Kid" Ory, in Shapiro and Hentoff, *Hear Me Talkin' to Ya*, 109.

12. James L. Dickerson, *Just for a Thrill: Lil Hardin Armstrong, First Lady of Jazz* (New York: Cooper Square Press, 2002), 130.

13. Christopher Hillman, Roy Middleton, and Hennie van Veelo, *Richard M. Jones: Forgotten Man of Jazz* (London: Cygnet Productions, 1997), 10.

14. Gene H. Anderson, *The Original Hot Five Recordings of Louis Armstrong* (New York: Pendragon Press, 2007), 57.

15. Ricky Riccardi, http://dippermouth.blogspot.co.uk/2011/02/heebie-jeebies.html.

16. Matrix numbers 80001 to 80198.

17. Brothers, *Louis Armstrong, Master of Modernism*, 212.

18. Charles Straight and Gene Greene, "King of the Bungaloos" (Chicago: Music House Laemmle, 1909), Mississippi State University Digital Collection; Gene Greene, "King of the Bungaloos," Columbia A-0994 (February 17, 1911); Victor 5854 (April 19, 1911); Emerson 7228 (December 1, 1916); Victor 18266 (March 9, 1917).

19. Ben Harney, "Cake Walk in the Sky" (New York: M. Witmark & Sons, 1899).

20. Stein, *Music Is My Life*, 1.

21. Louis Armstrong, "Interview for *Voice of America*," 1956. http://dippermouth.blogspot.co.uk/2011/02/heebie-jeebies.html.

22. *Esquire's World of Jazz*, 1951; Brothers, *Louis Armstrong, in His Own Words*, 133.

23. Anderson, *The Original Hot Five Recordings of Louis Armstrong*, 55.

24. Louis Armstrong and His Hot Five, "Heebie Jeebies" (Chicago: OKeh 8300, February 26, 1926).

25. Berrett, *Louis Armstrong and Paul Whiteman: Two Kings of Jazz*, 83.

26. Ferdinand "Jelly Roll" Morton, "Transcript of the 1938 Library of Congress Recordings of Jelly Roll Morton," ed. John Szwed, CD set (Washington, DC: Library of Congress, 2006), 51. A February 27, 1958, *Chicago Defender* obituary for Joe Simms (or Sims) confirms his Vicksburg nativity, and states that he was active in the profession by 1905. Simms was in New Orleans as early as 1909, when he appeared at the Temple Theater singing "Don't Dog Me Around." Abbott and Seroff, "'They Cert'ly Sound Good to Me,'" 413.

27. Louis Armstrong, "Interview May 5, 1970," in William Russell Jazz Collection MSS 519, ed. William Russell (New Orleans: Williams Research Center, Historic New Orleans Collection).

28. Armstrong, "Interview May 5, 1970."

29. Nadine George-Graves, *The Royalty of Negro Vaudeville: The Whitman Sisters and the Negotiation of Race, Gender and Class in African American Theater, 1900–1940* (New York: St. Martin's Press, 2000), 44.

30. Henry T. Sampson, *Blacks in Blackface: A Source Book on Early Black Musical Shows* (Metuchen, NJ: Scarecrow Press, 1980), 351.

31. Sampson, *Blacks in Blackface*.

32. Bernard L. Paterson Jr., *Profiles of African American Stage Performers and Theater People 1816–1960* (London: Greenwood Press, 2001), 45.

33. Marshall and Jean Stearns, *Jazz Dance: The Story of American Dance* (New York: Da Capo, 1968; repr., Berkeley, CA: Perseus Books Group, 1994), 27.

34. Stearns, *Jazz Dance: The Story of American Dance*.

35. Doug Seroff and Lynn Abbott, "The Life and Death of Pioneer Bluesman Butler 'String Beans' May: 'Been Here, Made His Quick Duck, and Got Away,'" *Journal of the Alabama Folklife Association* 5 (2002): 9, 47.

36. Seroff and Abbott, "The Life and Death of Pioneer Bluesman Butler 'String Beans' May," 11.

37. Seroff and Abbott, "The Life and Death of Pioneer Bluesman Butler 'String Beans' May," 43, 42–43.

38. Seroff and Abbott, "The Life and Death of Pioneer Bluesman Butler 'String Beans' May," 43, 43.

39. Rust, *Jazz Records 1897–1942*, 213.

40. Handy, *Father of the Blues*.

41. W. C. Handy, *Blues: An Anthology* (New York: Albert & Charles Boni, 1926; repr., New York: Macmillan, 1974), 10–11.

42. Handy, *Blues: An Anthology*, 11. The term "swipe" is described by Sigmund Spaeth as harmony "stolen from the altar of the gods"; Spaeth, *Barber Shop Ballads and How to Sing Them*, 9.

43. W. C. Handy in Dr. Ysaye Maria Barnwell, *W. C. Handy's Blues* (Public Radio International) www.wchandyblues.org.

44. Handy, *Blues: An Anthology*, 11; Dr. Ysaye Maria Barnwell, *W. C. Handy's Blues* (Public Radio International) www.wchandyblues.org.

45. Handy, *Father of the Blues*, 142.

46. Handy, *Father of the Blues*, 143. In his autobiography, Handy calls the tune "Got No More Home Than a Dog."

47. Handy, *Father of the Blues*; W. C. Handy, "Interview Transcript May 9, 1938," in Folklife Collection (Washington, DC: Library of Congress). Handy published the same song titled "Got No Mo' Home Dan a Dog," and adapted it to become "Friendless Blues" (1926).

48. Handy, *Blues: An Anthology*, 30.

49. Handy, *Blues: An Anthology*, 30.

50. Handy, *Blues: An Anthology*, 30.

51. "W. C. Handy Interview with George Avakian," on *Louis Armstrong Plays W. C. Handy* (Columbia CD, CL591); Berrett, *Louis Armstrong and Paul Whiteman: Two Kings of Jazz*, 184.

52. "W. C. Handy Interview with George Avakian."

53. Dorothy Scarborough, "The 'Blues' as Folk Song," *Folklore Society of Texas*, 1916; Karl Koenig, *Evolution of Ragtime and Blues to Jazz* (Running Springs, CA: Basin Street, undated), 117–18.

54. James Poling, "New Sounds from the Crib House," in *Esquire's World of Jazz*, 27.

55. E. C. Perrow, "Songs and Rhymes from the South," *Journal of American Folklore* 28, no. 108 (1915): 147.

56. Clarinet and cornet player Wooden Joe Nicholas (b. New Orleans, 1883) believed that Bolden may have composed the song himself. Joseph "Wooden Joe" Nicholas, "Interview Digest, November 12, 1956," in *Oral History Files*, ed. William Russell and Charlie DeVore (New Orleans: William Ransom Hogan Jazz Archive, Tulane University).

57. Handy, *Blues: An Anthology*, 55, 75.

58. "W. C. Handy Interview with George Avakian."

59. "W. C. Handy Interview with George Avakian."

60. "W. C. Handy Interview with George Avakian."

61. "W. C. Handy Interview with George Avakian." Handy made a similar comment on the "pride of race" about Mamie Smith's recording of "Crazy Blues" (1920). Dr. Ysaye Maria Barnwell, W. C. Handy's Blues, *Public Radio International*, www.wchandyblues.org.

62. Bessie Smith, "Careless Love" (New York: Columbia 14083D, May 26, 1925); Rust, *Jazz Records 1897–1942*, 1565.

63. Hobson, *Creating Jazz Counterpoint*, 67–70.

CHAPTER 14: LIL'S HOT SHOTS

1. Gerhard Kubik, *Africa and the Blues* (Jackson: University Press of Mississippi, 1999), 105.

2. Hodeir, *Jazz: Its Evolution and Essence*, 143.

3. Schuller, *Early Jazz: Its Roots and Musical Development*, 38.

4. Schuller, *Early Jazz: Its Roots and Musical Development*, 39.

5. Joshua Berrett, "Louis Armstrong and Opera," *Musical Quarterly* 76, no. 2 (1992); Peter Ecklund, "'Louis Licks' and Nineteenth-Century Cornet Etudes: The Roots of Melodic Improvisation as Seen in the Jazz Style of Louis Armstrong," *Historic Brass Society Journal* 13, no. 1 (2001).

6. Ecklund, "'Louis Licks' and Nineteenth-Century Cornet Etudes."

7. Ecklund, "'Louis Licks' and Nineteenth-Century Cornet Etudes."

8. Ecklund, "'Louis Licks' and Nineteenth-Century Cornet Etudes," 90.

9. Meryman, *Louis Armstrong: A Self Portrait*, 17.

10. Meryman, *Louis Armstrong: A Self Portrait*, 55.

11. Van Der Merwe, *Origins of the Popular Style*, 264–66.

12. Riccardi, "You've Got to Appreciate All Kinds of Music: Review of Thomas Brothers, *Louis Armstrong: Master of Modernism*," 80.

13. Armstrong, "The First Complete Pictorial Life Story of Louis Armstrong as Told to Inez Caveanaugh," 18.

14. Riccardi, "You've Got to Appreciate All Kinds of Music: Review of Thomas Brothers, *Louis Armstrong: Master of Modernism*," 81; see also Riccardi, *What a Wonderful World: The Magic of Louis Armstrong's Later Years*, 49.

15. Armstrong, *Swing That Music*, 70. In *Horn of Plenty*, Hardin was playing at the Dreamland when Armstrong first played with Oliver at the Lincoln Garden, and she subsequently joined the band. Goffin, *Horn of Plenty*, 164–65.

16. Armstrong, *Swing That Music*, 71.

17. Lillian Hardin-Armstrong, "Interview Digest July 1, 1959," in *Oral History*, ed. William Russell (New Orleans: William Ransom Hogan Jazz Archive, Tulane University).

18. *Twelfth Census of the United States, 1900*, Memphis, Tennessee, Ward 10, Supervisor's District 10, Enumeration District 94, sheet 5B; *Thirteenth Census of the United States, 1910*, Memphis City, Tennessee, Ward 10, Supervisor's District 10, Enumeration District 168, sheet 1B (Ancestry.com).

19. Hardin-Armstrong, "Interview Digest July 1, 1959."

20. Hardin-Armstrong, "Interview Digest July 1, 1959."

21. Hardin-Armstrong, "Interview Digest July 1, 1959."

22. Hardin-Armstrong, "Interview Digest July 1, 1959."

23. Dickerson, *Just for a Thrill: Lil Hardin Armstrong, First Lady of Jazz*, 26–27.

24. Dickerson, *Just for a Thrill: Lil Hardin Armstrong, First Lady of Jazz*, 135; *Chicago Defender*, June 9, 1928, 6; Harker, *Louis Armstrong's Hot Five and Hot Seven Recordings*, 77.

25. Armstrong, *Swing That Music*, 71.

26. Hardin-Armstrong, "*Jazzmen* Interviews."

27. Berrett, *Louis Armstrong and Paul Whiteman: Two Kings of Jazz*, 70.

28. Preston Jackson, in Shapiro and Hentoff, *Hear Me Talkin' to Ya*, 102.

29. Gushee, "The Improvisation of Louis Armstrong," 298, fn., 327.

30. Gushee, "The Improvisation of Louis Armstrong," 298.

31. This knowledge may also have been gained in part from other New Orleans musicians. Alfred Williams said that Armstrong admired Buddy Petit's use of "diminishes" with reference to the closing measures of "Cornet Chop Suey." In fact, the runs on Armstrong's recording are minor and not diminished, but it does suggest that there was an awareness among some New Orleans musicians of the significance of diminished harmony in Armstrong's playing. Alfred Williams, "Interview Summary October 13, 1961," in *Oral History Files*, ed. Richard B. Allen (New Orleans: William Ransom Hogan Jazz Archive, Tulane University).

32. Osgood, *So This Is Jazz*, 57.

33. Arnold Schoenberg, *Theory of Harmony* (Vienna: Universal Editions, 1911; repr., London: Faber & Faber, 1978), 193.

34. According to Schoenberg, diminished chords were often used in classical music to represent "pain, excitement, anger, or some other strong feeling." They would continue to be used in this capacity by pianists accompanying silent films.

35. Gushee, "The Improvisation of Louis Armstrong," 298.

36. Armstrong, *Satchmo: My Life in New Orleans*, 76.

37. Eva Taylor with Clarence Williams' Blue Five, "Coal Cart Blues" (New York: OKeh 8245, October 8, 1925). Transcribed by Scott Sproxton.
38. Gushee, "The Improvisation of Louis Armstrong," 298.
39. Harker, *Louis Armstrong's Hot Five and Hot Seven Recordings*, 121.
40. Harker, *Louis Armstrong's Hot Five and Hot Seven Recordings*.
41. Spaeth, *Barber Shop Ballads: A Book of Close Harmony*, 19.
42. Sargeant, *Jazz: Hot and Hybrid*, 163.
43. David Evans, "Musical Innovation in the Blues of Blind Lemon Jefferson," *Black Music Research Journal* 20, no. 1 (2000): 89.
44. Schuller, *Early Jazz: Its Roots and Musical Development*, 105; Berrett, *Louis Armstrong and Paul Whiteman: Two Kings of Jazz*, 73.
45. Berrett, *Louis Armstrong and Paul Whiteman: Two Kings of Jazz*, 74.
46. Brothers, *Louis Armstrong, in His Own Words*, xviii.
47. Anderson, *The Original Hot Five Recordings of Louis Armstrong*, 117; Louis Armstrong and His Hot Five, "Skid-Dat-De-Dat" (Chicago: OKeh 8436, November 16, 1925).
48. Wolfgang A. Mozart, "Symphony No. 41 in C major K551 'Jupiter'" (Leipzig: Eulenburg Study Edition, 1985). The harmony of the second measure could also be interpreted as a F6 chord with the third omitted.
49. Schuller, *Early Jazz: Its Roots and Musical Development*, 105.
50. Schuller, *Early Jazz: Its Roots and Musical Development*, 105–6.
51. William Bauer, "Louis Armstrong's 'Skid Dat De Dat': Timbral Organization in an Early Scat Solo," *Jazz Perspectives* 1, no. 2 (2007): 133.
52. Bauer, "Louis Armstrong's 'Skid Dat De Dat': Timbral Organization in an Early Scat Solo,"134.
53. Bauer, "Louis Armstrong's 'Skid Dat De Dat': Timbral Organization in an Early Scat Solo,"154; Louis Armstrong and His Hot Five, "Skid-Dat-De-Dat."
54. *Esquire's World of Jazz*, 1951, Brothers, *Louis Armstrong, in His Own Words*, 131.
55. Berrett, *Louis Armstrong and Paul Whiteman: Two Kings of Jazz*, 72–73.
56. Frank Tirro, *Jazz: A History* (New York: W.W. Norton, 1993), 192.
57. Berrett, *Louis Armstrong and Paul Whiteman: Two Kings of Jazz*, 72.
58. Sargeant, *Jazz: Hot and Hybrid*, 155.

CHAPTER 15: THE HOT FIVE AND SEVEN

1. Gene H. Anderson, "The Origin of Armstrong's Hot Fives and Hot Sevens," *College Music Symposium* 43 (2003): 14. Ralph Peer claimed to have coined the term "race record." Anderson, "The Origin of Armstrong's Hot Fives and Hot Sevens," 17.
2. Anderson, "The Origin of Armstrong's Hot Fives and Hot Sevens."
3. Ralph Peer, "Interview with Ralph Peer" by Liliane Borgeson (Library of the University of North Carolina); Anderson, "The Origin of Armstrong's Hot Fives and Hot Sevens."
4. Clarence Williams' Blue Five recording sessions with Louis Armstrong for OKeh, October 17, 1924; November 6, 1924; November 25, 1924; November 28, 1924; January 8, 1925; March 4, 1925; October 6, 1925; October 8, 1925; October 26, 1925.

5. Edward "Kid" Ory, in Shapiro and Hentoff, *Hear Me Talkin' to Ya*, 109. Peer's involvement with the Clarence Williams and Armstrong Hot Five recordings is borne out by Barry Mazor, *Ralph Peer and the Making of Popular Roots Music* (Chicago: Chicago Review Press, 2015), 63–67.

6. Anderson, "The Origin of Armstrong's Hot Fives and Hot Sevens," 17.

7. Anderson, "The Origin of Armstrong's Hot Fives and Hot Sevens."

8. Anderson, *The Original Hot Five Recordings of Louis Armstrong*, 75.

9. Anderson, "The Origin of Armstrong's Hot Fives and Hot Sevens," 17.

10. Ory, "The Hot Five Sessions," 17, 45; McCusker, *Creole Trombone*, 160–61.

11. Ory, "The Hot Five Sessions," 17, 45.

12. Ory, "The Hot Five Sessions," 17, 45.

13. Ory, "The Hot Five Sessions," 17, 45.

14. Ory, "The Hot Five Sessions," 17, 45.

15. Ory, "The Hot Five Sessions," 17, 45.

16. The discussion around Armstrong's "Gut Bucket Blues" solo is expanded in Hobson, *Creating Jazz Counterpoint*, 124–25.

17. St. Cyr, "Interview January 31, 1969."

18. St. Cyr, "Interview Digest, August 27, 1958."

19. For a transcription of St. Cyr's introductory chorus, see Anderson, "The Origin of Armstrong's Hot Fives and Hot Sevens," 20.

20. Louis Armstrong and His Hot Five, "Gut Bucket Blues" (Chicago: OKeh 8261, November 12, 1925). Transcribed in Peter Ecklund, *Great Trumpet Solos of Louis Armstrong* (New York: Chas. Colin Publications, undated). For further transcriptions of Armstrong's solo and comparison with, Ory's, Hardin's, and Dodds's solos, see Anderson, "The Origin of Armstrong's Hot Fives and Hot Sevens," 23.

21. It could be that Johnny St. Cyr on banjo actually played an A diminished chord (see Ex. 30, m. 9).

22. Spaeth, *Barber Shop Ballads and How to Sing Them*, 6. Spaeth numbered the fundamental cadences slightly differently in his two books on barbershop harmony. The principle was still the same: it was the tenor and baritone voices that changed their notes.

23. Harker, *Louis Armstrong's Hot Five and Hot Seven Recordings*, 124.

24. Sippie Wallace, "Have You Ever Been Down?" (Chicago: OKeh 8499, May 6, 1927). Transcribed by Brian Harker.

25. Transposed from G major; Spaeth, *Barber Shop Ballads and How to Sing Them*, 14.

26. Transposed from F major.

27. Louis Armstrong and His Hot Seven, "Gully Low Blues" (Chicago: OKeh 8474, May 14, 1927). Transcribed in Ecklund, *Great Trumpet Solos of Louis Armstrong*, 18.

28. Armstrong and Seven. Transcribed in Ecklund, *Great Trumpet Solos of Louis Armstrong*, 18.

29. Louis Armstrong and His Hot Five, "I'm Not Rough" (Chicago: OKeh 8551, December 10, 1927).

30. Schuller, *Early Jazz: Its Roots and Musical Development*, 85–86.

31. Anderson's footnote: "Edward 'Kid' Ory and Lester Koenig, 'The Hot Five Sessions,'" *The Record Changer* (July-August 1950), 17." "The Savoy Ballroom complex, including the Regal Theater, was opened on Thanksgiving night in 1927 at 47th Street and South Parkway (currently Martin Luther King Drive), and the Regal Theater opened on February 4, 1928." William Howland Kenney, *Chicago Jazz: A Cultural History, 1904–1930* (New York: Oxford University Press, 1993), 162.

32. McCusker, *Creole Trombone*, 160–61; Ory, "The Hot Five Sessions," 17, 45.

33. Gushee, "The Improvisation of Louis Armstrong," 307.

34. Louis Armstrong and His Hot Five, "Savoy Blues" (Chicago: OKeh 8535, December 13, 1927). Transcribed in Ecklund, *Great Trumpet Solos of Louis Armstrong*, 24.

35. Hugues Panassié, *Louis Armstrong* (New York: Da Capo, 1971), 49.

36. Panassié, *Louis Armstrong*.

37. Harker, *Louis Armstrong's Hot Five and Hot Seven Recordings*, 74–75.

38. Collier, *Louis Armstrong: An American Genius*, 178.

CHAPTER 16: "I FIGURE SINGING AND PLAYING IS THE SAME"

1. Louis Armstrong and His Hot Five, "Muskrat Ramble" (Chicago: OKeh 8300, February 26, 1926). Transcribed in Ecklund, *Great Trumpet Solos of Louis Armstrong*, 9.

2. Schuller, *Early Jazz: Its Roots and Musical Development*, 99.

3. Hodeir, *Jazz: Its Evolution and Essence*, 58.

4. Tirro, *Jazz: A History*, 176.

5. Schuller, *Early Jazz: Its Roots and Musical Development*, 104.

6. Lisa Mae Alix. Her name is sometimes spelled May Alix.

7. Stanley Dance, *The World of Earl Hines* (Boston: Crescendo, 1977), 49.

8. Louis Armstrong and His Hot Five, "Big Butter and Egg Man" (Chicago: OKeh 8423, November 16, 1926). Transcribed in Ecklund, *Great Trumpet Solos of Louis Armstrong*, 12.

9. For further discussion of chord extensions of sixths and ninths, see Gushee, "The Improvisation of Louis Armstrong," 291–334.

10. Brothers, *Louis Armstrong, Master of Modernism*, 257.

11. Hodeir, *Jazz: Its Evolution and Essence*, 56.

12. Berrett, *Louis Armstrong and Paul Whiteman: Two Kings of Jazz*, 81.

13. Schuller, *Early Jazz: Its Roots and Musical Development*, 105.

14. Dance, *The World of Earl Hines*.

15. Brian Harker, "Louis Armstrong, Eccentric Dance, and the Evolution of Jazz on the Eve of Swing," *Journal of the American Musicological Society* 61, no. 1 (2008): 67.

16. Stearns, *Jazz Dance: The Story of American Dance*.

17. Harker, "Louis Armstrong, Eccentric Dance, and the Evolution of Jazz on the Eve of Swing," 97.

18. Harker, "Louis Armstrong, Eccentric Dance, and the Evolution of Jazz on the Eve of Swing," 98.

19. Harker suggests that the rhythm of the second half of the bridge may also be inspired by Brown and McGraw. He argues, "The lengthy succession of eight-quarter-eight

figures (mm. 20–22), though atypical for Armstrong and other jazz soloists of this time, was a standard combination among tap dancers." Harker, *Louis Armstrong's Hot Five and Hot Seven Recordings*, 62.

20. Van Der Merwe, *Origins of the Popular Style*, 251.
21. Sargeant, *Jazz: Hot and Hybrid*, 200.
22. Sargeant, *Jazz: Hot and Hybrid*, 198.
23. Samuel B. Charters, *The Country Blues* (New York: Rinehart, 1959; repr., London: Jazz Book Club, 1961), 25.
24. *Ada Evening News* January 4, 1905 (Ancestry.Com).
25. Charters, *The Country Blues*, 25. Charters did not explain how he got this information, but it is possible that he was able to interview Wand, as he lived until 1961.
26. Charters, *The Country Blues*, 26. Copyright was granted on September 6, 1912 (United States Copyright Office, Library of Congress).
27. Hart A. Wand, "The Dallas Blues" (1912), thirteenth edition (Performing Arts Reading Room, Library of Congress).
28. Peter C. Muir, *Long Lost Blues: Popular Blues in America, 1850–1920* (Chicago: University of Illinois Press, 2010), 76.
29. Harker, *Louis Armstrong's Hot Five and Hot Seven Recordings*, 68.
30. Harker, *Louis Armstrong's Hot Five and Hot Seven Recordings*, 68–69.
31. Harker, *Louis Armstrong's Hot Five and Hot Seven Recordings*, 68–69.
32. Harker, *Louis Armstrong's Hot Five and Hot Seven Recordings*, 69.
33. *Esquire's World of Jazz*, 1951; Brothers, *Louis Armstrong, in His Own Words*, 128.
34. Louis Armstrong and His Hot Five, "Potato Head Blues" (Chicago: OKeh 8503, May 10, 1927). Transcribed in Ecklund, *Great Trumpet Solos of Louis Armstrong*, 16–17.
35. Jones and Chilton, *Louis: The Louis Armstrong Story 1900–1971*, 214–15.
36. F-minor six and D-minor seventh flatted fifth are inversions of the same chord, as they contain the same chord tones.
37. Sampson, *Blacks in Blackface*, 448.
38. Sampson, *Blacks in Blackface*, 448.
39. *Esquire's World of Jazz*, 1951; Brothers, *Louis Armstrong, in His Own Words*, 135.
40. Brooks, *The Young Louis Armstrong on Record*, 465.
41. Brooks, *The Young Louis Armstrong on Record*, 505.
42. Brooks, *The Young Louis Armstrong on Record*, 465; Louis Armstrong and His Orchestra, "Basin Street Blues" (Chicago: OKeh 8690, December 4, 1928).
43. Schuller, *Early Jazz: Its Roots and Musical Development*, 130.
44. Louis Armstrong and His Orchestra, "Basin Street Blues." Author's transcription.
45. Dance, *The World of Earl Hines*, 7.
46. Dance, *The World of Earl Hines*, 10.
47. Dance, *The World of Earl Hines*, 9.
48. Dance, *The World of Earl Hines*, 14.
49. Dance, *The World of Earl Hines*.
50. Dance, *The World of Earl Hines*.
51. Dance, *The World of Earl Hines*, 13.

52. Dance, *The World of Earl Hines*.
53. Dance, *The World of Earl Hines*, 14.
54. Dance, *The World of Earl Hines*, 23.
55. Armstrong, *Swing That Music*, 87.
56. Armstrong, *Swing That Music*.
57. Val Hicks, *The Six Roots of Barbershop Harmony* (Nashville, TN: Barbershop Harmony Society, 2003), 52. SEBSQSA is now known as the Barbershop Harmony Society.
58. Louis Armstrong, Interview with Richard Hadlock (San Francisco, February 1962), in Berrett, *Louis Armstrong Companion: Eight Decades of Commentary*, 26.
59. Sargeant, *Jazz: Hot and Hybrid*, 197–98.
60. Engel, "Jazz: A Musical Discussion." http://www.theatlantic.com/past/docs/unbound/jazz/cengel.htm.
61. Locke, *The Negro and His Music*, 79.
62. Dean Snyder, "Chautauqua and Male Quartets," *The Harmonizer*, January–February 1968, with reference to Harrison and Detzer, *Culture under Canvas*, in Hicks, 9.
63. Averill, *Four Parts, No Waiting*, 98–99.
64. Abbott, "'Play That Barber Shop Chord'"; Hobson, "Plantation Song: Delius, Barbershop, and the Blues."
65. Frédéric Döhl, "From Harmonic Style to Genre: The Early History (1890s–1940s) of the Uniquely American Musical Term Barbershop," *American Music* 32, no. 2 (2014): 155; Abbott and Seroff, *Out of Sight: The Rise of African American Popular Music 1889–1895*, 301.
66. Döhl, "From Harmonic Style to Genre: The Early History (1890s–1940s) of the Uniquely American Musical Term Barbershop," 133.

BIBLIOGRAPHY

BOOKS

Abbott, Lynn, and Doug Seroff. *Out of Sight: The Rise of African American Popular Music 1889–1895.* Jackson: University Press of Mississippi, 2002.

———. *Ragged but Right: Black Travelling Shows, "Coon Songs," and the Dark Pathway to Blues and Jazz.* Jackson: University Press of Mississippi, 2007.

———. *To Do This, You Must Know How.* Kindle ed. Jackson: University Press of Mississippi, 2013.

Allen, Walter C. *Hendersonia: The Music of Fletcher Henderson and His Musicians.* Highland Park, NJ: Walter C. Allen, 1973.

Allen, William Francis, Charles Pickard Ware, and Lucy McKim Garrison. *Slave Songs of the United States.* New York: A. Simpson & Co., 1867. New York: Dover, 1995.

Anderson, Gene H. *The Original Hot Five Recordings of Louis Armstrong.* New York: Pendragon Press, 2007.

Armstrong, Louis. *Louis Armstrong's 50 Hot Choruses for Cornet.* Chicago: Melrose Brothers, 1927.

———. *Louis Armstrong's 44 Trumpet Solos and 125 Jazz Breaks.* New York: Charles Hansen Music and Books, 1951.

———. *Louis Armstrong, in His Own Words: Selected Writings.* Edited by Thomas Brothers. Oxford: Oxford University Press, 2001.

———. *Satchmo: My Life in New Orleans.* London: Peter Davies, 1955. London: Sedgwick & Jackson, 1957.

———. *Swing That Music.* New York: Longmans, Green, 1936. New York: Da Capo, 1995.

Asbury, Herbert. *The French Quarter: An Informal History of the New Orleans Underworld.* London: Alfred A. Knopf, 1936. London: Basic Books, 2008.

Asher, Sally. *Stories from the St. Louis Cemeteries of New Orleans.* Charleston, SC: History Press, 2015.

Averill, Gage. *Four Parts, No Waiting: A Social History of Barbershop Harmony.* New York: Oxford University Press, 2003.

Badger, R. Reid. *A Life in Ragtime: A Biography of James Reese Europe.* New York: Oxford University Press, 1995.

Bechet, Sidney. *Treat It Gentle: An Autobiography.* Kindle ed. London: Cassell, 1960. New York: Da Capo, 1978.

Bergreen, Lawrence. *Louis Armstrong: An Extravagant Life.* London: Harper Collins, 1997.

Berrett, Joshua. *Louis Armstrong and Paul Whiteman: Two Kings of Jazz*. New Haven: Yale University Press, 2004.

———, ed. *Louis Armstrong Companion: Eight Decades of Commentary*. New York: Schirmer Books, 1999.

Bigard, Barney. *With Louis and the Duke: The Autobiography of a Jazz Clarinetist*. Edited by Barry Martyn. London: Macmillan, 1985.

Blesh, Rudi. *Shining Trumpets: A History of Jazz*. London: Cassell, 1949. Fourth edition, enlarged, 1958.

Brooks, Edward. *The Young Louis Armstrong on Record: A Critical Survey of the Early Recordings, 1923–1928*. Lanham, MD: Scarecrow Press, 2002.

Brooks, Tim. *Lost Sounds: Blacks and the Birth of the Recording Industry, 1890–1919*. Urbana and Chicago: University of Illinois Press, 2004.

Brothers, Thomas. *Louis Armstrong's New Orleans*. New York: W. W. Norton, 2006.

———. *Louis Armstrong, Master of Modernism*. New York: W. W. Norton, 2014.

———, ed. *Louis Armstrong, in His Own Words: Selected Writings*. New York: Oxford University Press, 1999.

Buckingham, William. "Musical Training and Early Jazz in New Orleans' Black Institutions of Education." Masters thesis, Tulane University, 2011.

Castle, Mr. and Mrs. Vernon. *Modern Dancing*. New York: Harper & Row, 1914. New York: Da Capo, 1980.

Charters, Samuel B. *The Country Blues*. New York: Rinehart, 1959. London: Jazz Book Club, 1961.

Chilton, John. *Sidney Bechet: The Wizard of Jazz*. London: Macmillan, 1987.

Collier, James Lincoln. *Louis Armstrong: An American Genius*. New York: Oxford University Press, 1983.

Condon, Eddie. *We Called It Music: A Generation of Jazz*. New York: H. Holt, 1947. New York: Da Capo, 1992.

Dance, Stanley. *The World of Earl Hines*. Boston: Crescendo, 1977.

Dickerson, James L. *Just for a Thrill: Lil Hardin Armstrong, First Lady of Jazz*. New York: Cooper Square Press, 2002.

Du Bois, W. E. B. *The Souls of Black Folk*. Chicago: A. C. McClurg, 1903. New York: Vintage, 1990.

Ecklund, Peter. *Great Trumpet Solos of Louis Armstrong*. New York: Chas. Colin Publications, undated.

Engel, Carl, ed. "Jazz: A Musical Discussion." In Karl Koenig, ed., *Jazz in Print (1859–1929): An Anthology of Selected Early Readings in Jazz History*. Hillsdale, NY: Pendragon Press, 2002.

Epstein, Dena. *Sinful Tunes and Spirituals: Black Folk Music to the Civil War*. Urbana: University of Illinois Press, 1977. Chicago: University of Illinois Press, 2003.

Esquire's World of Jazz. Edited by Lewis W. Gillenson. New York: Thomas Y. Crowell, 1975.

Faux, William. *Memorable Days in America*. London: W. Simpkins and R. Marshall, 1832.

Gammond, Peter. *Scott Joplin and the Ragtime Era*. Aylesbury, UK: Abacus, 1975.

Gara, Larry. *The Baby Dodds Story: As Told to Larry Gara*. Baton Rouge: Louisiana State University, 1992.

George-Graves, Nadine. *The Royalty of Negro Vaudeville: The Whitman Sisters and the Negotiation of Race, Gender and Class in African American Theater, 1900–1940*. New York: St. Martin's Press, 2000.

Giddins, Gary. *Satchmo: The Genius of Louis Armstrong*. Kindle ed. New York: Perseus, 2009.

Goffin, Robert. *Horn of Plenty: The Story of Louis Armstrong*. Translated by James F. Bezou. New York: Allen, Towne & Heath, 1947.

——. *La Nouvelle-Orléans Capital Du Jazz*. New York: Éditions De La Maison Française, 1946.

Gushee, Lawrence. "The Improvisation of Louis Armstrong." In Bruno Nettl and Malinda Russell, eds., *In the Course of Performance: Studies in the World of Musical Improvisation*. Chicago: University of Chicago Press, 1989.

Handy, W. C. *Blues: An Anthology*. New York: Albert & Charles Boni, 1926. New York: Macmillan, 1974.

——. *Father of the Blues*. New York: Macmillan, 1941. London: Sedgwick & Jackson, 1961.

Harker, Brian. *Louis Armstrong's Hot Five and Hot Seven Recordings*. New York: Oxford University Press, 2011.

Harrison, Harry P., and Karl Detzer. *Culture under Canvas*. New York: Hastings House, 1958.

Hazeldine, Mike, and Barry Martyn. *Bunk Johnson: Song of the Wanderer*. New Orleans: Jazzology Press, 2000.

Hennick, Louis C., and E. Harper Charlton. *The Streetcars of New Orleans*. Gretna, LA: Jackson Square Press, 1975, 32.

Henry, James Earl. "The Origins of Barbershop Harmony: A Study of Barbershop's Musical Link to Other African American Musics as Evidenced through Recordings and Arrangements of Early Black and White Quartets." PhD diss., Washington University, 2000.

Hersch, Charles. *Subversive Sounds: Race and the Birth of Jazz in New Orleans*. Chicago: University of Chicago Press, 2007.

Hicks, Val. *The Six Roots of Barbershop Harmony*. Nashville, TN: Barbershop Harmony Society, 2003.

Hillman, Christopher, Roy Middleton, and Hennie van Veelo. *Richard M. Jones: Forgotten Man of Jazz*. London: Cygnet Productions, 1997.

Hobson, Vic. *Creating Jazz Counterpoint: New Orleans, Barbershop Harmony, and the Blues*. Jackson: University Press of Mississippi, 2014.

Hodeir, Andre. *Jazz: Its Evolution and Essence*. New York: Grove Press, 1956.

Huggins, Nathan. *Harlem Renaissance*. New York: Oxford University Press, 1971.

Jones, Max, and John Chilton. *Louis: The Louis Armstrong Story 1900–1971*. Boston: Little, Brown, 1971.

Kennedy, Al. *Chord Changes on the Chalkboard: How Public School Teachers Shaped Jazz and the Music of New Orleans*. Langham, MD: Scarecrow Press, 2002.

Kennedy, R. Emmet. *Mellows: A Chronicle of Unknown Singers*. New York: Albert & Charles Boni, 1925.
———. *Remnants of Noah's Ham (According to Genesis)*. New Orleans: Myers' Printing House, 1910.
———. *The Songs of Aengus*. New Orleans: Myers' Printing House, 1910.
Kenney, William Howland. *Jazz on the River*. Chicago: University of Chicago Press, 2005.
———. *Chicago Jazz: A Cultural History, 1904–1930*. New York: Oxford University Press, 1993.
King, Leon. *Leon King Memoir: Jazz in the St. Louis Area: An Oral History Project*. Evansville: Southern Illinois University, 1982.
Koenig, Karl. *Evolution of Ragtime and Blues to Jazz*. Running Springs, CA: Basin Street, undated.
———. *The Scrap Book of R. Emmet Kennedy*. Running Springs, CA: Basin Street, 2007.
———. *Trinity of Early Jazz Leaders: John Robichaux, "Toots" Johnson, Claiborne Williams*. Running Springs, CA: Basin Street, undated.
Krehbiel, Henry Edward. *Afro-American Folksong: A Study in Racial and National Music*. New York: G. Schirmer, 1914.
Kubik, Gerhard. *Africa and the Blues*. Jackson: University Press of Mississippi, 1999.
Lambert, G. E. *Johnny Dodds (Kings of Jazz #10)*. New York: Barnes, 1961.
Lange, Arthur. *Arranging for the Modern Dance Orchestra*. New York: Robbins Music, 1926.
Leonard, Neil. *Jazz and the White Americans: The Acceptance of a New Art Form*. Chicago: University of Chicago Press, 1962. Jazz Book Club, 1964.
Locke, Alain. *The Negro and His Music*. Washington, DC: Associates in Negro Folk Education, 1936. New York: Arno Press, 1969.
Locke, Alain, and Winold Reiss. *The New Negro: An Interpretation*. New York: Albert & Charles Boni, 1925.
Magee, Jeffrey. *The Uncrowned King of Swing: Fletcher Henderson and Big Band Jazz*. New York: Oxford University Press, 2005.
Manual of Music Work: New Orleans Public School. New Orleans: Maubrret's Printing House, 1902.
Martin, Deac. *Martin's Book of Musical America*. Englewood Cliffs, NJ: Prentice-Hall, 1970.
Mazor, Barry. *Ralph Peer and the Making of Popular Roots Music*. Chicago: Chicago Review Press, 2015.
McCusker, John. *Creole Trombone: Kid Ory and the Early Years of Jazz*. Jackson: University Press of Mississippi, 2012.
Meryman, Richard. *Louis Armstrong: A Self Portrait*. New York: Eakins Press, 1966.
Moton, Robert. *What the Negro Thinks*. Garden City, NY: Doubleday, Doran, 1929.
Muir, Peter C. *Long Lost Blues: Popular Blues in America, 1850–1920*. Chicago: University of Illinois Press, 2010.
Newhart, Sally. *The Original Tuxedo Jazz Band: More Than a Century of a New Orleans Icon*. Kindle ed. Charleston, SC: History Press, 2013.
Ogren, Kathy J. *The Jazz Revolution: Twenties America and the Meaning of Jazz*. New York: Oxford University Press, 1989.

Osgood, Henry O. *So This Is Jazz*. Boston: Little, Brown, 1926.
Ostransky, Leroy. *Understanding Jazz*. Englewood Cliffs, NJ: Prentice-Hall, 1977.
Ottley, Roi, and William J. Weatherby. *The Negro in New York: An Informal Social History*. New York: Oceana Publications, 1967.
Panassié, Hugues. *Louis Armstrong*. New York: Da Capo, 1971.
———. *The Real Jazz*. New York: Smith & Durrell, 1942. New York: A. S. Barnes, 1960.
Paterson Jr., Bernard L. *Profiles of African American Stage Performers and Theater People 1816–1960*. London: Greenwood Press, 2001.
Poling, James. "New Sounds from the Crib House." In *Esquire's World of Jazz*. London: Arthur Baker, 1962.
Porter, Lewis, Michael Ullman, and Edward Hazell. *Jazz: From Its Origins to the Present*. Englewood Cliffs, NJ: Prentice-Hall, 1993.
Riccardi, Ricky. *What a Wonderful World: The Magic of Louis Armstrong's Later Years*. New York: Pantheon, 2011.
Robertson, David. *W. C. Handy: The Life and Times of the Man Who Made the Blues*. New York: Alfred A. Knopf, 2009.
Rose, Al. *I Remember Jazz: Six Decades among the Great Jazzmen*. Baton Rouge: Louisiana State University Press, 1987.
Rose, Al, and Edmond Souchon. *New Orleans Jazz: A Family Album*. 3rd ed. Baton Rouge: Louisiana State University Press, 1984.
Rust, Brian. *Jazz Records 1897–1942*. Chigwell, UK: Storyville, 1969. New York: Arlington House, 1978.
Sampson, Henry T. *Blacks in Blackface: A Source Book on Early Black Musical Shows*. Metuchen, NJ: Scarecrow Press, 1980.
Sargeant, Winthrop. *Jazz: Hot and Hybrid*. New York: Arrows Editions, 1938. New York: Da Capo, 1976.
Saxon, Lyle, Edward Dreyer, and Robert Tallant, eds. *Gumbo Ya-Ya: Folk Tales of Louisiana*. Gretna, LA: Pelican, 1945. Reprint, 1991.
Schoenberg, Arnold. *Theory of Harmony*. Vienna: Universal Editions, 1911. London: Faber & Faber, 1978.
Schuller, Gunther. *Early Jazz: Its Roots and Musical Development*. New York: Oxford University Press, 1986.
———. *The Swing Era: The Development of Jazz, 1930–1945*. New York: Oxford University Press, 1989.
Shapiro, Nat, and Nat Hentoff, eds. *Hear Me Talkin' to Ya: The Story of Jazz by the Men Who Made It*. New York: Rinehart, 1955. Reprint, Dover, 1966.
Sims, Alexander Dromgoole. *A View of Slavery, Moral and Political*. Charleston: Miller, 1834.
Smith, Eleanor. *The Eleanor Smith Music Course: Book 1*. New York: American Book Company, 1908. Kessinger Legacy Reprints.
Spaeth, Sigmund. *Barber Shop Ballads and How to Sing Them*. New York: Prentice-Hall, 1940.

———. *Barber Shop Ballads: A Book of Close Harmony*. New York: Simon and Schuster, 1925.

Spencer, Frederick J. *Jazz and Death: Medical Profiles of Jazz Greats*. Jackson: University Press of Mississippi, 2002.

Starr, S. Frederick. *Inventing New Orleans: Writings of Lafcadio Hearn*. Jackson: University Press of Mississippi, 2001.

Stearns, Marshall and Jean. *Jazz Dance: The Story of American Dance*. New York: Da Capo, 1968. Berkeley, CA: Perseus Books Group, 1994.

Stein, Daniel. *Music Is My Life: Louis Armstrong, Autobiography, and American Jazz*. Kindle ed. Ann Arbor: University of Michigan Press, 2012.

Stoddard, Tom. *Pops Foster: The Autobiography of a New Orleans Jazzman*. Berkeley: University of California Press, 1971. San Francisco: Backbeat Books, 2005.

Teachout, Terry. *Pops: A Life of Louis Armstrong*. New York: Houghton Mifflin Harcourt, 2009.

Tirro, Frank. *Jazz: A History*. New York: W.W. Norton, 1993.

Van Der Merwe, Peter. *Origins of the Popular Style*. Oxford: Clarendon Press, 1989.

Waters, Ethel. *His Eye Is on the Sparrow: An Autobiography by Ethel Waters and Charles Samuels*. New York: Doubleday, 1951. Westport, CT: Greenwood Press, 1978.

Work II, John W. *Folk Song of the American Negro*. Nashville, TN: F. A. McKenzie, 1915.

Work III, John W. *American Negro Songs and Spirituals: 230 Folk Songs and Spirituals, Religious and Secular*. New York: Bonanza, 1940. New York: Dover, 1998.

JOURNALS

Abbott, Lynn. "'For Ofays Only': An Annotated Calendar of Midnight Frolics at the Lyric Theater (Part 1)." *Jazz Archivist: A Newsletter of the William Hogan Jazz Archive* XVII (2003): 1–29.

———. "'Play That Barber Shop Chord': A Case for the African-American Origin of Barbershop Harmony." *American Music* 10, no. 3 (1992): 289–325.

———. "Remembering Mr. E. Belfield Spriggins: First Man of Jazzology." *78 Quarterly* 1, no. 10: 13–51.

Abbott, Lynn, and Doug Seroff. "'They Cert'ly Sound Good to Me': Sheet Music, Southern Vaudeville, and the Commercial Ascendancy of the Blues." *American Music* 14, no. 4 (Winter 1996): 402–54.

Albinder, Frank, and Jeremy D. Jones. "Male Choirs: A Brief Historical Overview of the European Tradition of Male Singing Societies and Their Influence of the Development of Collegiate Glee Clubs in America (Part 2)." *Choral Journal* 49, no. 4 (2008): 87–90.

Anderson, Gene H. "The Origin of Armstrong's Hot Fives and Hot Sevens." *College Music Symposium* 43 (2003): 13–24.

Bauer, William. "Louis Armstrong's 'Skid Dat De Dat': Timbral Organization in an Early Scat Solo." *Jazz Perspectives* 1, no. 2 (2007): 133–65.

Berrett, Joshua. "Louis Armstrong and Opera." *Musical Quarterly* 76, no. 2 (1992): 216–41.

Buckingham, Will. "Louis Armstrong and the Waifs' Home." *Jazz Archivist: A Newsletter of the William Ransom Hogan Jazz Archive* XXIV (2011): 2–15.

Campbell, Brun. "From Rags to Ragtime Riches." *Jazz Journal* (July 1949).

Chevan, David. "Riverboat Music from St. Louis and the Streckfus Steamboat Line." *Black Music Research Journal* 9, no. 2 (1989): 153–80.

Döhl, Frédéric. "From Harmonic Style to Genre: The Early History (1890s-1940s) of the Uniquely American Musical Term Barbershop." *American Music* 32, no. 2 (2014): 123–71.

Ecklund, Peter. "'Louis Licks' and Nineteenth-Century Cornet Etudes: The Roots of Melodic Improvisation as Seen in the Jazz Style of Louis Armstrong." *Historic Brass Society Journal* 13, no. 1 (2001): 90–101.

Evans, David. "Musical Innovation in the Blues of Blind Lemon Jefferson." *Black Music Research Journal* 20, no. 1 (2000): 83–116.

Gussow, Adam. "'Shoot Myself a Cop': Mamie Smith's 'Crazy Blues' as Social Text." *Callaloo* 25, no. 1 (2002): 8–44.

Harker, Brian. "Louis Armstrong and Clarinet." *American Music* 21, no. 2 (2003): 137–58.

———. "Louis Armstrong, Eccentric Dance, and the Evolution of Jazz on the Eve of Swing." *Journal of the American Musicological Society* 61, no. 1 (2008): 67–121.

Hobson, Vic. "Buddy Bolden's Blues." *Jazz Archivist: A Newsletter of the William Ransom Hogan Jazz Archive* XXI (2008): 1–18.

———. "Plantation Song: Delius, Barbershop, and the Blues." *American Music* 31, no. 3 (2013): 314–39.

Johns, Donald. "Funnel Tonality in American Popular Music, Ca. 1900–70." *American Music* 11, no. 4 (1993): 458–72.

Knapp, J. Merrill. "Samuel Webbe and the Glee." *Music and Letters* 33, no. 4 (1952): 346–51.

Magee, Jeffrey. "Before Louis: When Fletcher Henderson Was the 'Paul Whiteman of the Race.'" *American Music* 18, no. 4 (2000): 391–425.

———. "Revisiting Fletcher Henderson's 'Copenhagen.'" *Journal of the American Musicological Society* 48, no. 1 (1995): 42–66.

Malcolm, Douglas. "'Myriad Subtleties': Subverting Racism through Irony in the Music of Duke Ellington and Dizzy Gillespie." *Black Music Research Journal* 5, no. 2 (2015): 185–227.

Nussbaum, Jeff, Niles Eldridge, and Robb Stewart. "Louis Armstrong's First Cornet?" *Historic Brass Society Journal* 15 (2003): 353–58.

Perrow, E. C. "Songs and Rhymes from the South." *Journal of American Folklore* 28, no. 108 (April-June 1915): 129–90.

Piper, Charles, and Judy Piper. "A Passport to History." *Jazz Archivist: A Newsletter of the William Ransom Hogan Jazz Archive* 23 (2010): 30–36.

Raeburn, Bruce Boyd. "Early New Orleans Jazz in Theaters." *Louisiana History: Journal of the Louisiana Historical Association* 43, no. 1 (2002): 41–52.

Riccardi, Ricky. "You've Got to Appreciate All Kinds of Music: Review of Thomas Brothers, Louis Armstrong: Master of Modernism." *Journal of Jazz Studies* 10, no. 1: 78–90.

Schenbeck, Lawrence. "Music, Gender, and 'Uplift' in the 'Chicago Defender,' 1927–1937." *Musical Quarterly* 81, no. 3 (1997): 244–370.

Seroff, Doug, and Lynn Abbott. "The Life and Death of Pioneer Bluesman Butler 'String Beans' May: 'Been Here, Made His Quick Duck, and Got Away.'" *Journal of the Alabama Folklife Association*, no. 5 (2002): 9–48.

Scarborough, Dorothy. "The 'Blues' as Folk Song." *Folklore Society of Texas*, 1916.

"Storyville." *Satchmo: Collector's Copy* (1971): 9–13.

Suisman, David. "Co-Workers in the Kingdom of Culture: Black Swan Records and the Political Economy of African American Music." *Journal of American History* 90, no. 4 (2004): 1295–324.

Waters, Edward N. "Gershwin's 'Rhapsody in Blue.'" *Quarterly Journal of Current Acquisitions* 4, no. 3 (1947): 65–66.

Youngren, William H. "Louis." *Hudson Review* 29, no. 2 (1976): 23–48.

PERIODICALS

Armstrong, Louis. "60-Year-Old 'Bunk' Johnson, Louis' Tutor, Sits in the Band." *Down Beat* (August 15, 1941): 11.

———. "Bunk Didn't Teach Me." *Record Changer* 9, no. 6–7 (1950): 30.

———. "The First Complete Pictorial Life Story of Louis Armstrong as Told to Inez Caveanaugh." *Band Leaders* (January 1945): 16–22.

———. "Joe Oliver Is Still King." *Record Changer* 9, no. 6–7 (1950): 10–11.

———. "Scanning the History of Jazz." *Jazz Review* 3, no. 6 (1960): 8–9.

Breck, Park. "This Isn't Bunk; Bunk Taught Louis." *Down Beat* 6, no. 6 (1939): 4.

Cavendish, John C. "Folk-Tunes as Material for Music." *American Mercury* January (1925): 79–82.

Crowder, Ed, and A. F. Niemoeller. "Norman Mason: Riverboat Jazzman." *Record Changer*, no. 2 (1952): 8, 19.

Engel, Carl. "Jazz: A Musical Discussion." *Atlantic Monthly* 130, no. 2 (1922): 182–89.

Feather, Leonard. "The Real Louis Armstrong." *Down Beat* 29, no. 5 (1962): 23.

Henderson, Fletcher. *The Scroll* 21, no. 4 (January 1917).

———. "He Made the Band Swing." *Record Changer* 9, no. 6–7 (1950): 15–16.

Jones, Max. "The Hit No One Wanted." *Melody Maker* (May 23, 1964): 3.

Manskleid, Felix. "Fletcher Henderson, as told to Felix Manskleid." *Jazz Monthly*, December 1957: 27.

Merrille, Art. "You Can Call Off the Search—for We've Found the Lost Chord." *Harmonizer* 10, no. 3 (1951): 27.

Morgenstern, Dan. "Roses for Satchmo." *Down Beat* 37, no. 13 (1970): 15–19.

Ory, Edward "Kid." "The Hot Five Sessions." *Record Changer* 9, no. 6–7 (1950): 17, 45.

Petters, John. "Louis Armstrong: The World's Greatest Jazz Vocalist." *Just Jazz* 40 (2001): 10.

Reagan, Maurice. "The Mechanics of Barbershop Harmony." *Harmonizer* 3, no. 3 (1943): 10.

Schoebel, Elmer, and Herman Openneer Jr. "The Elmer Schoebel Story." *Doctor Jazz* 32 (1968): 6–7.

Singleton, Zutty. "Zutty First Saw Louis in Amateur Tent Show." *Down Beat* (July 14, 1950): 6.
Snyder, Dean. "Chautauqua and Male Quartets." *The Harmonizer* (January–February 1968).
Souchon, Edmond. "King Oliver: A Very Personal Memory." *Jazz Review* 3, no. 4 (May 1960): 6–11.
Tonk Bros. Inc. Catalogue, No. 47, 1930. http://www.acousticmusic.org/userfiles/file/pdfs/historical-data/Musical%20Distributors/Tonk%20Bros%201930%20Catalog%2047.pdf.
Tompkins, Les. "Playing with King Oliver Was Still the Real High Spot." *Crescendo* 3, no. 12 (1965): 20–22.

NEWSPAPER ARTICLES

Chicago Defender, June 9, 1928, 6.
Karst, James. "Armstrong Already the Leader of Waifs' Home Band at 11." New Orleans *Times-Picayune*, December 21, 2014.
———. "Secrets of Satchmo." New Orleans *Times-Picayune*, December 21, 2014.
"Lively Music Provided." *New Orleans Times-Democrat*, December 27, 1913.
Mencken, H. L. "Negros' Contribution to Music Condensed in a Book of Spirituals," unidentified publication, 1925.
"Playground Dedicated: First in the South for the Use of Negro Children." New Orleans *Times-Picayune*, August 29, 1915.
Rink, Janet. "Satchmo Comes Home." *Dixie*, October 31, 1965.
Spaeth, Sigmund. "Famous Tune Detective, Says Many Music Lovers Are Hypocrites." *Cornell Daily Sun*, January 7, 1935.
"To Dedicate First Negro Playgrounds: Thorny [sic] Lafon Recreation Center to Be Formally Opened Saturday." *New Orleans Item*, August 28, 1915.
Manuscripts and Letters
Armstrong, Louis. "Typescript for Satchmo: Life Story of Louis Armstrong." New Jersey: Institute of Jazz Studies, Rutgers University.
Jackson, Preston. "Autobiography." In William Russell Jazz Collection, MSS 519. New Orleans: Williams Research Center, Historic New Orleans Collection.
Johnson, Bunk. "Letter from Bunk Johnson to William Russell." In William Russell Collection, MSS 501. New Orleans: Williams Research Center, Historic New Orleans Collection, undated.
Schacht, Beulah. "Riverboat Jazz and the Story of a Legendary St. Louisian Who Made It Click." *St. Louis Globe-Democrat*, July 22, 1945.
Streckfus, Joseph. "Manuscript, February 20, 1958." In Vertical Files. New Orleans: William Ransom Hogan Jazz Archive, Tulane University.
———. "Manuscript, March 18, 1958." In Vertical Files. New Orleans: William Ransom Hogan Jazz Archive, Tulane University.
Tate, Erskine. "Erskine Tate's Vendome Symphony Orchestra Including a Review of his Chicago Recording Sessions 1923 & 1926."
"Tulane University 'Jelly Roll Morton Symposium' May 7, 1982." Dixon Hall.

INTERVIEWS

Angrum, Steve. "Interview Digest, August 8, 1961." In *Oral History Files*, edited by William Russell and Ralph Collins. New Orleans: William Ransom Hogan Jazz Archive, Tulane University.

Armstrong, Louis. "Armstrong Heritage T.V. Program Part 1, August 2, 1960." In *Audio Collection*, edited by Robert McCully and Adam Lynch. New Orleans: William Ransom Hogan Jazz Archive, Tulane University.

———. "Armstrong Heritage T.V. Program, Part 2, August 9, 1960." In *Audio Collection*, edited by Robert McCully and Adam Lynch. New Orleans: William Ransom Hogan Jazz Archive, Tulane University.

———. "Armstrong Heritage T.V. Program, Part 4, August 23, 1960." In *Audio Collection*, edited by Robert McCully and Adam Lynch. New Orleans: William Ransom Hogan Jazz Archive, Tulane University.

———. "Interview May 5, 1970." In William Russell Jazz Collection, MSS 519, edited by William Russell. New Orleans: Williams Research Center, Historic New Orleans Collection.

———. "Jazzmen Interviews." In Papers of Frederic Ramsey Jr., MSS 559. New Orleans: Williams Research Center, Historic New Orleans Collection.

Barker, Danny. "Interview Digest June 30, 1959." In *Oral History Files*, edited by Richard B. Allen. New Orleans: William Ransom Hogan Jazz Archive, Tulane University.

Beaulieu, Paul. "Interview Summary, June 11, 1960." In *Oral History Files*, edited by William Russell and Ralph Collins. New Orleans: William Ransom Hogan Jazz Archive, Tulane University.

Bocage, Peter. "Interview Transcript, January 29, 1959." In *Oral History Files*, edited by Richard B. Allen and William Russell. New Orleans: William Ransom Hogan Jazz Archive, Tulane University.

Brown, Steve. "Interview Transcript, April 22, 1958." In *Oral History Files*, edited by Richard Allen and William Russell. New Orleans: William Ransom Hogan Jazz Archive, Tulane University.

Casimir, John. "Interview, January 17, 1959." In *Oral History Files*, edited by Richard B. Allen. New Orleans: William Ransom Hogan Jazz Archive, Tulane University.

DeDroit, Johnny. "Interview, December 4, 1969." In *Oral History Files*, edited by Betty B. Rankin, Richard B. Allen, and Keith V. Abramson. New Orleans: William Ransom Hogan Jazz Archive, Tulane University.

Foster, George "Pops." "Interview Digest, April 21, 1957 (for *Life Magazine*)." In *Oral History Files*, edited by Nesuhi Ertegun and Robert Campbell. New Orleans: William Ransom Hogan Jazz Archive, Tulane University.

French, Morris, and Ernest "Punch" Miller. "Interview Digest, June 24, 1960." In *Oral History Files*, edited by Richard B. Allen and Marjorie T. Zander. New Orleans: William Ransom Hogan Jazz Archive, Tulane University.

Garland, Ed "Montudi." "Interview April 16, 1957." In *Oral History Files*, edited by Nesuhi Ertegun and Robert Campbell. New Orleans: William Ransom Hogan Jazz Archive, Tulane University.

———. "Interview April 21, 1957." In *Oral History Files*, edited by Nesuhi Ertegun and Robert Campbell. New Orleans: William Ransom Hogan Jazz Archive, Tulane University.

Glenny, Albert. "Interview Transcript, March 27, 1957." In *Oral History Files*, edited by Richard B. Allen and Nesuhi Ertegun. New Orleans: William Ransom Hogan Jazz Archive, Tulane University.

Handy, W. C. "Interview Transcript May 9, 1938." In Folklife Collection. Washington, DC: Library of Congress.

Hardin-Armstrong, Lillian. "Interview Digest July 1, 1959." In *Oral History*, edited by William Russell. New Orleans: William Ransom Hogan Jazz Archive, Tulane University.

———. "Jazzmen Interviews." In Papers of Frederic Ramsey Jr., MSS 559. New Orleans: Williams Research Center, Historic New Orleans Collection.

Humphrey (the elder), Willie E., and Willie J. Humphrey (the younger). "Interview Digest, March 15, 1959." In *Oral History Files*, edited by William Russell and Ralph Collins. New Orleans: William Ransom Hogan Jazz Archive, Tulane University.

Jackson, Preston. "Interview June 2, 1958." In *Oral History Files*. New Orleans: William Ransom Hogan Jazz Archive, Tulane University.

Jones, Louis, and Edmund Wise. "Interview Transcript, June 4, 1954." In Papers of Frederic Ramsey Jr., MSS 559. New Orleans: Williams Research Center, Historic New Orleans Collection.

Keppard, Louis. "Interview Transcript, December 25, 1969." In William Russell Jazz Collection, MSS 519. New Orleans: Williams Research Center, Historic New Orleans Collection.

Laine, "Papa" Jack. "Interview Transcript, March 26, 1957." In *Oral History Files*, edited by William Russell and Richard B. Allen. New Orleans: William Ransom Hogan Jazz Archive, Tulane University.

Madison, Kid Shots. "Interview with Bill Russell August 8, 1944." In William Russell Jazz Collection, MSS 536. New Orleans: Williams Research Center, Historic New Orleans Collection.

Manetta, Manuel. "Interview Digest, March 28, 1957." In *Oral History Files*, edited by William Russell, Robert Campbell, Nesuhi Ertegun, and Richard B. Allen. New Orleans: William Ransom Hogan Jazz Archive, Tulane University.

McBride, Billy, and Mary McBride. "Interview November 23, 1970." In William Russell Jazz Collection, MSS 506. New Orleans: Williams Research Center, Historic New Orleans Collection.

Miller, Ernest "Punch." "Interview, September 25, 1959." In *Oral History Files*, edited by Richard B. Allen. New Orleans: William Ransom Hogan Jazz Archive, Tulane University.

Morton, Ferdinand "Jelly Roll." "Transcript of the 1938 Library of Congress Recordings of Jelly Roll Morton." CD box set edited by John Szwed. Washington, DC: Library of Congress, 2006.

Nicholas, Joseph "Wooden Joe." "Interview Digest, November 12, 1956." In *Oral History Files*, edited by William Russell and Charlie DeVore. New Orleans: William Ransom Hogan Jazz Archive, Tulane University.

Oliver, Stella. "Interview Digest, April 22, 1959." In *Oral History Files*, edited by William Russell and Ralph Collins. New Orleans: William Ransom Hogan Jazz Archive, Tulane University.

Ory, Edward "Kid." "Interview Transcript, April 20, 1957 (for *Life Magazine*)." In *Oral History Files*, edited by Nesuhi Ertegun and Robert Campbell. New Orleans: William Ransom Hogan Jazz Archive, Tulane University.

Ory, Edward "Kid," and Manuel "Fess" Manetta. "August 26, 1958." In *Oral History Files*, edited by William Russell, Richard B. Allen, and Ralph Adamo. New Orleans: William Ransom Hogan Jazz Archive, Tulane University.

Peer, Ralph. "Interview with Ralph Peer by Liliane Borgeson." Library of the University of North Carolina.

Phillips, Berenice. "Interview September 3, 1960." In *Oral History Files*, edited by Richard B. Allen. New Orleans: William Ransom Hogan Jazz Archive, Tulane University.

Rene, Joe. "Interview April 7, 1960." In *Oral History Files*. New Orleans: William Ransom Hogan Jazz Archive, Tulane University.

René, Joseph. "Interview Digest September 8, 1960." In *Oral History Files*, edited by Richard B. Allen and Majorie Zander. New Orleans: William Ransom Hogan Jazz Archive, Tulane University.

Ridgley, William "Baba." "Interview Summary June 2, 1959." In *Oral History Files*, edited by Betty B. Rankin, Elizabeth Snapp, Marjorie T. Zander, and Richard B. Allen. New Orleans: William Ransom Hogan Jazz Archive, Tulane University.

———. "Interview Summary, April 11, 1961." In *Oral History Files*, edited by John Handy, Richard B. Allen, and Marjorie T. Zander. New Orleans: William Ransom Hogan Jazz Archive, Tulane University.

———. "Interview, April 7, 1961." In *Oral History Files*, edited by Richard B. Allen and Dave Dutcher. New Orleans: William Ransom Hogan Jazz Archive, Tulane University.

Singleton, Zutty. "Jazzmen Interview Notes." In Papers of Frederic Ramsey Jr., MSS 559. New Orleans: Williams Research Center, Historic New Orleans Collection.

Souchon, Edmond "Doc." "Interview February 17, 1962." In *Oral History Files*, edited by William Russell. New Orleans: William Ransom Hogan Jazz Archive, Tulane University.

St., Cyr, Johnny. "Interview August 27, 1958." In *Oral History Files*, edited by William Russell. New Orleans: William Ransom Hogan Jazz Archive, Tulane University.

———. "Interview January 31, 1969." In William Russell Jazz Collection, MSS 519, edited by William Russell. New Orleans: Williams Research Center, Historic New Orleans Collection.

Streckfus, Verne. "Digest September 22, 1960." In *Oral History Files*, edited by Paul R. Crawford and Richard B. Allen. New Orleans: William Ransom Hogan Jazz Archive, Tulane University.

Valentine, "Kid" Thomas. "Interview Digest, March 22, 1957 (for *Life Magazine*)." In *Oral History Files*, edited by William Russell and Nesuhi Ertegun. New Orleans: William Ransom Hogan Jazz Archive, Tulane University.

———. "Interview with Richard B. Allen, January 27, 1969." In *Oral History Files*, edited by Kay L. Wicker and Richard B. Allen. New Orleans: William Ransom Hogan Jazz Archive, Tulane University.

Vincent, Clarence "Little Dad." "Interview Digest, January 21, 1960." In *Oral History Files*, edited by Richard B. Allen and Ralph Collins. New Orleans: William Ransom Hogan Jazz Archive, Tulane University.

"W. C. Handy Interview with George Avakian." *Louis Armstrong Plays W. C. Handy*. Columbia CD CL591, 1954.

Wiggs, John. "Interview Digest August 26, 1962." In *Oral History Files*, edited by William Russell and Betty Hyman. New Orleans: William Ransom Hogan Jazz Archive, Tulane University.

Williams, Alfred. "Interview Summary October 13, 1961." In *Oral History Files*, edited by Richard B. Allen. New Orleans: William Ransom Hogan Jazz Archive, Tulane University.

DISCOGRAPHY

Armstrong, Louis, and His Hot Five. "Big Butter and Egg Man." Chicago: OKeh 8423, November 16, 1926.
———. "Gut Bucket Blues." Chicago: OKeh 8261, November 12, 1925.
———. "Heebie Jeebies." Chicago: OKeh 8300, February 26, 1926.
———. "I'm Not Rough." Chicago: OKeh 8551, December 10, 1927.
———. "Muskrat Ramble." Chicago: OKeh 8300, February 26, 1926.
———. "Potato Head Blues." Chicago: OKeh 8503, May 10, 1927.
———. "Savoy Blues." Chicago: OKeh 8535, December 13, 1927.
———. "Skid-Dat-De-Dat." Chicago: OKeh 8436, November 16, 1925.
Armstrong, Louis, and His Orchestra. "Basin Street Blues." Chicago: OKeh 8690, December 4, 1928.
Armstrong, Louis, and His Dixieland Seven. "Maryland My Maryland." *New Orleans* (film). Los Angeles: United Artists, 1946.
Armstrong, Louis, and His Hot Seven. "Gully Low Blues." Chicago: OKeh 8474, May 14, 1927.
Barnwell, Dr. Ysaye Maria. *W. C. Handy's Blues*. Public Radio International. www.wchandyblues.org.
Greene, Gene. "King of the Bungaloos." Columbia A-0994, February 17, 1911.
———. "King of the Bungaloos." Victor 5854, April 19, 1911.
———. "King of the Bungaloos." Emerson 7228, December 1, 1916.
———. "King of the Bungaloos." Victor 18266, March 9, 1917.
Henderson, Fletcher, and His Orchestra. "Copenhagen." New York: Vocalion 14926, master 13929, October 30, 1924.
———. "Copenhagen." New York: Vocalion 14926, master 13928, October 30, 1924.
Hickman, Art, Orchestra. "Love Nest." New York: Columbia A2955, June 11, 1920.
———. "A Young Man's Fancy." New York: Columbia A2970, July 10, 1920.
———. "Avalon." New York: Columbia A3322, October 1, 1920.

Marable, Fate, Society Syncopators. "Frankie and Johnny." New Orleans: OKeh 40113. March 16, 1924.

Oliver, King, and the Creole Jazz Band. "Dippermouth Blues." Richmond, IN: Gennett 5132, April 6, 1923.

———. "Dippermouth Blues." Chicago: OKeh 8402-A, June 23, 1923.

Smith, Bessie. "Careless Love." New York: Columbia 14083D, May 26, 1925.

Taylor, Eva, with Clarence Williams' Blue Five. "Coal Cart Blues." New York: OKeh 8245, October 8, 1925.

Wallace, Sippie. "Have You Ever Been Down?" Chicago: OKeh 8499, May 6, 1927.

SHEET MUSIC

Cadman, Charles Wakefield. *The Vision of Sir Launfal.* New York: G. Schirmer, 1910.

Foster, S. C. "Old Folks at Home." Edited by William G. Smith. Boston: Oliver Ditson & Co., 1887.

Gumble, Albert, and Jack Yellen, "Circus Day in Dixie." New York: Jerome H. Remick, 1915.

Handy, Will. "Oh! Didn't He Ramble." New York: Jos. Stern & Co., 1902.

Harney, Ben. "Cake Walk in the Sky." New York: M. Witmark & Sons, 1899.

Johnson, Billy. "Down on the Amazon." New York: Dowling Sutton Music Publishing Co., 1903.

Jolson, Al, and Vincent Rose. "Avalon: Fox Trot Song." New York: Jerome H. Remick & Co., 1920.

Joplin, Scott. "Please Say You Will." New York, M. L. Mantell, 1895.

Lessing, Edith Maida, and Jimmie V. Monaco. "Oh, You Circus Day." Chicago: Will Rossiter, 1912.

Mozart, Wolfgang A. "Symphony No. 41 in C major K551 'Jupiter.'" Leipzig: Eulenburg Study Edition, 1985.

Muir, Lewis F., and William Tracy. "Play That Barber Shop Chord." New York: J. Fred Helf Co., 1910.

Mygrant, W. S. "My Maryland." Edited by Maurice F. Smith. New York: Leo Feist, 1906.

Smith, Chris, and Jim Burris. "Ballin' the Jack." New York: Jos. W. Stern, 1913.

Straight, Charles, and Gene Greene. "King of the Bungaloos." Chicago: Music House Laemmle, 1909.

Wand, Hart A. "The Dallas Blues." Oklahoma: self-published, 1912.

Whiting, Richard A., and Raymond B. Egan. "The Japanese Sandman." New York: Jerome H. Remick, 1920.

INDEX

Abbott, Lynn, xii, 41, 130
Acme Packet Company, 81
Adderley, Cannonball, 3
Alix, Mae, 155, 158
Allen, Walter C., 115
Allen, William, *Slave Songs of the United States*, 29
Ancoin, A. M., 39
Anderson, Archie, 39
Anderson, Gene H., 129; *The Original Hot Five Recordings of Louis Armstrong*, 141
Anderson, Tom, 66, 94–95, 124
Anderson, William "Cat," 3
Andrews Coal Yard, 57–58, 59, 60, 61, 66, 76, 139
Angrum, Steve, 25
Armstrong, Louis: in Chicago, 4, 17, 98–101, 107, 109, 126–27, 145; church singing, 27, 32, 41; connection between singing and playing, 8–9, 142, 161–62, 170–71; early career, 60–63, 64–66, 68, 69–70; early musical education, 35–37; education, 33–35; juvenile record, 39–41, 42, 47; in New York, 116, 123, 124–25; OKeh sessions, 146–47; quartet singing, 8–9, 11–12, 13, 14, 15, 21–22, 24, 41, 42, 51; role as an African American, 4–6; *Satchmo*, 12, 18, 49, 56; singing, 3–4, 6–8, 127, 128–29, 142–43, 169–70; *Swing That Music*, 6, 11; at Waifs' Home, 39–40, 47, 48–52, 54, 59; work on riverboats, 81, 83, 84–88, 89–90, 92–93, 94–95, 96
Armstrong, Mama Lucy, 27, 59
Art Hickman's Orchestra, 90, 91, 94

Atkins, Boyd, 127, 130
"Avalon," 90, 91–92, 93, 154

Bailey, William C. "Buster," 99, 123–24
Barbarin, Paul, 49
barbershop chord, 14, 178n
Barbershop Harmony Society, 172
barbershop revival, 43, 44, 170, 172
Barker, Danny, 73
Bart, Wilhelmina, 63
Barth, Wilhelmina, 74
Bartlett, Buddy. *See* Haywood, Joseph
"Basin Street Blues," xiii, 166–68, 169–70
Bauer, William, 142
bebop, 5, 137, 171, 173
Bechet, Joseph, 74
Bechet, Leonard, 73, 74
Bechet, Sidney, 22–23, 73, 74–75, 76, 78, 171
Beiderbecke, Bix, 85, 120
Benny, Black, 61–62, 76
Bergreen, Lawrence, 60
Bernhardt, Clyde, 98
Berrett, Joshua, 129, 141, 144
Bigard, Barney, 7, 54, 63, 73, 95
Bigard, Emile, 63
"Big Butter and Egg Man," 155–59, 160, 161, 163, 167, 170
Black Swan Records, 112, 113–14, 115
Black Swan Troubadours, 114, 115
Blake, E. B., 86
Blesh, Rudi, 95, 120
Blue Five, 145
blues tonality, xii, 9, 20, 21, 24, 45, 102, 104, 106, 118, 140, 141, 147, 149, 162, 171
Blumberg, Jerry, 78

230

Bocage, Peter, 77, 84, 86, 107–8
Bolden, Charles "Buddy," 23, 26, 48, 60, 71, 72, 74, 77, 133, 138, 171, 172
Bolton, James William Red Head "Happy," 11, 12, 13, 14, 22, 51, 56
Boogus, 65
Boyd, Ella S., 53
Bradford, Perry, "The Bull Frog Hop," 130
Brookins, Tommy, 108–9
Brooks, Edward, 120, 167
Brothers, Thomas, 71, 128, 157; *Louis Armstrong's New Orleans*, 18
Brown, James, 48
Brown, Steve, 26
Brown and McGraw, 158, 213n
Butterbeans and Susie. *See* Edwards, Jodie and Susan
Buttermilk Man, 19, 20, 144

Calloway, Blanche, 145
"Careless Love," 133, 134
Carey, Mutt, 26, 38, 62, 63, 108, 124
Carney, Harry, 3
Carr, Mancy, 167, 169
Carter, Benny, 3
Carter, Robert, 93
Cash, O. C., 172
Casimir, John, 54
Castle, Vernon and Irene, *Modern Dance*, 91
Cavendish, John C., 15, 16, 17
Celestin, Papa, 69
Centilivere, John, 39
"Coal Cart Blues," 138–41
Collier, James Lincoln, 48, 152
Condon, Eddie, 109
Cook, Ann, 25
Cooke, Charles M., 128
"Copenhagen," 118–22, 123, 149
Cornish, Willie, 23, 71
Cosey, William M., 26, 182n

Dabney, Ford, 5
Dance, Stanley, 7

Dantonio, John, 39
Davis, Charlie, 118, 120
Davis, Peter, 48, 49, 50, 51, 52, 54, 61
DeDroit, Johnny, 93, 199n
Dekemel, "Buglin' Sam," 21
Demaselière, Alfred, 74
Deppe, Lois, 169
Desvigne, Sidney, 74
Dett, R. Nathaniel, 112
Dickerson, Carroll, 151, 169
Dickerson, James L., 138
"Dippermouth Blues," 100, 101, 102–3, 104–5, 106, 107, 108, 139, 164
Dodds, Johnny, 63, 64, 77, 84, 99, 104–5, 106, 123, 124, 145, 163, 171
Dodds, Warren "Baby," 64, 84, 85, 86, 87, 88–89, 95, 99, 100
"Down on the Amazon," 42, 43, 44, 159, 170
Drob, Harold, 78
Du Bois, W. E. B., 111; *The Souls of Black Folk*, 112
Dusen, Frankie, 77
Dvořák, *New World Symphony*, 28

Eagle Band, 72, 77
Eagle Orchestra, 74, 76
Eagle Packet Company, 82
Ecklund, Peter, 136–37
Edwards, Jodie and Susan, 130–31
Eleanor Smith Music Course, 36–37, 51, 185n
Elder, Clarence W., 94
Engel, Carl, 117–18, 171
Evans, David, 140

Fearn, Elmer A., 130, 145
Feather, Leonard, 6
Ferguson, Ollie, 82
Fisk, Abijah, 33, 183n
Fogarty, John J., 47
Foster, George "Pops," 60, 62, 63, 64, 77, 84–86, 95
Foster, Stephen, "Old Folks at Home," 14, 15

fox trot, 90–91, 93, 94, 121
"Frankie and Johnny," 89, 93
French, Morris, 69
funnel tonality, 44, 45, 46

Gande, Al, 120
Garbie, Sonny, 65
Garland, Ed "Montudi," 21, 22
George-Graves, Nadine, *The Royalty of Negro Vaudeville*, 130
Gershwin, George, *Rhapsody in Blue*, 117
Giddins, Gary, 8
Gillespie, Dizzy, 3, 5
Glaser, Joe, 7
glee clubs, 110–11
Glenny, Albert, 22
Goffin, Robert, 47, 48, 52, 74; *Horn of Plenty*, 11, 22, 56, 57, 66
"Got No More Home than a Dog," 131–32
Gray, Georgie, 11, 13, 22
Greene, Gene, "King of the Bungaloos," 128
Greenfield, Elizabeth Taylor, 112
Gregson, Harry, 40
Grofé, Ferde, 117
"Gully Low Blues," 149–50
Gumbo Ya-Ya: Folktales of Louisiana, 18
Gushee, Lawrence, 138–39, 151
"Gut Bucket Blues," 147–48

Hall, Herb, 3
Hall, Rupert, 172
Hammerstein, Oscar, 166
Handy, W. C., 15, 111–12, 131–34, 135; *Blues: An Anthology*, 132; *Father of the Blues*, 131; "Memphis Blues," 124; "St. Louis Blues," 89
Hardin, Lillian Beatrice "Lil," 99, 116, 125, 126, 128, 137–38, 139, 140, 141, 142, 143, 144, 145
Harker, Brian, 8, 140, 149, 158, 163
Harney, Ben, "Cake Walk in the Sky," 128

Harris, Jeffrey, 48
Harrison, Lou, 103, 104, 107
Haywood, Joseph, 60, 75
Hearn, Lafcadio, 18
"Heebie Jeebies," 127, 128, 129, 130, 131
"Hello Dolly," 6–7, 8
Henderson, Fletcher Hamilton, Jr., 3–4, 100, 110, 113, 114–15, 116, 117, 118, 121, 123, 124–25, 126, 133, 145
Henderson, Fletcher Hamilton, Sr., 110
Henry, James Earl, xii, 19
Higgins, Nathan, 113
Hightower, Willie, 84
Hill, Bertha "Chippie," 145
Hines, Earl, 155, 158, 167, 168–69
Hobson, Vic, *Creating Jazz Counterpoint*, xii
Hodeir, André, 31, 136, 155, 157
Holy Roller churches, 26
Hot Five, 4, 6, 17, 122, 145, 146–47, 156, 169
Hot Seven, 4, 146, 147, 151, 156
Howard, Joe, 69, 86, 94, 95, 98
Humphrey, Jim, 68
Humphrey, Willie E., 81

"I'm Not Rough," 150–51

Jackson, Franz, 3
Jackson, Preston, 23, 52, 95, 97, 98, 100, 108
"Japanese Sandman," 90, 91, 199n
Jazzmen, 71, 116, 138
Jazz Singer, The, 4
Jefferson, Blind Lemon, 140
Johns, Donald, 44
Johnson, Billy, "Down on the Amazon," 42, 43
Johnson, Bunk, 48, 65, 70, 71, 72–73, 74, 75–79, 80, 134
Johnson, Lonnie, 134
Johnson, Sam, 50
Jolson, Al, 90
Jones, David, 86, 87–88

Jones, Joseph, 47–48, 50, 52, 61, 75
Jones, Phil, 131
Jones, Richard M., 97, 128, 145
Jones, Thad, 3
Joplin, Scott, 46

Karnofsky, David, 59
Karnofsky, Louis, 59
Karnofsky, Morris, 59
Karnofsky family, 55–57, 58–59
Kennedy, R. Emmet, 19, 27–28, 30, 32; *Mellows*, 29; *Remnants of Noah's Ham*, 29; *The Songs of Aengus*, 28–29
Kennedy, William, 39
Kent, James, 39
Keppard, Louis, 23–24, 60–61
Kid Ory's Orchestra, 81, 84, 85, 124
King, Leon, 94
Krehbiel, Henry Edward, 30–31
Kubik, Gerhard, 136

Lacoumbe, Emile "Stale Bread," 22
Lafon, Thomy, 52
Laine, Papa Jack, 23
Lala, Pete, 66, 80
Landreaux, Elizabeth. *See* Miles, Lizzie
Lange, Arthur, *Arranging for the Modern Dance Orchestra*, 121
Lanin, Sam, 116
Lauzetta Quartet, 131
"LaVeda," 94
Lead Belly, 134–35
Leneries, Zeb, 69
Liszt, "Liebestraum," 46, 159, 170
Little Mack, 12, 13, 74, 76
Locke, Alain, 32, 112, 118, 171; *The Negro and His Music*, 113
Lomax, Alan, 129, 131
Louis Armstrong's 50 Hot Choruses for Cornet, 101
"Loveless Love," 133, 134
Lynch, Adam, 41

"Mack the Knife," 7
MacNeal, James Williams, 33
MacNeal, Wendell Phillips, 33
Madison, Louis "Kid Shots," 51
Magee, Jeffrey, 117, 121, 123
Manetta, Manuel, 61, 64–65
Mannes, David, 112
Marable, Fate, 77, 81–82, 83–84, 85, 86, 88, 89, 93, 94, 95
Marrero, Simon, 74
Martin, Alice, 34
Martin, Carmelite, 34
Martin, Deac, 42, 44
Martin, Henry, 34
Martin, Orleania, 34
Martin, Wilhelmina, 34
"Maryland My Maryland," 53, 54
Mason, Norman, 86–87, 94, 95, 98
Matranga, Henry, 65, 66
May, Butler "String Beans," 130, 131
McBride, Billy and Mary, 12
McCully, Robert, 41
McPherson, Cecile, 5
Mellon, Charles, 39
Melody Maker, 6–7
Melrose, Walter, 102
Melrose Brothers Music Company, 101, 118, 119, 120
"Memphis Blues, The," 15
Mencken, H. L., 31
Meryman, Richard, 123
Metcalf, Louis, 121, 122
Miles, Flora, 57
Miles, Lizzie, 25, 74
Mills, Charlie, 81
Moore, Eddie, 39
Morton, Jelly Roll, 18–19, 23, 129, 130, 172
Moton, Robert Russa, 5
Mozart, *Jupiter Symphony*, 141–42
Muir, Peter, 161
Mumford, Brock, 23
"Muskrat Ramble," 153–54, 157
"My Brazilian Beauty," 40–42, 43, 44, 45

National Association for the Advancement of Colored People (NAACP), 111, 112
New Orleans, 54
New Orleans Cotton Pickers, 82
Nicholas, Albert, 95
Nicholas, Joseph "Wooden Joe," 134
Noone, Jimmy, 66

OKeh Records, 145, 146, 147
Oliver, Joe "King," 3–4, 25, 48, 60, 61, 65, 66–67, 78–80, 85, 88, 96, 97–100, 101, 102–3, 104, 105, 107–9, 116, 123, 126, 137, 163–64, 169
Oliver, Stella Dominique, 25, 66, 97
Original Dixieland Jazz Band, 72, 172
Ory, Edward "Kid," 26, 50, 54, 61–62, 63–64, 65, 66, 67–68, 81, 84, 85, 128, 145–46, 151, 163, 171
Ose, Viéjas, 47, 49
Osgood, Henry O., 139; *So This Is Jazz*, 22
Ostransky, Leroy, *Understanding Jazz*, 45

Pace, Harry H., 111–12, 114
Pace and Handy Music Company, 111
Panassié, Hugues, 152; *Le Jazz Hot*, *The Real Jazz*, 117
Peer, Ralph, 145
Petters, John, 6
Phillips, Berenice, 25
Piron, Armand J., 84, 124
Porter, Lewis, Michael Ullman, and Edward Hazell, 104; *Jazz*, 7–8
"Potato Head Blues," 163, 164–65, 166

Rabbit's Foot Minstrels, 86
Rainey, Ma, 140
Randolph, Zilner, 36
Reagan, Maurice, 43–44
Redman, Don, 117, 118–19, 121, 123, 128
Rena, Kid, 48, 50, 51. *See also* René, Henry "Kid"
Rena, Louis, 52

René, Henry "Kid," 23, 25, 48, 50, 52
René, Joe, 23, 25
Rhapsody in Black and Blue, 4, 5
Ridgley, William "Baba," 68, 85, 95
Robbins, Annabelle, 161
Roberts, Clarence, 39
Robichaux, John, 116
Robinson, Red, 82
"Rock Mount Sinai," 29, 30, 31–32, 139
Rose, Al, *New Orleans Jazz*, 22
Roseland Ballroom, 116, 117, 122, 123
Russell, Bill, 12, 72, 127, 129, 130
Russell, Luis, 95

Sabrier, Anthony, 39
Sampson, Henry T., *Blacks in Blackface*, 130
Sansovich, Mike, 39
Sargeant, Winthrop, 103–4, 106, 107, 140, 144, 159–60, 161, 171; *Jazz Hot and Hybrid*, 45
"Savoy Blues," 151–52
scat singing, 3, 5, 127, 128–29, 130
Schoebel, Elmer, 102
Schoenberg, Arnold, *Theory of Harmony*, 139
Schoeppe, Franz, 124
Schuller, Gunther, 7, 93, 118, 136, 142, 151, 155, 158, 167
Scott, Bud, 26
Seroff, Doug, 130
"Shine," 4, 5, 6
Sims, Joe, 130
Singleton, Zutty, 12–13, 49, 54, 83, 115–16, 142, 169
"Skid-Dat-De-Dat," 141, 142–43
Smith, Bessie, 114, 122–23, 134, 140
Smith, Henry, 39
Smith, Joseph Emery, 122
Smith, Mamie, "Crazy Blues," 114
Smith, Wilson G., 14
Smooth, Isaac, 48
"Sobbin' Blues," 88

Society for the Preservation and Encouragement of Barbershop Quartet Singing in America (SPEBSQSA), 170, 172
Souchon, Edmond "Doc," *New Orleans Jazz*, 22
Spaeth, Sigmund, 14, 17, 101, 105, 106, 140, 148, 149, 160, 161, 162, 164; *Barber Shop Ballads*, 13, 100; "Blues Progression," 19–20, 104, 122, 142
Sparks, Julie, 27, 29
Sparks, Sammy and Johnny, 27
spasm bands, 22, 23, 24, 32
Spriggins, Naomi, 51, 52
St. Cyr, Johnny, 21, 25, 86, 127, 145, 147
Stein, Daniel, 128
Storyville, 40, 65, 80, 124, 166; closure of, 66, 67, 185n
Streckfus, John, Jr., 82, 83
Streckfus, John, Sr., 81, 82–83, 84, 94
Streckfus, Joseph, 82, 83, 89–90, 91, 92–93, 94
Streckfus, Roy, 82, 83
Streckfus, Verne, 82, 83, 84, 85, 94
Streckfus brothers, 85, 88, 89, 93
Streckfus Steamboat Line, 82
"Struttin' with Some Barbecue," 143–44
"Sugarfoot Stomp," 100
"Swanee River," 14–17, 24, 32, 49, 66, 100, 111, 139, 166
"Sweet Adeline," 162–63
"Sweet Georgia Brown," 45–46

Tate, Erskine, 124, 126, 127, 133, 155
Tate, James, 127
Teachout, Terry, 5
Telfry, Willie, 39
"That's Why They Call Me Shine," 5
Tirro, Frank, 143, 155
Tonk Brothers (Charles J. and William), 61, 65
Tuxedo Orchestra, 68–69, 81, 85; marching brass band, 94

Ukelele Ike, 128
Utopian Quartet, 171

Valentine, "Kid" Thomas, 22
Vallée, Rudy, 6
Vance, J. Madison, 53
Van der Merwe, Peter, 45–46
Van Zan, Gus, 48
Venable, Percy, 157, 159
Vendome Theater (Chicago), 4, 124, 126, 131, 133
Vincent, Clarence "Little Dad," 22

Waifs' Home, 11, 13, 25, 34, 35, 39–40, 51, 56, 57, 59, 60, 61, 62, 64, 65, 70, 75, 76, 78, 171; Band, 49, 52, 53, 54; Brass Band, 50; Orchestra, 47–48, 49, 81
Wallace, Sippie, "Have You Ever Been Down?," 148–49
Wand, Hart A., "Dallas Blues," 160–61
Waters, Ethel, 115, 122; "Down Home Blues," 114
"West End Blues," 8
"When It's Sleepy Time Down South," 5; lyrics, 6
White, Lulu, 166
Whiteman, Paul, 98, 117
Williams, Arthur P., 33
Williams, Bert, 166
Williams, Clarence, 124, 139, 145
Williams, Cootie, 3
Williams, Spencer, "Basin Street Blues," 166
Wiggs, John, 21
Wise, Edmund, 23
Wolverine Orchestra, 118–20, 121
Work, John, III, *American Negro Songs and Spirituals*, 92

Youngren, William H., 123

Zeno, Henry, 63